THE
ALLIED
BOMBER
WAR
1939-45

THE
ALLIED
BOMBER
WAR
1939-45

MAURICE HARVEY

BCA
LONDON · NEW YORK · SYDNEY · TORONTO

This edition published in 1992 by
Book Club Associates
by arrangement with
Spellmount Ltd
12 Dene Way, Speldhurst
Tunbridge Wells, Kent TN3 0NX

CN 4213

Designed by Words & Images, Speldhurst, Kent
Typesetting by Vitaset, Paddock Wood, Kent
Printed and bound in Great Britain by
Biddles Ltd, Guildford and King's Lynn

Half title page
A Stirling Mk 1 of No 7 Squadron being 'bombed up'.　　　RAFM

Title page: A Lancaster at night.

Opposite page
*The 8th Air Force was able to range widely over Germany towards the
end of 1944 with little interference from the Luftwaffe. These are
B-17Fs.*　　　IWM

Page six
*Top: A Lancaster of No 617 Squadron breaches the Mohne Dam on
the 16th May 1943.*　　From a painting by Jean Clark
Below: A German flak tower at Hamburg.
　　　From a painting by Muller of 1943

CONTENTS

FOREWORD

GROUP CAPTAIN HAMISH MAHADDIE, DSO, DFC, AFC, Cz.MC, C.Eng, FRAeS

I devoured this manuscript at one sitting within hours of its arrival. There has never been a more comprehensive treatment of the *Allied* Bomber War, for whilst Bomber Command has been the subject of in-depth research and the 8th Air Force has also been faithfully recorded, there have been few attempts to bring both strands of the Combined Bomber Offensive together in one book, and particularly one which pays such careful attention to the difficulties of each command at the time of its greatest trial.

Looking at Bomber Command operations in the first half of the strategic offensive, we are left with a crystal clear view of how the Chief of Staff's directives were tackled, and sadly failed, leading eventually to Lord Cherwell's inspired Butt report which some felt at this time was even over generous to bomber crews. But probably the main result of the Butt report, which coincided with the arrival of Sir Arthur Harris to command the bomber offensive, was a positive move by the Army and the Navy to carve-up his new command since the former were desperate for bombers in the Western Desert and the latter were fighting a losing battle in the Atlantic Western Approaches. Harris, however, was well aware of this not so secret ploy and was determined to out-manoeuvre the soldiers and sailors at the earliest possible moment. Unfortunately, he had available at this time only some 300 mainly twin engine bombers and a handful of Stirlings. Nevertheless, within three months he was able to muster sufficient aircraft to mount his 'thousand bomber raid' to demonstrate to the faint hearts that the bomber could devastate a target despite the lack of scientific aids. The plan was an enormous success and got the Army and the Navy off his back so that he could concentrate on building-up his Command to the 3,500 bombers he had been promised. I have described the 'thousand plan' in Harris' presence as the greatest confidence trick of the war, but it only raised one of his wry chuckles.

The advent of the Pathfinder Force after the hesitant beginning was the main feature of 1942 although it only really got into the battle in mid 1943. But at least Don Bennett was now getting some help from the scientists with the ever improving H2S and Oboe, although both depended almost entirely for success on the skill of the operator. We nearly did not have a PFF in spite of the entreaties from the Air Staff because Harris refused to entertain a 'corps d'elite' which in fact

he later set-up in 5 Group with 617 Squadron. I am quite sure he regretted his comment at the time when he told the CAS that 'this was yet another example of a Commander in Chief in the field being dictated to by a junior officer at the Ministry'. The author deals with the PFF with much sympathy and is strictly fair, as he does with the question of 'Gardening' – the laying of sea mines from the air.

The Ruhr is also clearly shown as the frightening place that it was. We are permitted the disappointment and tears of the early 40s and the elation when Oboe opened-up targets like the Krupp factory and other 'impossible' targets. Guy Gibson and the saga of the dams is discussed as a success despite the many snide observations from ill-informed sources that not all the dams were breached. In my daily round throughout the Command I was keenly aware of the enormous impact it had on morale amongst the squadrons in all the groups. I have found, however, when lecturing in the United States that I have yet to convince the Americans that we actually did have a bomb which walked on water! The great firestorm of Hamburg follows and we should remember that, despite what Harris' critics have claimed, Albert Speer said that 'six more Hamburgs and we are out of the war'. Bomber Command, however, could not support six more raids at this intensity and the opportunity was lost. I was reminded by this excellent description of an earlier raid on Hamburg in March 1943 when I mismarked the aiming point. This was one of the earlier sorties using H2S and we forgot, if we were ever told, that the Elbe was tidal and we marked a huge tank farm to the west of Hamburg. Whenever I met Harris in later years he always enquired with his characteristic chuckle 'have you been to Hamburg recently Hamish?' The July Hamburg raids can truly be termed the watershed of Bomber Command.

I found a great deal of sympathy with the author's careful research into the interweaving of the technological battle between the two opponents. He paints a rare picture of the incessant endeavour on both sides to out-wit each other in the field of tactics and radar counter-measures and one is left with the impression that the enemy was usually one step ahead of ourselves until the final months of the war.

Whilst Bomber Command was struggling with the early build-up of the heavy bomber force, the USAAF was suffering all the trials of a determined daylight force to come to grips with the lethal enemy day fighters. Whilst the 8th Air Force found early ventures into France were sustainable, their first visits to Germany were a disaster and a severe shock to the crews. However they recovered from these constant maulings and were ever changing their tactics. In mid 1944 I was seconded by Sir Arthur Harris to General Jimmy Doolittle as a pathfinder advisor in the hope that the 'Mighty Eighth' would throw in their lot with Bomber Command and fly with us at night. This plea by Harris was, however, rejected out of hand by the Americans despite their fatal missions against the ball bearing factories at Schweinfurt. Oddly enough, the morale of the Americans was not unduly affected by their visits to Schweinfurt. I saw this at first hand since several bases in General Doolittle's command were very near to my own airfield at Warboys. But at this stage of the Combined Bomber Offensive we both seemed to suffer from a failure to sustain the promised build-up, which was made worse by the losses which both commands were suffering at this time.

The sad saga of Berlin must, regretfully, be considered a failure despite Harris' boast to Churchill that 'the Big City could be wrecked from end to end'. What I found personally amazing during this Berlin phase was how buoyant aircrew morale remained despite the debilitating losses of nearly a thousand aircraft. I believe the Berlin plan was feasible, but in retrospect it could have waited until a later stage when the formidable B-17/Mustang combination could have joined Bomber Command in a grand finale. But Berlin was a target that Harris had to have in his time and his own way, and this only fuelled the charges laid at his door of which many still persist.

The author illustrates how well the Mosquito was used as an independent bomber. Don Bennett's plea to get some 'Mossies' was at first rejected by the Command Staff, but he had his way, after a protracted debate with Harris, and the Light Night Striking Force was born. At this time I was his Training Inspector and I was soon to see the value of this new wing of the PFF when used in spoof attacks along the route of the main force. Many may recall Richard Dimbleby's historic broadcast over Berlin when the pilot, having lost an engine on the outward leg, asked him if he wanted to go on and he replied with the classic PFF battle cry 'Press on regardless'.

Air Marshal Sir Arthur Harris in the Operations Room at Bomber Command Headquarters at High Wycombe in October 1943.

From a painting by Herbert Oliver

I feel I must return briefly to the sad story of Nuremberg which may be known as the lost battle of Bomber Command. I have gone to considerable lengths to research the decision to mount this unfortunate mission which should never have been allowed to happen. After ˙a telebroadcast to Group Commanders on the results of the met reconnaissance flight, Don Bennett, supported strongly by Roddy Carr (4 Group), pressed to scrub that night. However, the Command plus the rest of the Group AOCs headed by 5 Group stressed equally strongly that the sortie should take place as planned, and this was the view of Command Met. Thus the day was carried by a majority vote. What I have never been able to accept is that this marginal decision was taken without due reference to Bennett's professional background – after all he was a Fellow of the Royal Meteorological Society.

I must end my appraisal of this unique study with a word about Sir Arthur Harris. After the end of the war he was hounded, unrewarded, to South Africa vowing never to return. But return he did only to fail to get recognition for an award for his ground crews who endured the rigours of six winters in all weathers maintaining and repairing bombers. But his plea was rejected and he died an embittered man, not because of the shabby treatment he received from the Government on the day after the war, but wholly on the question of a ground crew award. We revelled in many happy hours at reunions and lunches at his Thameside home after the war. On one occasion when about to embark on an overseas lecturing tour, I asked him for a couple of sentences to spice some after-dinner speech in my round of Australia and New Zealand. I beg leave to include at least some extracts from the long letter he sent me in reply.

Uncheddie

When Hitler's urgent messenger Albert Speer reached Sepp Dietrich's Headquarters and said 'the Fuehrer's orders are that you must not stop, you must go on at all costs', Dietrich replied, 'Go on! How can we go on? We have no ammunition left and all our supply lines have been cut by air attack'.

In the atrocious weather during those critical few days and nights only the bombers of Bomber Command were in continuous action, or at times at all. Sepp Dietrich confirmed it to Albert Speer that night as they listened to the continuous roar of heavy four-engined bombers overhead in the dark and mist by saying 'people don't realise that not even the best troops can stand up to this heavy bombing! After an experience of it they lose all fighting spirit'. The General who surrendered Boulogne with 8,000 fit men also confirmed that by writing in his Diary which was captured with him, 'Can anyone survive when a carpet of bombs has fallen. One is driven to despair when at the mercy of the RAF without defence. All our fighting seems hopeless, all our casualties in vain'. Eisenhower also described Bomber Command as 'one of the most effective parts of his whole organisation, always seeking new ways of using their types of aircraft to help the Armies forward'.

As for Goebbels, he and Albert Speer repeatedly assert in their writings that the strategic bombing was 'the cause of all our set backs' and Speer further asserts that all the Allied war books he has read miss that obvious fact and conclusion. He refers to the Strategic Bombing as, for Germany, 'The greatest lost Battle of all'.

In the air, bombing prevented the Germans from ever building up a worthwhile bombing force and made them con-centrate almost entirely on the production of fighters and the training of day and night fighter pilots in a despairing effort, which failed, to protect the Fatherland. The anti-aircraft defence of Germany deprived the German armies on all fronts of half their vitally needed anti-tank/anti-aircraft guns and the 900,000 fit men needed to man those guns in Germany, men who would otherwise have manned those essential anti-tank weapons on every enemy front. Railway repairs to bomb damage kept another 80,000 fit skilled men fully employed in Germany and thousands more for repairs to bomb damage to essential war industries. All of those men, but for the bomber offensive, would have been additional highly skilled soldiers in the German armies in the field.

Speer also states that it was the very heavy RAF bombs that did the 'irreparable damage' to industrial plants and he has also expressed his astonishment at the extraordinary and ever-increasing accuracy of the RAF bombers on such small targets as Benzole plants, sometimes bombed blind through thousands of feet of cloud, during the final stages of the war.

Official history describes the result of the bombing of Berlin as 'not a failure, but a defeat'. Before any Allied soldier got within 50 miles of Berlin the Central Government of Germany had been virtually reduced by that bombing to two maniacs – Hitler and Goebbels – cowering deep underground beneath the widespread ruin of the capital city, issuing voluminous orders to practically phantom armies which either no longer existed or were in such position and condition as to make obedience to such orders impossible. If London and the Government of England had been reduced by German bomb-ing to similar conditions and, say, Winston Churchill and Brendan Bracken to the same state (which is of course inconceivable), I wonder if any German official history would describe that bombing as 'not a failure, but a defeat'!

I leave that to your judgment; and to the verdict of history. My warmest regards to you all,

Arthur T. Harris

PREFACE

It is nice to be associated with this publication: I send my very warmest wishes for its success.

[signature: Leonard Cheshire]

Group Captain Lord G. Leonard Cheshire VC, OM, DSO, DFC

The strategic bomber offensive in the Second World War was an immense undertaking. With the exception of the 'Battle of the Atlantic, it was the only major operation which ran without interruption from the very first day of the war right through to its dying moments nearly six years later. It was a campaign marked by periods of intense disappointment, intermittent controversy, frantic reappraisal and steady consolidation; it developed in its final year into a machine of awesome power and destruction which laid waste the very heart of Germany's economic structure. Furthermore, the strategic bombing campaign had to labour in the beginning under the shadow of a philosophy which some believed would revolutionise the whole pattern of warfare. It was, however, a doctrine which had been adumbrated only in theory in the interwar years and never put to the test; and as so often, theory and practice were separated by a gulf which took several years to bridge.

After the conflict had finally drawn to a close, Bomber Command was enveloped in an almost embarrassing silence. There was no public recognition of its endeavours or its leaders, not even a campaign medal for its participants. The politicians and journalists who had so readily lauded its achievements and criticised its weaknesses during the dark days of war now preferred to ignore it altogether. It is I think revealing that Sir Winston Churchill in his massive history of the Second World War (Volume VI – Triumph and Tragedy) devotes little more than a single rather inconsequential paragraph to the strategic bombing offensive in the nearly 600 pages in which he describes the last year of the war. It is as though he preferred to forget, or at least minimise, the massive contribution that Bomber Command and the 8th Air Force had made to the final subjection of Germany. The shadow of Dresden and Hiroshima had suddenly appeared in some quarters to transform the bombing offensive into an act of shame.

In later years, the official history (The Strategic Air Offensive Against Germany 1939-1945 – Sir Charles Webster and Dr Noble Frankland) fairly and dispassionately set-out the record in great detail to which all later historians are greatly indebted. Other authors have given their own interpretations of these fateful years, often with little consensus of view of what the bombing offensive actually achieved. Polemics have too often taken precedence over facts and sober analysis. Most, however, have been fulsome in their praise of the

determination, courage and fortitude of those who fought and died in the bomber campaign – this can hardly be in doubt – but many have been in varying degrees critical of the strategies and tactics adopted in those years. It is only too easy with hindsight to identify the mistakes which were made, and there were indeed several, but it is also important to recognise the constraints of equipment, manpower, intelligence, and perhaps above all, preconceived ideas, which impacted on the decision making of people who were working under great pressure and stress at the time. The armchair author is susceptible only to a critic's unfavourable review; those actually fighting the war carry a far weightier burden. I too shall express or infer criticism of the direction of the campaign from time to time, but I have tried, and so should the reader, to place these into the context of the time.

In writing this book, I was constantly aware of the limitations of space. This is an enormous subject and I am conscious that many of those who participated in the campaign will look in vain for mention of their particular highlights of the war. I fully recognise that I have done scant justice to the efforts of the 9th and 15th Air Forces and to the Middle East Air Force squadrons who contributed to the bombing of Germany from their bases in Italy from 1944 onwards. My aim in the first part of the book is to describe the aircraft, men, infrastructure and doctrine with which the campaign was fought, for this is essential in understanding the many disappointments which marked the opening three years of the war. The second part describes the events as they unfolded and the policies which drove them. I have highlighted individual raids as examples of the developing strategies or tactics, but the reader must always bear in mind the immense scale of the bomber effort: in the last year of the war Bomber Command and 8th Air Force were both able to dispatch over a thousand bombers almost daily to all corners of Germany and the occupied territories.

I am indebted to many people in the writing of this book. In particular I would like to acknowledge the invaluable assistance of Group Captain Ian Madelin and his staff in the Air Historical Branch of the Ministry of Defence and also to David Brown of the Naval Historical Branch who was very helpful in respect of that much undervalued contribution of Bomber Command in aerial minelaying. Air Commodore M.J. Milligan provided useful information and advice on air navigation systems in use

Bomber Command had a close association with Lincolnshire. This painting shows a Lancaster overflying Lincoln Cathedral.

during the war. The staff of the MoD Central Library were invariably extremely helpful in directing me to published sources and the comprehensive library of the Royal United Services Institute was also very useful. I would also like to thank Mr Edgar Spridgeon, the Chairman of the Uxbridge Branch of the Aircrew Association, who put me in touch with many Bomber Command personnel who fought in the war. I am very much indebted to all the many people who wrote to me, often at considerable length, to describe their experiences. I am only sorry that I could not include more of them in the limited space available. In help with the selection of the photographs, I am grateful to David Parry and his colleagues at the Imperial War Museum, to Andrew Renwick at the Royal Air Force Museum and to Paul Lincoln of the Wartime Watton Experience, a museum at the old bomber station at Watton in Norfolk which is well worth a visit. I am also indebted to the Commander in Chief Strike Command and the Station Commander RAF Wadding-ton for permission to reproduce paintings in their charge.

I am particularly grateful to Bob Murray who provided the excellent original paintings which grace this book and to Group Captain Hamish Mahaddie who contributed the Foreword. Group Captain Mahaddie was a distinguished bomber pilot throughout the war who flew a Whitley on a leaflet raid on the very first night of the conflict, was later a founder member of the Pathfinder Force and finally a bomber station commander. He is himself a prominent author and lecturer on the bomber offensive. I would finally like to give my sincere thanks to Tina Dauncey who typed the manuscript, to Andrew Potts who drew the maps, to James Hoseason who supplied references to US Bombers and to Diane Drummond who designed the layout of the book. My wife, as before, was a constant source of encouragement and support.

Maurice Harvey   Ruscombe, Berks, 1991

In less than a generation, the strategic bombing threat had evolved from the slow and ungainly airship to the sleek and powerful Lancasters. The German Naval Airship L12 was commissioned on the 21st June 1915 and damaged by gunfire over England on the 10th August that year. The Lancaster, over Lincoln Cathedral, is the RAF's preserved example of this legendary bomber of the later conflict.

CHAPTER ONE

Strategy or Delusion

The Fledgling Bomber

The image of the bird as a precursor of manned flight is commonplace, but it may seem strange, even bizarre, to commence an account of the Allied bomber war between 1939 and 1945 with the adventures of Sinbad the Sailor from the Arabian Nights. But Sinbad was the victim of the first recorded bombardment from the air when two giant rocs carrying huge boulders in their claws swept from the sky and released their improvised weapons directly over his ship: one narrowly missed, but the other hit unerringly amidships 'splintering it into a thousand pieces'. On a less ethereal plane, the first use of the manned bomber occurred on the 1st November 1911 during the Turkish-Italian War when Lieutenant Gavotti dropped four 4½lb bombs on a Turkish camp in Libya. No significant damage resulted, but there was a strident if somewhat illogical outcry at this novel form of warfare which has persisted with varying degrees of intensity ever since.

From this very first employment of aerial bombardment there inexorably unfolded a doctrine for the use of the aeroplane in an offensive role. It was a doctrine which the traditionalists of military theory were at first, as is so often the case, slow to embrace but then did so with an intensity which was hardly substantiated by the actual practice of war. The First World War was well underway before the various strands began to coalesce, but stimulated by the first civilian casualties from this new form of warfare, a web of theory began to evolve around the strategic use of the manned bomber. We need, therefore, to briefly follow the development of this doctrine, for it was in many respects responsible for the difficulties and disappointments which confronted the Allied Air Forces for at least the first half of the Second World War.

In the 1914-18 conflict, it was the Royal Naval Air Service (RNAS) which first took an interest in long range bombing, albeit of a defensive nature. There was considerable concern in Britain in 1914 as to how Germany might use her small force of Zeppelin airships and the RNAS lost no time in seeking to constrain her options. On the 22nd September 1914 four aircraft from Antwerp attacked the Zeppelin sheds at Cologne and Dusseldorf with mixed results. By November they were ranging even farther afield with a successful attack by diminutive Avro 504s against the Zeppelin factory at Friedrichshafen on Lake Constance. The Admiralty never lost its interest in strategic bombing, but was continually thwarted by the Army who claimed the highest priority for the more capable machines emerging from the expanding aircraft factories. By contrast, the Royal Flying Corps in France was firmly attached to the British Expeditionary Force structure, each Corps having its own integrated Air Wing. Inevitably, therefore, the primary use of the aeroplane was regarded as reconnaissance and artillery spotting although, not unexpectedly perhaps, some of the pilots soon looked for ways to adopt a more belligerent posture. The war was less than a month old when Lieutenant Conran of No 3 Squadron tried dropping hand grenades over the side of his aircraft on an enemy column: little damage was caused to the troops but the noise stampeded the horses. At about the same time, Captain Strange of No 6 Squadron experimented with a crude form of petrol bomb with which he deftly destroyed two German canvas topped trucks.

It was Captain Strange again who carried out the first properly planned bombing sortie on 11th March 1915. His B.E.2c was specially modified to carry externally four 20lb bombs, released by a cable from the cockpit. The target, which was out of range of the artillery, was the railway station at Coutrai through which German reinforcements were streaming into the battle of Neuve-Chapelle. With no bomb sight the attack had to be pressed home at low level against small arms fire, but a train in the station was hit with a reported 75 casualties. That same afternoon Captain Carmichael of No 5 Squadron flying a Martinsyde S.1 carrying a single 100lb bomb attacked a railway junction at Menin with some success, but suffered severe damage in return and was lucky to stagger home. The euphoria generated by these early successes was not to be sustained. Some four months later, with casualties becoming unacceptably high, this first phase of tactical bombing was suspended after 141 attacks of which only three were judged successful. Nevertheless, the pattern for the development of an offensive air doctrine was already set in train.

The air war was resumed in September 1915 in support of the battle of Loos. A primitive bomb site had by now been introduced, but given the puny bomb loads that could then be carried, the effort was insufficiently concentrated to achieve any worthwhile results. By 1916 the benefits of concentration were recognised, but the fragmented command and control structure

The German Gotha bomber posed a rather more credible threat to Britain than the Zeppelin. This line-up of Gothas belonging to 'The Englandgeschwader' is at Gontrode, near Ghent, in Belgium.

IWM

negated the scale of effort required. Later that same year, the first specialised bomber aircraft at last arrived in France, and with them a change of policy. It was already accepted that air superiority in the battle zone had to be achieved if tactical support of the Army was to be freely enjoyed, and thus the bombers were turned against the enemy airfields in an attempt to reduce the number of opposing fighters. But once again the raids were not sufficiently concentrated to achieve worthwhile results and casualties were high. Tactical misuse of the available resources contributed at least as much as the inadequate aircraft and weapons to the disappointing results achieved during these first three years of aerial bombardment.

Although the Royal Flying Corps had so far concentrated exclusively on tactical bombing in direct support of the land battle, the Germans had already turned towards using aircraft in a strategic role. In an unseasonal Christmas gesture in December 1914, a German seaplane penetrated as far as the London suburbs before it was driven off by a F.B.5 and jettisoned its bombs near Cliffe in Kent. The strategic mantle was then assumed by the Zeppelins which first reached London on the 31st May 1915, causing little damage but creating widespread alarm. By mid 1916 the Zeppelin menace had been largely contained, but a far more sinister threat developed the next year with the Gotha bomber. After two abortive attacks, 14 Gothas reached the capital on the 13th June, and despite being intercepted, killed 158 civilians.

The most important aspect of these early raids, however, was not the damage or casualties they actually caused – these were by no means heavy – but the perception it imprinted upon the minds of both government and public alike. It stimulated a hysteria and revulsion of air bombardment which had a major impact on the development of strategic and political thinking over the next 20 years, a perception which was to prove in many respects without foundation as events actually unfolded between 1939 and 1945.

The lessons of the German offensive were not lost in either London or France and the first strategic bombing attack by the Royal Flying Corps occurred on the 17th October 1917 against a factory at Saarbrucken. A Government commissioned report soon led to the introduction in France of an Independent Air Force of long range bomber aircraft under Major General Hugh Trenchard equipped with the D.H.4 and D.H.9 which had a radius of action of about 100 miles carrying up to 500lbs of bombs. Their objectives were industrial and communications centres in the Ruhr and Rhineland and plans were even afoot in Britain to develop an aircraft which could reach Berlin. This was the Handley Page V. 1500, by the standards of the time a huge four engine aircraft for which a 1,650lb bomb was also developed. However, the Armistice was signed before it could be employed in anger.

General Jan Smuts, an erstwhile opponent from the South African War, was in large part responsible for the creation of an independent air force within Britain and the catalyst for the development of strategic bombing theory.

The Handley Page V.1500 was designed towards the end of the First World War as a strategic bomber capable of reaching Berlin. This is the second form of the first prototype.   IWM

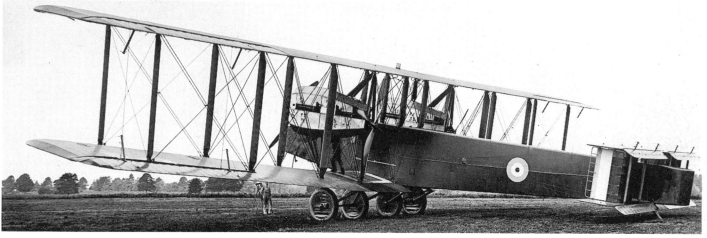

The Development of a Strategic Doctrine

The aeroplane had come of age by 1918, but its use had been mainly tactical and the results of the brief strategic offensive and the isolated forays of the RNAS into Germany were at best inconclusive. It was nevertheless the strategic aspects of bombing that were to dominate thinking over the next 20 years even though many of the lessons that might have been learned in its application had been exaggerated, forgotten, or misunderstood by 1939.

The Gotha raids on London in 1917 had generated a public outcry for protection against this new menace from the skies and demands by incensed Members of Parliament for retaliation in kind. In response to this general if disproportionate alarm, the Government asked General Jan Christiaan Smuts, a shrewd, energetic and greatly respected South African, to review the whole question of the use of air power. The report he submitted on the 17th August 1917 was to have profound implications not only for the future of the Royal Flying Corps, but on the development of strategic thinking into the Second World War.

In essence Smuts agreed with Trenchard that the counter offensive was the best form of defence. But he was ahead of Trenchard at this stage in recognising that this doctrine could only be achieved if the air arm was separated from the control of the Army and the Navy and was so organised that the essential attributes of air power – concentration of effort and flexibility of employment – could be used to maximum advantage. He advocated an independent Air Service embracing the army and naval air arms with its own general staff, its own organisation and the ability to develop its own strategy of the air. On the 1st April 1918 the Royal Air Force was born and Major General Hugh Trenchard was nominated as its first Chief of Air Staff (CAS). Athough the latter is widely regarded as the 'Father of the Royal Air Force', its actual genesis owes much more to General Smuts, a visionary ahead of his time.

Smuts also strongly advocated the creation of a large strategic bombing force which led directly to the creation of the Independent Air Force in France. But there was insufficient time to prove or disprove Smut's prophetic view of its potential:

> Air power can be used as an independent means of war operations. Nobody that witnessed the attack on London on 7th July could have any doubt on that point. Unlike artillery, an air fleet can conduct extensive operations far from, and independently of, both Army and Navy. As far as can at present be foreseen there is absolutely no limit to the scale of its future independent war use. And the day may not be far off when aerial operations with their devastation of enemy lands and destruction of industrial and populous centres on a vast scale may become the principal operation of war, to which the older forms of military operations may become secondary and subordinate.

Predictably, the Army and the Navy did not see the future in quite the same light, but as the strategic bombing offensive was at the forefront of the principles which brought the RAF into being, it is not surprising that it formed the basis of its strategic

Gothas being loaded with 25 and 50Kg bombs before a raid on England in 1917.   IWM

thinking throughout the next 20 years. In many ways this concentration by the RAF upon a single doctrine was detrimental to a balanced overall strategy. In the inter-war years the very real benefits of army co-operation tended to be forgotten and the RAF was ill prepared to provide tactical support for the Army in the field in 1940, as was well demonstrated in Norway and the Low Countries. Equally, the Royal Navy which was now dependent upon the RAF for naval air support was ill served by the collection of obsolete aircraft which it inherited when the Fleet Air Arm was belatedly created in 1937.

The development of the RAF in its early years was beset with immediate difficulties. Trenchard only remained in post as CAS designate for a few months before political disagreement and intrigue rent apart the Air Ministry and he returned to France to command the Independent Air Force. On his return as CAS in 1919, he was preoccupied for years in protecting his fledgling service from the predatory instincts of the Army and the Navy. He only just succeeded, but in the general euphoria of disarmament, the strategic bombing force was dismantled and the RAF adopted a new role of colonial policing, far distant from the ideals which had brought it into existence.

But the strategic doctrine was not forgotten even though the means to implement it had temporarily disappeared. Trenchard had already recognised two strands of thought: strategic bombing could be used either to destroy the enemy's resources for waging war by striking at the heart of its industrial and economic power, or it could be directed at the morale of the population, destroying their will to resist. One of Trenchards' oft quoted dictums was 'the moral effect of bombing stands undoubtedly to the material effect in a proportion of 20 to 1.' In fact, Trenchard did not see these two strands as conflicting aims; he believed the application of the first would lead to the latter, he did not envisage a direct attack on the civilian population as such although he recognised that many civilians would be killed in the process.

The strategic argument was carried forward by General Giulio Douhet of the Italian Air Force who published in 1921 an influential although widely reviled and misquoted book called 'The Command of the Air'. He preached the doctrine of total war – 'the battlefield will be limited only by the boundaries of the nations at war, and all their citizens will become combatants.' He believed that the concentration of effort in time and place which strategic air forces could bring to bear made air defence difficult if not impossible. It contributed to the widely held philosophy eventually articulated by the British Prime Minister Stanley Baldwin that 'the bomber will always get through'. But this dictum sat uncomfortably with the civilian population who recognised that it applied equally to the air force of a potential enemy, and thus the concept of the strategic bomber as a deterrent force was born long before the advent of nuclear weapons made it a realisable aim.

In the United States the proponents of an independent Air Force, led by Brigadier General 'Billy' Mitchell, were unsuccessful. Mitchell pressed his views so strongly that he was eventually court martialled and suspended from duty for five years: he resigned from the Army shortly thereafter. But the theory of an independent bombing force lived on, harried and frustrated though it was by Army control of the Air Corps, and in 1933 Congress approved the development of a long range bomber aircraft.

The principle that strategic bombing in isolation could win any future war was not widely held except by its most vociferous proponents. There were varying views on the ability of the bomber to find and destroy precise targets either by night or day

Major General Hugh Trenchard commanded the Independent Air Force in France before becoming Chief of the Air Staff. He was to have a significant impact on the development of the strategic doctrine of the Royal Air Force in its formative years.

RAFM

and the effect on the morale of the population was a matter for conjecture. It was certainly never accepted as a universal panacea by the combined Chiefs of Staff even though the First World War had totally removed any inclination to engage in the future in a 'slogging match in the trenches'. For politicians, however, always mindful of the financial burden of armed forces in peacetime, it proved a useful expedient to reconcile supposedly adequate means of defence with economic parsimony.

As the shadows of renewed conflict lengthened over Europe, confidence in the strategic bombing doctrine began to waver. It was increasingly recognised that against a revitalised Germany, rearming at a much faster rate than its potential enemies, the deterrent effect of a strategic bombing force was becoming less credible. That the RAF did not actually possess such a force capable of curbing German aggression sufficiently quickly to influence the course of the war became a powerful constraint on the strategic doctrine still prevalent in the Air Ministry. On the other hand the fear, irrational though it was in many ways, that the Luftwaffe could mount a devastating first strike on Britain led to an increasing interest in air defence and a consequential move of resources in that direction. It was somewhat ironic, therefore, that the principles that had led to the formation of the RAF in 1918 and sustained it throughout the inter-war years had proved wanting when the time came once again to face the new dictator. The belief, not only held within the portals of the Air Ministry, that a strategic bombing offensive would change the whole character of war was in the end a delusion.

Rearmament

Although the newly created Royal Air Force was quite resolute in upholding its strategy of the counter offensive, it had little hardware to show for it for another 20 years. In November 1918, the RAF comprised 188 front line squadrons, but these were soon whittled away by 1925 to a mere 27, of which 22 were based overseas. In the struggle to maintain an independent Air Force Trenchard preferred to spend what little money was available on creating a sound infrastructure of buildings, training schools and research facilities to support an expanded Service at some time in the future.

Ironically, it was growing friction with Britain's wartime ally France in 1923 which enabled Trenchard to propose the establishment by 1928 of 52 front line squadrons, of which two thirds would be bombers. This division between offence and defence was by no means uncontested; the RAF's vision of an offensive force designed to strike at a potential enemy nation rather than merely at its armed services was contrary to the defensive or even pacific posture fashionable in political and public circles in the aftermath of the war. The spirit of international co-operation, which found formal expression in the Treaties of Locarno in 1926, dominated political thinking and militated against the provision of an offensive air arm even hidden under the guise of self defence. The pernicious Ten Year Rule, first advanced by the Cabinet in 1919, assumed that

Britain would not be involved in a major war for ten years, and allied with economic stringency, was sufficient to ensure that progress in re-armament was slow. By 1930, although all 17 fighter squadrons envisaged in the Trenchard plan had been formed, only 12 bomber squadrons were in existence, eight of which consisted of light bombers which did not meet the role envisaged by the counter offensive strategy.

In 1928 the Chancellor of the Exchequer, Winston Churchill, reaffirmed the Ten Year Rule in even more stringent form, and disarmament came to the forefront of international deliberations. The League of Nations took the lead in exploring the opportunities for a General Disarmament Conference, but was weakened by the absence of both the USA and Russia from its counsels. The world economic crisis which began in 1929 gave greater impetus to the negotiations and the League of Nations Disarmament Conference at last assembled in Geneva in 1932. Britain was at the forefront in seeking to prohibit bombardment from the air, with some reservations concerning colonial policing, and to impose a maximum size for aircraft of 6600lbs weight. As well as the politicians, the armies and navies of many countries welcomed this development which sought to put back the clock and reassert their power base in international warfare. But the development of the aeroplane for civil aviation was irrevocable and its conversion to military use comparatively straight forward: any attempt to constrain its employment was as doomed to failure as was the attempt to ban gunpowder in the fourteenth century.

The clouds were already gathering on the horizon in the first years of the new decade. Japan had taken hostile action against China and both France and Germany, for differing reasons, were increasingly stifling progress in the disarmament negotiations. The advent of Hitler as Chancellor of Germany and the resignation of Japan from the League, both in January 1933, began the slow process of disintegration of this first attempt to establish a world forum for co-operation. The Disarmament Conference itself collapsed in May 1934 with no agreement whatsoever. A decade of idealism and retrenchment was laid to rest, to be succeeded, albeit hesitantly, by realism and rearmament.

The catalyst for rearmament was of course the re-emergence of Germany as a military power, and the breakdown of the Disarmament Conference was the immediate spur for the first proposal for the future development of the RAF to counter the threat. (See Page 77 for the rise of the Luftwaffe). Announced in July 1934 and known as Scheme 'A', this was the first of many new plans in the succeeding five years sequentially designated by the letters of the alphabet. Although progress was painfully slow, a significant turning point had already been reached when Prime Minister Stanley Baldwin announced to the House of Commons in March 1934 that 'in air strength and air power this country shall no longer be in a position inferior to any country within striking distance of our shores.' At that time, however, these were words bereft of real meaning, for economic stringency still in practice ruled the actions of the Government.

Tension was increased in March 1935 when two British Ministers, Sir John Simon and Anthony Eden, returned from a visit to Berlin to announce that Hitler had told them that the German Air Force had already reached parity with the homebased RAF and was expanding still further to match that of France. Although at this time not strictly correct, it was sufficient to provoke the Government to announce Scheme 'C' in May 1935 followed by Scheme 'F' in February 1936. (The intervening Schemes were moribund and quickly abandoned).

Europe was now in the throes of a new wave of instability. In October 1935 Italy invaded Abyssinia and the League of Nations proved powerless to prevent it either by direct intervention or economic sanctions. Tension in Spain was mounting between the Republicans in power and a Nationalist element led by General Franco. In March 1936, Hitler dispatched German troops into the demilitarised Rhineland, a flagrant breach of Versailles which provoked no more than diplomatic protest. As the shadows of Fascism lengthened, the years of neglect came increasingly to haunt the Government and public conscience.

The Air Staff had not lost faith in its policy of strategic offence, but the wish alone was not the father of the deed. The design and development of new modern fighter aircraft was ahead of that of the bomber and, significantly, fighters were cheaper than bombers and thus more aircraft could be produced with the resources available. The Government was by this stage obsessed with numerical parity and the number of aircraft produced came to be more important than their capability or role. Nevertheless, Scheme 'F' proposed 990 bombers in 68 squadrons and, more importantly, embraced the provision of medium and heavy bombers with adequate reserves. In the meantime, however, light bombers continued to be produced as the larger more capable aircraft were still on the drawing board.

It soon became apparent that Scheme 'F' was inadequate in terms of numerical parity and so Schemes 'G' and 'H' were announced, but in general they merely redistributed aircraft yet to be built from the reserves to the front line. The continuing worsening of the political situation and the prospect that the Germans might take over airfields in neutral Belgium, thus bringing their bombers and escort fighters well within range of the British mainland, led to a change of direction. Sir Thomas Inskip, newly appointed Minister for the Co-ordination of Defence instituted a review of future needs which led to an Air Staff proposal that production must henceforth concentrate on the new long range heavy bombers which would keep the RAF a qualitative step ahead of the Luftwaffe. Inskip did not support this proposal, recommending instead that emphasis should be given to the production of fighter aircraft at the expense of bombers which would take much longer to materialise. The Air Ministry were aghast at this heretical view, but the Cabinet agreed with Inskip and all future schemes favoured the production of increasing numbers of Hurricanes and Spitfires.

The rape of Austria and Chamberlain's meeting with Hitler at Munich followed in quick succession, as did yet further schemes for re-equipment. But as war now rapidly approached, the pieces with which it would be contested were already on the board. Looking at its Battles, Blenheims, Whitleys and

Expansion Schemes – Metropolitan Air Force – 1934 to 1939

	Pre-Expansion Strength	Scheme 'A'	Scheme 'C'	Scheme 'F'
Approved		Jul 34	May 35	Feb 36
Date for completion		Mar 39	Mar 37	Mar 39
Bomber Squadrons	28	41	68	68
Bomber Aircraft	316	476	816	990
Fighter Squadrons	13	28	35	30
Fighter Aircraft	156	336	420	420
Other Aircraft	75	148	276	326

	Scheme 'H'	Scheme 'J'	Scheme 'K'	Scheme 'L'
Approved	Jan 37	Not approved	Not approved	April 38
Date for completion	As soon as possible	Mar 41	Mar 41	Mar 41
Bomber Squadrons	90	90	77	77
Bomber Aircraft	1,659	1,442	1,360	1,360
Fighter Squadrons	34	38	38	38
Fighter Aircraft	476	532	532	608
Other Aircraft	357	413	413	413

	Scheme 'M'			
Approved	Nov 38			
Date for completion	Mar 39	Mar 40	Mar 41	Jan 42
Bomber Squadrons	57	70	82	85
Bomber Aircraft	812	1,352	1,360	1,360 (all heavy bombers)
Fighter Squadrons	40	40	50	50
Fighter Aircraft	638	640	800	800
Other Aircraft	330	389	389	389

The early rearmament schemes were more concerned with achieving numerical parity with Germany than with the establishment of a balanced and adequately equipped air force.

The Handley Page Harrow was the most modern aircraft the RAF could produce for the Empire Air Day in 1937. It still remained in the RAF's front line inventory on the outbreak of war, but did not see operational service in Europe.

RAFM

Harrows at the end of 1938, even the Air Ministry acknowledged that a counter offensive by Bomber Command could do little in the time available to stem a German attack and that the task of defending Britain must, for the time being, rest with Fighter Command. Nevertheless, the bomber force, such as it was, could not be left sitting on the ground in the event of war with Germany and we now need to look at the developing plans in the final years of peace for its employment.

The Collapse of a Strategic Plan

The RAF tried to remain true to the doctrine of the counter offensive even when the means to implement it were not yet available. But a strategy is not sufficient in itself, there must be detailed plans to put it into effect, and it is in the formulation of precise objectives for Bomber Command that difficulties arose. The strategy itself was in one important sense ambiguous – should the bombers be seeking to destroy the material resources necessary for the enemy to pursue the war, or should they be unleashed directly at the people in an effort to destroy their will to continue the fight? Largely for reasons of moral sensitivity, this issue had never been squarely faced, and the dilemma was compounded by the fact that the other two Services had never accepted the basic tenets of the strategy anyway.

The issue came to the fore in 1934 in the scramble by all three Services for the extra funds to be devoted to defence. The Joint Planning Committee, a subordinate group to the Chiefs of Staff Committee which had been set up in 1927, was tasked with examining strategic priorities. The three Services found little common ground upon which to build and their final report was not completed until 1936; even then it was hedged with uncertainty and buttressed with compromise.

To the Government and general public, the threat of concentrated air attack in an attempt to knock Britain out of the war loomed large. Recollection of the Gotha raids of 1917 exaggerated estimates of the civilian casualties which would be incurred and thus it was deemed that the first objective of the RAF should be to counter this threat. That the Luftwaffe was mainly designed for army co-operation and not able to mount an effective attack from airfields in Germany was largely ignored. As little confidence at this period rested in air defence, it was thought that the bomber forces should therefore be concentrated against the German airfields and maintenance depots to destroy or disrupt their striking capability. On the other hand, a German offensive might consist of a land attack against the Low Countries and France, in which case the bombers should be used against German communications to disrupt their advance. Already the basic principles of the strategic offensive were being subordinated to the realities of actually planning to fight a war. Only after this essentially defensive phase had run its course could the bomber forces be turned onto the offensive, the attack against German industry.

The Air Ministry was now in a position to prepare the detailed plans to meet the newly formulated priorities. These objectives, of course, had to be within the capability of the

Western Air Plans – September 1939	
W.A.1	Attack on the German Air Striking Force and its maintenance organisation (including aircraft industry).
W.A.2	Reconnaissance in co-operation with the Navy in Home Waters and the eastern Atlantic.
W.A.3	Close co-operation with the Navy in convoy protection in Home Waters and the eastern Atlantic.
W.A.4	Attack on German military rail, canal and road communications.
W.A.5	Attack on German manufacturing resources.
W.A.6	Attack on Italian manufacturing resources.
W.A.7	Counter-offensive action in defence of seaborne trade in co-operation with the Navy, i.e. attack on the Fleet or on the bases of enemy surface, submarine and air forces operating against our trade.
W.A.8	Attack on specially important depots or accumulations of warlike stores other than air, in enemy country.
W.A.9	Putting the Kiel Canal out of action.
W.A.10	Destruction of enemy shipping and facilities in German mercantile ports – precedence to be given to the Baltic.
W.A.11	Attack on forests.
W.A.12	Attacking the German Fleet or a section thereof at sea.
W.A.13	Attack on enemy's headquarters and administrative offices in Berlin and elsewhere.
W.A.14	Dropping propaganda leaflets.
W.A.15	Operations against enemy shipping by magnetic mine in concert with the Navy.
W.A.16	Bouyancy mine attack against German waterways.

The 'Western Air Plans' were formulated in 1937 for the employment of the newly created Bomber Command.

newly formed Bomber Command, and as the study progressed the limitations of the bomber force at this time became increasingly apparent. Although plans for the new generation of bombers – Hampdens, Wellingtons and Whitleys – were now well advanced, the Command was actually equipped with a motley assembly of obsolete machines which had little capability to undertake any of the tasks envisaged. Furthermore, it was recognised that even by 1939-40, the RAF would not be in a position to make any substantial contribution to either the defensive or the offensive strategy formulated in the Joint Planning Committee's report.

The Air Staffs, nevertheless, got down to work and by October 1937 a list of sixteen plans, called Western Air (W.A.) 1, 2, 3 etc, were sent to Bomber Command with instructions to concentrate on the tactical development of three in particular:

(1) W.A.1 – The attack on the German Air Force and its maintenance organisations.
(2) W.A.4 – The attack on road, rail and canal communications within Germany and the Low Countries.
(3) W.A.5 – The attack on German industry in the Ruhr, Rhineland and Saar.

The Bomber Command response in late 1938 was pessimistic. In respect of W.A.1, it was considered that these targets would be difficult to pinpoint and hit, and it was unlikely that unescorted bombers would be able to penetrate far into Germany without sustaining unacceptable losses. In any case, the bombers would have to be based in France which would take time, certainly longer than that needed to counter the 'knock-out blow'. Staff discussions with France had not even been authorised at this stage. W.A.4 presented 'political' as well as other difficulties. It would, for all practical purposes, mean subordinating the bomber force to the Army Commander-in-Chief – a heretical thought for those airmen nurtured on the milk of Trenchard's seminal doctrine of the independent air force. Nor could agreement be reached with the General Staff as to which type of target would best accomplish the aim. No such problem of principle confronted W.A.5, and despite the inconsistencies with their objection to W.A.1, it was proposed that the most profitable employment of Bomber Command would be against the energy industry of the Ruhr. But no such policy could be pursued until the Command was equipped with heavy bombers capable of making attacks against precision targets in daylight, and as this could not be achieved until 1941, the immediate aim of Bomber Command in the event of war starting earlier should be to conserve its forces, particularly its trained aircrews. Mr Chamberlain was passing through a crisis of confidence at this time on the morality of attacking targets which might cause death or injury to civilians, and it was in 1938 that the Government at last changed direction towards the emphasis on air defence.

It was at this time also that the CinC Bomber Command first mooted the idea of using the bombers to drop propaganda leaflets rather than bombs on enemy cities (W.A.14) and serious consideration was also given to attacking naval objectives (W.A.7) which did not break the Prime Minister's ban on bombing land targets. But as war broke out, the counter offensive doctrine so long and vigorously advocated between the wars was almost entirely in tatters – the realities of inadequate equipment and unimaginative training had left Bomber Command close to being a broken reed in 1939. It was in this unhappy situation that the Command went to war in September 1939, but before tracing the progress of bomber operations throughout the war, it is first appropriate to look at the inventory and infrastructure of the Command and that of its eventual ally, the United States Army Air Corps.

CHAPTER TWO

The Aircraft

Years of Retrenchment

The First World War spawned a rapid rise in the number of firms building 'war planes', with many of the early pioneers of flight like A.V. Roe, Geoffrey de Havilland and C.S. Rolls taking advantage of the boom conditions to create companies which by 1945 had become household names. But the cessation of hostilities in 1918 and the drastic reduction in the size of the RAF which followed led inevitably to what would now be called rationalisation of the industry; some firms went out of business altogether and others concentrated on the slowly expanding civil market. Nevertheless, an interest remained in the bomber aircraft, stimulated perhaps in the 1920s more by theory than practice as the RAF declined to little more than 20 squadrons, mostly overseas. In the circumstances, a surprising number of prototypes emerged from the drawing boards before rearmament started in earnest in the early 1930s, but as the emphasis in the RAF had turned towards colonial policing, the particular requirements of that role influenced the design of bomber aircraft and the larger types, the successors to the H.P.V.1500, tended at first to be used rather more in a transport than an offensive role.

Some of the most senior commanders of the Second World War, such as Arthur Harris and Charles Portal, were squadron commanders during this difficult period who recognised the wider potential of these larger aircraft even in the colonial environment, and with the initiative that was allowed to comparatively junior officers in those days exploited their capability for bomber operations both by day and night. The Air Ministry played its part in keeping interest alive by issuing a steady flow of specifications which were intended to stimulate manufacturers to seek new lines of technical development even though few of their products in those parsimonious days would reach the production line. Progress in engine design and aerodynamics was also greatly encouraged by such well publicised events as the Schneider Trophy, and the experience and expertise thereby gained by firms like Vickers, De Havilland and Rolls Royce were invaluable in later years.

Some firms became well established in the bomber field between the wars. Vickers with the Vernon, Victoria and Valentia transport/bombers was perhaps in the lead, but

A Handley Page Heyford. The first production model of this aircraft did not fly until mid 1933 and it was obsolete almost as soon as it entered operational service. RAFM

Another bomber/transport, the Bristol Bombay, which first flew as late as 1935 and which was destined to have no role to play in a European war only four years later.

RAFM

Handley Page, Bristol and Boulton Paul all maintained a lively interest. Hawker, Fairey and De Havilland tended to concentrate on the more agile medium or light bomber designs. Irrespective of size, most aircraft produced in the 1920s and early 30s were biplanes of all metal construction except for moving surfaces, with open cockpits and a top speed of not much over 125 mph. One only has to look at a photograph of an aircraft such as the Handley Page Heyford, the first production model of which did not fly until the 21st June 1933, to recognise the dramatic improvements in aircraft design which were to materialise in the next few years, culminating in the Lancaster, the outstanding heavy bomber of the war which first flew just eight years later.

The pace began to step-up with the turn of the decade. In many respects design criteria were advanced by the modern civil airliner embodying twin engine monoplane construction, variable pitch propellers, retractable undercarriage and flaps. In this context, much valuable work was undertaken in the United States with companies like Boeing setting a vigorous lead. As the 1930s progressed, specifications overtook each other in the search for ever better performance and payload. Prototypes were often recognised to be obsolescent even before they had flown: the Bristol Bombay did not fly until June 23rd 1935 when the Wellington was already in design. Furthermore, the decision to order from the drawing board meant that some of these obsolete aircraft were often produced in quite large numbers; partly for political reasons in the obsessive quest for numerical parity and partly for practical reasons in that factories geared-up for one type could not switch readily to a new design. The aircraft industry itself expanded rapidly in these years with the bold and imaginative creation of shadow factories in 1936 which were designed to enable the motor and other industries to switch rapidly to aircraft production. Even so, when war broke

Although the limitations of the Whitley were by then well recognised, this production line was still running strongly at the end of 1940. IWM

out in 1939, the RAF still had a shortfall in both quantity and quality, and it was not until 1942 that the outflow of heavy bombers from the factories began to redress the situation.

The Light Bombers – The Battle and Blenheim

Air bombardment in the First World War had of necessity to depend upon the single engined light bomber, principally the D.H.4 and D.H.9, and these were followed by derivatives in the inter-war years designed mainly for a colonial policing role. There was thus a long tradition of light bombers in the RAF and the Fairey Battle followed naturally in that role. In 1932 the Air Ministry set in motion plans to replace the latest of the light bombers, the Hawker Hart. However, the first seeds of doubt regarding the effectiveness of this conventional design were apparent in the decision to produce two parallel requirements for comparative evaluation, P27/32 for a single engine light bomber and B9/32 for a twin engine medium bomber. The latter led to the production of the Hampden and the Wellington, both, with all their limitations, immeasurably more effective than the Battle.

Fairey Aviation won the order to meet specification P27/32 with a design submitted by the Belgian Marcel Lobelle, the Company's chief designer. In many respects it was an ingenious and advanced design for a low wing, two seat monoplane powered by the Company's own engine, the Prince. From the outset the Battle was a victim of its specification: a single engine could not produce the power necessary to provide speed and manoeuvrability commensurate with a reasonable payload and radius of action. This was recognised by the Company who at an early stage wished to convert the design to a twin engine aircraft, but the Air Ministry instead changed the specification to include a third crew position, a dedicated bomb aimer, which with the additional weight simply exacerbated the design limitations.

A large order for 155 aircraft was placed in mid 1935, mainly for political reasons, even before the first flight of the prototype. This was the period when the dramatic expansion of the Luftwaffe first impinged upon the Government and the public conscience and numerical parity was the cry of the hour. In terms of current development, the Battle was the most advanced of the possible contenders for bomber rearmament.

The Prince engine having been discarded in favour of a Rolls Royce Merlin, the Battle made its first flight in the hands of Chris Staniland from the Company's airfield at Northolt, close to the modern Heathrow airport, on the 10th March 1936:

performance was predictably disappointing. As the capability of the modern fighter became ever more evident, it was now universally recognised that the Battle was too slow and inadequately armed. It had only a single fixed Browning 0.3in forward firing gun and another single Vickers gun of the same calibre mounted in the rear cockpit. Orders nevertheless continued to flow from the Air Ministry: not only did the Battle make-up the numbers, however inadequately, but it kept the factories in being for the production of more advanced types when released from the drawing board. The Battle entered service with No 63 Squadron in March 1937. After a short and disastrous career with the Advanced Air Striking Force in France, it was soon generally relegated to training duties. It is one of the most tragic examples of the inadequacy of pre-war rearmament planning.

The Bristol Blenheim had an altogether different pedigree. It was designed in 1933 by Frank Barnwell as a twin engine light commercial transport carrying two pilots and six passengers. The influential press baron, Lord Rothermere, supported the project and ordered one, the 'Britain First', for his own personal

Fairey Battle[1]	
Engine	Rolls Royce Merlin II
Max Speed	241 mph at 13,000 feet
Economical Cruise	200 mph at 15,000 feet
Service Ceiling	26,000 feet
Range	1018 miles with max load
Max Bomb Load	1500lbs (1000lbs internally)
Crew	3
Number Built	2201

[1] Note
Performance figures vary with the mark of aircraft, and it must be said, according to the source from which they are derived. The figures in this chapter are taken from the Ministry of Production Manual wherever possible. The Service Ceiling figure is at maxweight, the aircraft could cruise climb to a higher altitude as the fuel was used. The range quoted is with a representative bomb load, but the radius of action would be rather less than half this figure to take account of reserves and operational considerations. Range could be increased considerably by reducing the bomb load.

Fairey Battles of No 218 Squadron. This slow and inadequately armed aircraft was no match for the Bf 109 in France in 1940. IWM

use. Designated the Type 142, this aircraft made its maiden flight at Bristol (Filton) nearly one year before the Battle on 12th April 1935 and immediately attracted attention by its outstanding performance. Finland was the first country to show an interest in a military version, but the Air Ministry soon recognised the potential of the Type 142 as a bomber. Learning of this interest, Rothermere presented the aircraft to the Government who continued its testing by the RAF at Martlesham Heath. Its superior performance was rapidly confirmed; with a top speed of over 300 mph, it was 50 mph faster than the latest fighter then in production.

Bristol quickly redesigned the aircraft for military use; the wing was raised to a mid position to incorporate a bomb bay, a dorsal gun turret was fitted and provision made for a bomb aimer's position in the nose. Now known as the Blenheim Mk 1, powered by Mercury engines and carrying a crew of three – pilot, wireless operator/air gunner and bomb aimer – the first production aircraft was delivered less than a year later in June 1936. By the end of that same year, the RAF had over 1,500 on order and production was extended to other companies including the car manufacturer Rootes who participated in the Governments' shadow factory scheme. The Blenheim Mk 1 was superceded by the Mk IV in 1938. Originally conceived as a reconnaissance aircraft for Coastal Command known as the Bolingbroke, this longer nosed variant was eventually developed as a bomber. By the outbreak of war, three production lines were producing 100 aircraft a month and the Mk IV had replaced the Mk 1s in Bomber Command, the latter being adapted, not very successfully, as a fighter. The early euphoria soon began to crumble; the early Blenheims were no better armed than the Battle and successive Service requirements had added to the weight and taken the edge off its top speed. Furthermore, its bomb load and range were very similar to the Battle. Despite, therefore, its initial high promise, the Blenheim was already outdated when hostilities broke-out and no match for the latest German fighters. Although it lasted in operational service in Western Europe for slightly longer than the Battle, most had been withdrawn from front line service in

A Blenheim Mk I of No 90 Squadron. This version had been largely superseded by the long nosed Mk IV by September 1939. RAFM

Bomber Command by the end of 1941. The RAF had to wait for the Mosquito before it acquired a high performance light bomber.

Bristol Blenheim Mk IV

Engine	Mercury XV × 2
Max Speed	266 mph at 11,800 feet
Economical Cruise	180 mph at 15,000 feet
Service Ceiling	22,000 feet
Range	1460 miles with max load
Max Bomb Load	1000lbs (internally)
Crew	3
Number Built	5374 (all marks)

The Mosquito

Alongside the Spitfire and the Lancaster, the Mosquito must surely rank as one of the outstanding British aircraft of the war, and like the Spitfire it received little official encouragement in its conception and early development. Although in the forefront of bomber production in the First World War, the De Havilland Aircraft Company of Hatfield specialised in light and commercial aircraft between the wars, but had already found fame and gained valuable experience in high speed flight with their Comet racer of 1934. Speed was to be the hallmark of their major contribution to the next war, the Mosquito.

In the years immediately before the war, however, the Air Ministry was moving in a totally different direction. From 1934 onwards it sought heavy, powerfully armed aircraft which could carry large bomb loads over long distances: inevitably thereby increasing their weight at the expense of speed, ceiling and manoeuvrability. Furthermore, such complex aircraft required a large crew, heightening the manpower shortage and increasing the cost of training. The specification P13/36 of August 1936, which led eventually to the Halifax and the Lancaster, was not therefore particularly attractive to the De Havilland Company's innovative design team lead by C.C. Walker and R.E. Bishop; their ideas containing two strikingly different concepts to that embraced by most other design teams who responded to this requirement. The first was to break away from the by now conventional practice of constructing aircraft entirely of light alloys which required materials and skills which might quickly become scarce under the exigencies of war time production. Secondly, they espoused a design which used speed and a high operating ceiling to render it immune to fighters and anti aircraft defences and which, therefore, would not need to carry weapons for self defence. Furthermore, their aircraft with a crew of two was economical in manpower.

In February 1938, the Air Ministry issued a specification, B18/38, which went some way towards De Havilland's concept, but in general there was little enthusiasm in official circles for this line of development. Fortunately, there were two lone but nevertheless influential voices which supported this revolutionary concept, now known officially as the D.H. 98.

The C-in-C Bomber Command, Air Chief Marshal Sir Edgar Ludlow-Hewitt called for a 'speed' bomber in March 1939 and, more importantly, the Air Member for Research, Development and Production, Air Chief Marshal Sir Wilfred Freeman issued a specification, B1/40, for a single aircraft at the end of the year. It was irreverently known as 'Freeman's Folly'.

The D.H. 98 was conceived as a mid wing aircraft of all wood construction powered by two Rolls Royce Merlin engines. It had an estimated top speed of about 420 mph and a ceiling of 30,000 feet: it was to carry a 1,000lb bomb load about 1,500 miles. Its potential was now more readily recognised in official circles and by early 1940 the order for the single prototype had been increased to 50, and its use as a fighter with four 20 mm canon had already been envisaged. The distinctive all yellow prototype was built at Salisbury Hall about 5 miles from the Company's base at Hatfield and eventually towed by road to the airfield for its maiden flight by Geoffrey de Havilland on 25 November 1940. The aircraft was basically constructed of balsa wood sandwiched between two skins of birch plywood and powered by the Merlin 21 engine. Like most prototypes, it had grown slightly in weight in the detailed design and its performance had consequently marginally deteriorated. Nevertheless, it achieved 388 mph at 22,000 feet and although somewhat sensitive on the controls, was generally considered pleasant to fly. The initial order of 50 aircraft was split after various contractual vacillations into three prototypes; nine photo reconnaissance aircraft, ten bombers and 28 fighters. It was now officially designated the Mosquito.

The first production bomber was the B Mk IV of which 300 were eventually built, the first being delivered to No 105 Squadron in November 1941. However, as a result of the German night raids on London, the emphasis had swung towards the production of the Mosquito as a night fighter and it was not until May 1942 that the bomber version was used

The Mosquito was justly famous for its versatility: this Mk IX, 'D' for 'Dolly', was used for meteorological reconnaissance.

IWM

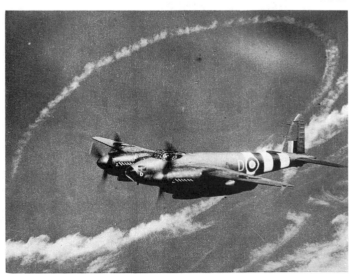

The first bomber version of the Mosquito was the B Mk IV. These aircraft pictured in December 1942 were from No 105 Squadron at Marham in Norfolk. RAFM

operationally with four individual sorties against Cologne in the wake of the first 1,000 bomber raid.

The early operations by the Mosquito were not conspicuously successful. Their introduction had coincided with the advent of the FW 190, which had only a marginally inferior performance at high level, and it had not yet been decided how best to use the potential of the new bomber – high level day/night or low level dawn/dusk. Efforts were nevertheless quickly directed towards improving the performance of the Mosquito to try to regain a flight envelope which would be invulnerable to fighter attack; this was, after all, the *raison d'etre* of the design concept.

Further development was mainly concerned with increasing the bomb load, the power output of the engines and the navigation fit. A first step was to provide a new universal wing with carriage points for two 500lb bombs or, alternatively, external fuel tanks. Later in 1943, the aircraft was again modified to carry one 4,000lb bomb known as the 'Cookie', but this was only partially successful as it tended to make the aircraft longtitudinally unstable. The higher bomb loads envisaged necessitated attention to the power plants if the essential performance criteria was to be maintained or even improved. A two stage Merlin engine was flown on the original prototype aircraft in June 1942, a later version of which eventually pushed the speed up to a maximum for the type of 437 mph. Another development was the fitting of a pressurised cabin to enable very high level operations to be conducted with greater comfort and safety: operations at 40,000 feet were now within reach.

The use of the Mosquito in specialised roles, particularly in the Pathfinder Force, also necessitated the fitting of more sophisticated navigation equipment, firstly Oboe which was superceded by G-H and eventually in January 1944 with H2S for radar bomb aiming. Flying at 30,000 feet at night, aircraft fitted with these equipments could mark targets precisely whilst remaining almost immune to enemy defences.

These improvements resulted in two new marks of Mosquito, the B Mk 1X and the B Mk XVI. The former incorporated the precision navigation aids but not the pressurised cabin and only 54 were delivered, mostly used by the Pathfinder Force. The Light Night Striking Force (LNSF) was eventually equipped with either the B Mk XVI or one of the Canadian variants, the B Mk XX or B Mk 25. As De Havillands already had a Canadian branch, it readily followed that the aircraft would also be built at its Toronto factory. Governmental agreement was reached in June 1941 and construction began with British supplied components. An indigenous Canadian version was quickly designed using Merlin engines constructed under licence by Packard. Deliveries of aircraft to Britain started in August 1943 and nearly 500 of the bomber versions were received before the end of the war. The final version of the Mosquito built in Britain was the B Mk 35 which first flew in March 1945 but did not see operational service.

Despite unexpectedly high losses in the early part of its operational life whilst a role for the aircraft was still being formulated and tactics evolved, the Mosquito eventually became statistically the safest aircraft operated by Bomber Command. The De Havilland Aircraft Company's foresight and courage in developing an aircraft for which very few people saw a role in the late 1930s had been overwhelmingly vindicated.

De Havilland Mosquito B Mk XVI	
Engine	Merlin 72 × 2
Max Speed	397 mph at 26,000 feet
Economical Cruise	245 mph at 15,000 feet
Service Ceiling	36,000 feet
Range	1485 miles with 3000lbs
Max Bomb Load	3000lbs (or one 4000lbs 'Cookie')
Crew	2
Number Built	7757 (all marks – 1684 bombers)

The Medium Bombers – Hampden, Wellington and Whitley

A production prototype of the Handley Page Hampden. Although soon outclassed as a bomber, this aircraft provided sterling service as a mine layer. IWM

Although the Geneva Disarmament Conference monopolised the political debate in 1932, the Air Ministry had to continue planning for the future as usual and a replacement aircraft was needed for the Boulton Paul Sidestrand biplane, now rapidly becoming obsolete in the light of advancing technology. However, the Ministry could not ignore the deliberations in Geneva, one feature of which was a proposal supported by the British Government to restrict the basic weight of new aircraft to 6,600lbs. This limitation constrained specification B9/32 which was issued in early 1933. In the event this restriction was soon forgotten, but by then it had led to design constraints, which were never really overcome, on the two aircraft selected for development to meet the specification – the Hampden and the Wellington.

The original specification was quite modest, requiring a twin engine aircraft for daylight bombing with a maximum speed of 190 mph and a range of 1,250 miles. The Handley Page response, led by chief designer Dr Gustav Lachmann, was quite a striking design with a short, very narrow, deep slab sided fuselage and a slim tail boom with twin fins. The aircraft was of all metal construction incorporating Handley Page's ingeniously designed wing slots for added lift at low speeds. Several engine designs were considered, but the choice eventually settled on the Bristol Pegasus supercharged radial. The prototype took rather a long time to construct and the first flight was not achieved until 21 June 1936 by Major J Cordes at the Company's Radlett airfield. The Air Ministry had by now relaxed the original weight restriction and the aircraft was substantially heavier than that envisaged by the Geneva limitation. The performance was also much improved and the prototype, known as the H.P. 52, reached a very respectable 265 mph. However, the narrow fuselage, although aerodynamically efficient, was creating difficulties in providing adequate defensive armament; a powered turret proved impracticable and in the end only four 0.3in machines were carried – single ventral and dorsal guns and two firing forward. This was a major handicap which left the Hampden extremely vulnerable to fighter attack, particularly from the beam, and soon precluded its operation by day.

The Air Ministry was, nevertheless, sufficiently satisfied to place a production order for the aircraft, 180 from Handley Page itself and a second order for 100 from one of the new shadow factories in Belfast. The latter's aircraft, powered by the Napier Dagger engine, was to prove a complete failure – the Hereford (a name chosen to differentiate it from the Pegasus Hampden) flew only one operational sortie before being relegated to training. Further contracts were let in 1938 including some in Canada which eventually contributed 160 aircraft to the total.

The first aircraft, now known officially as the Hampden, reached Bomber Command in September 1938 replacing the Hawker Hind biplanes of No 49 Squadron. It is a telling comment on the inadequacy of the Command at this stage, coincident as it was with Chamberlain's Munich meeting with Hitler, that front line squadrons were still equipped with the obsolete Hind. Eventually ten squadrons were equipped with the Hampden, all in No 5 Group. The Hampden as delivered had quite a reasonable performance; it could carry a 2,000lb bombload nearly 2,000 miles and was quite fast, but its Achille's heel remained its defensive armament.

As a day bomber, the Hampden soon proved hopelessly inadequate, as indeed did its more famous counterpart the Wellington, and was soon generally relegated to subsidiary operations, mostly at night. It did, however, find one niche for which it was well suited, the laying of mines at sea, a practice known as 'Gardening'. Efforts continued to improve its armament and throughout 1941 and 42 the Hampden continued to make-up the numbers in the large scale raids, participating in the first 1,000 bomber raid on Cologne and early attacks on Berlin. Hampden operations in Bomber Command gradually wound down, finishing altogether in mid September 1942, although the aircraft found a new lease of life in Coastal Command as a torpedo bomber. Overall, its performance as a bomber could only be regarded as barely adequate.

By far the most successful of the British medium bombers, the prototype Wellington first flew in June 1936.   **IWM**

Handley Page Hampden	
Engine	Pegasus XVIII × 2
Max Speed	254 mph at 13,800 feet
Economical Cruise	155 mph at 15,000 feet
Service Ceiling	20,000 feet
Range	1200 miles with max load
Max Bomb Load	4000lbs
Crew	4
Number Built	1432 (plus 150 Herefords)

The Wellington, designed by the Vickers Aircraft Company arose from the same specification as the Hampden. It was altogether a more capable and versatile aircraft, and whilst not in the same league as the Lancaster, was certainly the outstanding medium bomber produced by British industry during the war. The chief designer at Vicker's Weybridge works was Rex Pierson, but the unique feature of the Wellington, its geodetic construction, was the brainchild of Dr Barnes Wallis who had pioneered the design in the Wellesley which flew about a year before the Wellington. The theory behind geodesics relates to the shortest line joining two points on a sphere which, translated into aircraft structural terms, forms the principle of construction for the load carrying members of the fuselage and wing. It required no internal bracing and had a very high strength in relation to its weight. The end result rather resembled a latticework garden fence.

Like the Hampden, the design was initially constrained by the 6,600lb weight limitation, but this was fortunately abandoned before the design of the production aircraft was finalised. The aircraft originally incorporated nose, tail and dorsal gun turrets, but the latter was soon dropped and replaced

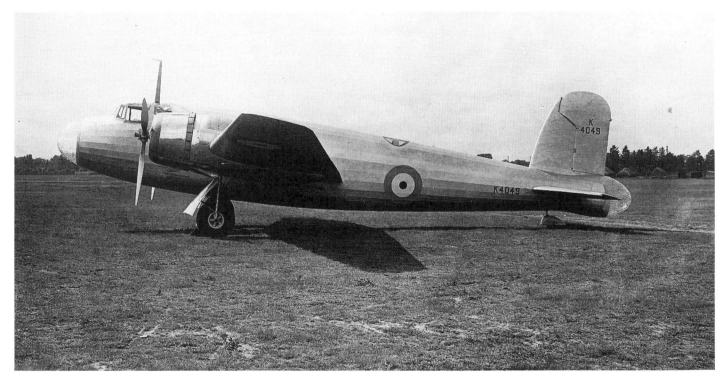

The Wellington B Mk II was the first version to be powered by the Rolls Royce Merlin engine. IWM

eventually by beam positions either side of the rear fuselage. The prototype Vickers Type 271 powered by Bristol Pegasus engines made its first flight, just nine days before the Hampden, on the 15th June 1936 in the hands of Captain Mutt Summers, Vicker's chief test pilot. At this stage the project was developing in step with its Handley Page counterpart, but the Wellington's overall performance proved vastly superior, the main advantage stemming from the latter's capacious fuselage which allowed a full bomb load to be carried internally leaving the wings free to hold fuel. The prototype could carry 4,500lbs well over 1,500 miles and the larger fuselage also gave more latitude in the design and installation of the gun turrets, always a problem on the Hampden. Contracts were rapidly signed for production aircraft to a modified specification, but flight trials disclosed a disturbing aerodynamic problem with the tailplane causing the prototype to crash. At this stage the dorsal turret was abandoned and design problems prevented the introduction of the alternative ventral turret: this was to have serious implications for the Wellington in its initial role as a day bomber.

No 99 Squadron at Mildenhall was the first unit to take the Wellington on charge in October 1938 and by the outbreak of war seven more squadrons had joined No 3 Group. The first Wellington daylight operation was flown on the second day of the war, but after the end of December, heavy losses sustained largely because of the lack of a gun which could fire to the beam resulted thereafter in the Wellington only normally being used at night: a role for which it had been neither designed nor

equipped. Nevertheless, its reliability, its sturdy construction and ability to withstand heavy punishment made it a deservedly popular aircraft, at least until the best of the heavy bombers came along.

Subsequent developments of the Wellington were generally concerned with a change of powerplant from the Pegasus XVIII. The Mk II was powered by the Rolls Royce Merlin, the Mk III by the Bristol Hercules and the Mk IV by the American Pratt and Whitney Twin Wasp. Substantial quantities of each mark were ordered and deficiencies in the Mk I were corrected in the later versions, particularly the introduction of self sealing petrol tanks, armour plating, and the provision of the much needed beam gun. One other interesting development was the proposal first made in 1938 to develop the Wellington as a high

Vickers Wellington Mk III	
Engine	Hercules XI × 2
Max Speed	261 mph at 12,500 feet
Economical Cruise	180 mph at 15,000 feet
Service Ceiling	19,500 feet
Range	1200 miles with max load
Max Bomb Load	4500lbs (9 × 500lbs)
Crew	6
Number Built	11,461 (all marks)

Hardly recognisable as a Wellington, the Mk V was provided with a pressure cabin for the crew for high altitude bombing. It saw very little operational service as the perceived role was taken over by the Mosquito. RAFM

altitude bomber with a pressurised chamber for the crew and a special bomb sight for use at heights up to 40,000 feet. This was a most strange looking aircraft with an enormous bulbous nose and a tiny spherical cupola for the pilot to view the outside world, making take off and landing in this tailwheeled aircraft a potentially hazardous affair. Only two of the 64 built saw operational service.

At the beginning of 1942 the Wellington was by far the most numerous aircraft in Bomber Command, comprising well over half of the aircraft involved in the first 1,000 bomber raid on Cologne in May. The new heavy bombers assumed the main strategic role within Bomber Command in the following year, but the Wellington continued in use in a number of special duty roles until their last operational sortie towards the end of 1944.

Whilst the Geneva discussions had restricted specification B9/32 which produced the Hampden and the Wellington, no such limitation impeded the next bomber specification, B3/34, which sired the Whitley. Nevertheless, the result was disappointing, the Whitley in some respects proving less satisfactory than the Hampden and certainly less so than the Wellington. B3/34 was nominally drawn-up for a heavy bomber, but the resulting Whitley can only be described as a medium and was eventually officially categorised as such. The specification itself was modest: a maximum speed of 225 mph at 15,000 feet and the ability to carry a mixed bomb load of 2,500lbs over 1,250 miles. Four companies were asked to submit designs, but financial considerations precluded the Air Ministry from following its normal practice of ordering two competing prototypes. Thus in September 1934, Armstrong Whitworth was commissioned to produce two prototypes of an aircraft

originally identified as the A.W.38: it was an ugly, slab sided aeroplane as ponderous in performance as it was inelegant in appearance.

After the collapse of the Geneva Conference in 1934, tension began to rise rapidly in Europe and the Air Ministry obtained Government approval to order the A.W.38 straight from the drawing board. Although this had definite advantages in reducing the timescale in which an aircraft could enter squadron service – the Whitley in this way gaining an advantage over the Hampden and the Wellington which had been conceived two years earlier – it could also prolong the operational service life of an aircraft which was less than satisfactory in performance. This was to be the fate of the Whitley.

The basic problem of the Whitley from the outset was the provision of a suitable engine. Armstrong Siddeley Tiger IX radials were chosen for the prototype which made its first flight on the 17th March 1936 in remarkably quick time from the letting of the contract. Although the aircraft was relatively docile to fly, its performance was poor, achieving a maximum speed of only 192 mph at 7,000 feet and a ceiling of 19,000 feet which it took a painfully long time to reach. The second prototype equipped with higher rated Tiger engines was only marginally better.

The first production Whitleys performed even worse than the prototypes when they entered RAF service with No 10

The Whitley was well liked by its crews despite its inelegant appearance and ponderous performance. This Mk III was powered by the inadequate Armstrong Siddeley Tiger VIII engine.

IWM

Squadron at Dishforth, Yorkshire, in March 1937. The top speed had dropped to 184 mph at 15,000 feet and the range with the normal bomb load of 5,000lbs was less than 1,400 miles. In an attempt to salvage something from this debacle, the Whitley progressed quickly through various marks from I to IV, but it was not until a change was at last made to the Rolls Royce Merlin engine with the Mk IV that any worthwhile improvements resulted. The Company had maintained a long and close association with Armstrong Siddeley, but this was one link which should have been severed more quickly.

Retaining the Merlin engine and with better defensive armament, the Whitley V soon replaced the earlier marks in the operational squadrons. Nearly 1,500 Whitley Vs were ordered and production continued whilst the factories awaited jigs for the newer Halifaxes and Lancasters long after the aircraft had been withdrawn from front line service.

In operational service, the Whitleys were concentrated in No 4 Group. Its poor performance ensured that the squadrons were confined to the night bombing role for which the aircraft was designed and initially they concentrated on leaflet dropping until restrictions were lifted on bombing the German mainland. The aircraft played a full part in the night offensive during 1940/41, but it was not widely lamented when it was withdrawn from front line service as early as April 1942 although Operational Training Unit aircraft occasionally continued to make-up the numbers in the larger raids for a little longer.

Most of the light and medium bombers attracted a remarkable loyalty from the crews destined to fly and fight with them; but in truth, the Mosquito and the Wellington apart, they were a poor lot. Although all were of advanced design at the time they were conceived, they were overtaken by later developments, particularly in the design of the modern fighter. It was a considerable tragedy that so many young men were condemned to endure the first three years of the war in aircraft as inadequate for their role as the first crop of so called strategic bombers. The Air Ministry could not be held responsible for this unfortunate development; the war arrived at the least convenient time in the development of the bomber aircraft.

Armstrong Whitworth Whitley Mk V

Engine	Merlin X × 2
Max Speed	222 mph at 17,000 feet
Economical Cruise	165 mph at 15,000 feet
Service Ceiling	17,600 feet
Range	1370 miles with 5500lbs
Max Bomb Load	8000lbs (2 × 2000, 2 × 500 and 12 × 250lbs)
Crew	5
Number Built	1812 (all marks)

The Heavy Bombers – Halifax and Stirling

Almost as soon as specifications had been issued for the light and medium bombers between 1932 and 1934, their limitations were recognised by the Air Ministry who progressively moved towards the true heavy bomber for the counter offensive role. It was a route which the Germans did not follow, for apart from the ill fated Heinkell He 177, they never proceeded beyond the twin engine medium bomber designed primarily for army co-operation, although soon used in a strategic role. Events were to prove that the Air Ministry decision to move in this direction, allied to a similar progression by the US Army Air Corps, was the most decisive factor in the eventual outcome of the war in the air.

The key specification was B12/36 for the four engined heavy bomber, but issued in the same year was P13/36 for a medium tactical bomber and it is to the latter specification that Handley Page responded with the aircraft which eventually became the Halifax. The Company had already been working on a specification, B1/35, for a twin engine aircraft to replace the Whitley which was known to be obsolescent even before it entered mass production. However, the Handley Page variant did not look too promising either, engines of sufficient power and/or reliability were simply not available in mid 1936 to achieve the performance required. The issue of P13/36 re-opened the door for Handley Page, for by waiting for more powerful engines – the Rolls Royce Vulture was initially the favoured powerplant – the later specification for a much larger aircraft could be met. This aircraft was designated the H.P.56 and was intended for day and night use in a variety of roles from bomber to troop transport. But the Vulture, although potentially a very powerful engine, was of complex design and by mid 1937 thought was already being given by designer George Volkert to converting the H.P.56 into a four engined aircraft. There was, however, one more snag; the RAF's standard hangar could only accept an aircraft with a 100 feet wingspan, and thus the H.P.57 eventually emerged with a less than optimum 99 feet span. In line with Government policy at this time of ordering straight from the drawing board, an initial contract for 100 aircraft was placed at the beginning of 1938.

Two prototypes were built at the Company's Cricklewood factory and the first made its maiden flight in the hands of Major J Cordes on the 25th October 1939. After its somewhat convoluted gestation, this aircraft was powered by four Rolls Royce Merlin engines, equipped like the Hampden with slots (soon discarded) and now carried a crew of six. Boulton Paul

The Halifax was almost as successful as the more celebrated Lancaster. This Mk I belongs to No 10 Squadron. IWM

turrets were selected for nose and tail positions fitted with Vickers or Browning 0.3in guns; a dorsal turret was soon fitted in production aircraft. The undercarriage and hydraulic systems were a continual source of problems on the Halifax from its very first flight and from time to time throughout its operational life. Nevertheless, the first squadron, No 35, formed at Boscombe Down towards the end of 1940 and the first operational mission was launched from Linton-on-Ouse on the 10th March 1941.

A multitude of modifications followed with bewildering frequency which it would be tiresome to detail, but perhaps the most significant was the change of engine from the Merlin to the Bristol Hercules with the Halifax Mk III. The aircraft operated in a wide range of roles including strategic night bomber, special duties operations and pathfinding. Although in all over 6,000 Halifaxes were built, the aircraft was always marginally less capable than the Lancaster. It was, however, significantly better in most respects than the other heavy bomber developed at the same time, the Stirling.

Handley Page Halifax Mk III	
Engine	Hercules XVI × 4
Max Speed	281 mph at 13,500 feet
Economical Cruise	225 mph at 20,000 feet
Service Ceiling	20,000 feet
Range	2005 miles with 6250lbs
Max Bomb Load	13,000lbs (2 × 2000, 6 × 1000 and 6 × 500lbs)
Crew	7
Number Built	6179

The Stirling was the first of the heavy bombers to enter service in 1940. This Mk I belongs to No 7 Squadron who mounted the first operational mission in February 1941. IWM

The Short Stirling was conceived from the outset as a four engined aircraft deriving from B12/36. It was the first of the true heavies to fly and enter into operational service, and to a large extent suffered from this distinction. B12/36 required an aircraft which had a maximum range of 3,000 miles and a bomb load capacity of a massive 14,000lbs, to be achieved it was thought at this time with some means of catapult assisted take-off. A crew of six was specified with all crew members except the first pilot having subsidiary roles; for example, the second pilot did the navigation and one air gunner acted as flight engineer. The specification was circulated to 19 companies of which five submitted proposals: only Short Brothers and Vickers Armstrong were asked to produce prototypes of which the former alone saw the light of day.

Short's designer Arthur Gouge soon decided upon the unusual and innovatory step of constructing a half size prototype for aerodynamic testing which John Lankester Parker first flew in September 1938 from the Company's Rochester factory. This led directly to one of the Stirling's most noticeable characteristics, the stalky undercarriage, which was fitted as an expedient to, in effect, increase the wing incidence for take off and landing. This miniature Stirling continued flying for test and development purposes until it eventually crashed in 1944.

Development meanwhile continued on the full size model fitted with Bristol Hercules engines leading to its first flight on the 14th May 1939. The maiden flight went well until the stalky undercarriage collapsed on landing causing the aircraft to be written-off. This inevitably led to redesign and delay and the second prototype did not fly until December. Production had already commenced to an initial order of 100 in 1937 and the first aircraft was ready for delivery by May 1940. The limitations which were to cloud the Stirling's reputation were already apparent, for like many developments at this time, the weight of the aircraft had moved decisively ahead of the available power output. The performance was most disappointing in almost every respect; take-off distance, the maximum and cruising speeds, rate of climb and operational ceiling were all deficient to a greater or lesser extent. The fact that the aircraft was pleasant to fly and quite manoeuvrable did not compensate for these overriding disadvantages. Another major limitation was that the aircraft, for structural reasons, was never able to carry anything larger than the 2,000lb bomb.

Nevertheless, the first squadron, No 7, formed at Leeming in August 1940 and made its operational debut on the 10th February 1941. It was hoped that the Stirling's heavier armament of eight 0.3in Browning machine guns might allow it to be operated in daylight, but experience soon dictated otherwise and the aircraft was normally restricted to night operations. As with most other bombers there were continual updates, particularly with the intention of improving engine performance and strengthening the defensive armament. The Stirling Mk III entered production at the end of 1942 with the Hercules VI engine, but the improvement in performance was only marginal and it was not long before the aircraft was relegated to subsidiary roles. The Stirling was used briefly by the Pathfinder Force and more successfully as a radar jammer with No 100 Group. It also performed extensively as a glider tug and transport. Nevertheless, the aircraft must be judged a failure overall; it was a little too far ahead of its time.

Short Stirling Mk III	
Engine	Hercules XVI × 4
Max Speed	270 mph at 14,500 feet
Economical Cruise	200 mph at 15,000 feet
Service Ceiling	17,000 feet
Range	2010 miles with 3575lbs
Max Bomb Load	14,000lbs (7 × 2000lbs)
Crew	7
Number Built	2437

Manchester and Lancaster

The Avro Manchester, like its 1918 predecessor of the same name which suffered from similar failings, would require only passing mention were it not for the fact that from it was derived the legendary Lancaster. The Manchester arose out of the same specification, P13/36, which ultimately gave rise to the Halifax, and like the other designs of this era, its wing span had to be restricted to 100 feet so that it would fit into a standard hangar. Furthermore, like the Stirling, it was intended to be launched by catapult at high operational weights. Avro responded to the specification with its Model 679 designed by Roy Chadwick and powered by two Rolls Royce Vultures, the engine which caused so many problems with the early development of the Halifax. Production contracts for 500 aircraft were signed by 1939, but 1,500 were planned to be in operation by 1942.

The Manchester made its maiden flight from Manchester

The first prototype of the Manchester, the undistinguished forbear of the Lancaster.   IWM

The Lancaster was undoubtedly the most successful of the heavy bombers and entered service in December 1941. This Mk I belongs to No 50 Squadron. RAFM

Ringway airfield in July 1939 and serious problems were soon apparent. The aircraft was underpowered from the outset, failing to meet the expected performance in speed or ceiling. Directional stability was also unsatisfactory leading initially to the installation of a central fin, soon replaced by two larger fins and rudders on an extended tailplane. Despite these severe difficulties, the operational version was soon flowing from the production line and No 207 Squadron formed at Waddington in November 1940. The aircraft's already chequered career persisted into Service life; the hydraulic system was unreliable as were the propellers, but most importantly of all, the Vulture engine was proving extremely temperamental. The aircraft was soon heartily distrusted by its crews and there were several accidents, particularly at night. These difficulties, however, did not halt the flow of aircraft from the production line and by early 1942 six squadrons had been re-equipped. Consideration was given to re-engining the Manchester with either Napier Sabre or Bristol Centaurus engines, but a much more promising line had already appeared, the provision of four Rolls Royce Merlins. The emergence of this aircraft, eventually known as the

Lancaster, led immediately to plans to withdraw the Manchester from operational service as soon as possible and by June 1942 it had been relegated to training units only. Even here it was barely tolerable because of its poor handling characteristics at heavy weights and on one engine.

Avro Manchester	
Engine	Vulture II × 2
Max Speed	273 mph at 17,000 feet
Economical Cruise	185 mph at 15,000 feet
Service Ceiling	19,200 feet
Range	1630 miles with 8000lbs
Max Bomb Load	10,350lbs
Crew	5
Number Built	199

The Lancaster Mk II powered by Hercules radial engines was significantly less successful than the far more numerous Merlin engined versions. IWM

The Lancaster was in an altogether different league to the Manchester; it soon became a firm favourite with the Bomber Command crews and was deservedly regarded as one of the outstanding aircraft of World War II. The twin engined Handley Page H.P.56 had set a precedent in 1937 with its conversion into the four engined Halifax, but it was not until much later that Roy Chadwick followed suit. Originally known as the Manchester Mk III, it was soon thought expedient to give it a new name as the reputation of the Manchester was already fading rapidly. There were several design changes, but the new aircraft incorporated the fuselage, tail unit and centre wing of its predecessor with new outer wing sections to carry the two additional engines. The prototype first flew from Woodford in the hands of Captain H.A. Brown on the 9th January 1941 and the early test flights confirmed that the aircraft promised a very good performance combined with docile handling characteristics. The early production aircraft had the same nose, ventral, dorsal and tail armament as the Manchester, incorporating altogether ten 0.3in machine guns. One major advantage that the Lancaster held over the Stirling which stemmed from its origin in the P13/36 specification was a very large bomb bay unimpeded by internal structural members, allowing the Lancaster to carry eventually the 22,000lb 'Grand Slam' bomb.

The Lancaster came into productive service remarkably quickly after the decision to opt for four engines which is a tribute to the basically sound design of the Manchester airframe. Furthermore, unlike its contemporaries, it was subjected to no major design modifications during its operational career which spanned the rest of the war. Not only was it pleasant to fly, it was also comparatively easy to maintain and repair, for each sub assembly could be transported in a standard RAF vehicle. It was, in summary, one of the few aeroplanes, like the Canberra and the Hunter of post war years, which looked and felt just right almost from the outset.

As a most welcome Christmas present, the first Lancasters for No 44 Squadron at Waddington arrived to replace their Hampdens on the 24th December 1941. There were some teething problems, two aircraft being lost as a result of structural design defects in the outer wing sections. The ventral turret was soon removed, which may have been regretted later when the Germans developed a technique of creeping-up unseen right under the belly of a bomber and using a specially designed gun which fired upwards at an angle of 45 degrees.

More powerful versions of the Merlin were fitted as they became available which allowed the aircraft to carry ever increasing loads over greater distances. Even from the outset the Lancaster had an overall superior performance to the Stirling and was marginally better in most respects than the Halifax. However, the success of the Merlin engine in a wide range of different aircraft types placed great demands on its production and it was soon decided to contract Armstrong Whitworth to build a Lancaster with the Bristol Hercules radial engine. This was not a very successful venture as the performance, particularly the service ceiling, was substantially inferior to the Merlin engined version. Only 300 Hercules Lancasters were actually built, but the standard Lancaster rolled-off the many production lines at an ever increasing rate reaching no less than 260 a month in 1944. As more and more aircraft entered operational service, many of its contemporaries were relegated to subsidiary tasks. This fate never befell the Lancaster which eventually equipped 57 front line squadrons and often made-up the full complement of the mass raids in the last 18 months of the war.

Later versions of the Lancaster, the Mk IV and V, were designated Lincolns, appropriately enough in view of the aircraft's close association with that county throughout its operational life, but they were too late to see operational service before the end of the war although continuing in use with the RAF until the mid 1950s. It is fitting that the only wartime heavy bomber still flying with the RAF's Battle of Britain Memorial Flight is a Lancaster, although this particular aircraft never saw operational service.

Avro Lancaster Mk III

Engine	Merlin 22/28/38 × 4
Max Speed	270 mph at 20,000 feet
Economical Cruise	216 mph at 20,000 feet
Service Ceiling	20,000 feet
Range	2250 miles with 10,000lbs
Max Bomb Load	14,000lbs (some aircraft modified to carry 22,000lbs 'Grand Slam')
Crew	7
Number Built	7194

The American Heavy Bombers – The B-17 Flying Fortress and The B-24 Liberator

It is one of those strange paradoxes which bestride military mythology that of the two American heavy bombers used in the European theatre, the B-17 Flying Fortress achieved an almost mystical and enduring reputation both inside the Air Force and with the general public whilst the much less highly regarded B-24 Liberator was in fact the more powerful and in some ways the more capable aircraft, and actually produced in far greater numbers. Nevertheless, the B-17 became symbolic of the 8th Air Force, the 'Mighty Eighth', and despite several serious setbacks throughout 1943, eventually emerged with the Lancaster in the last 18 months of the war to at least partially vindicate those pre-war prophets of the invincibility of the strategic bomber. In fact, the B-17, which was conceived in the early 1930s in an atmosphere of virulent feuding between the Army and the Navy as to the purpose of the Air Corps, had been the catalyst of much of the argument between the protagonists of the strategic and the tactical role for the bomber aircraft.

The forerunner of the B-17 was the Model 294, a development contract for which was placed with the Boeing Aircraft Company of Seattle under the design leadership of Edward Wells in 1934. This was followed in the same year by the Model 299, a synthesis of the 294 and an earlier civil transport aircraft, the Model 247. This aircraft was already christened the Flying Fortress when it made its first flight in July 1935 and at that time was the most advanced strategic bomber in the world. A low wing, sleek and elegant aircraft powered by four Pratt and Whitney Hornet radial engines, it quickly proved capable of meeting its demanding specification. But disaster soon followed, for in the hands of the Army Air Corps just three months later, the prototype was destroyed after taking-off with locked controls. Although the aircraft was blameless, its many opponents quickly seized the opportunity to enforce the abandonment of the production line and authority was given for only 13 development aircraft, now known as YIB-17s.

Entering service in 1937 with the 2nd Bombardment Group under the enterprising command of Lieutenant Colonel Bob Olds, a programme of record breaking and publicity seeking flights was immediately set in train to attract the attention of the public, the Army and most crucial of all the Senate. The legend of the Flying Fortress was born. Despite their undoubted success, it was actually the crisis of Munich which revived the fortunes of the strategic bomber and with it an order for another 39 B-17Bs. Even so, the prevarication led to the Army Air Corps having only 23 B-17s in its inventory when conflict finally broke-out in Europe.

The B-17 was always intended as a day bomber and its proven bombing accuracy made possible by the advanced Norden gyro-stabilised bomb sight attracted widespread interest. The American penchant for inspired publicity this time produced the 'pickle barrel' legend in which the B-17 was claimed to be able to place a bomb in a barrel from 30,000 feet. Alas, this was not to prove so simple in the more rigorous examination of a European winter. The aircraft first saw active service with the RAF when 20 B-17Cs were allocated under Lend Lease to No 90 Squadron at West Raynham in May 1941. The Army Air Corp's B-17s were first used operationally in the Pacific theatre where its defensive limitations were soon exposed by the Japanese Zero fighters, confirming the experience of the RAF over Germany. Extensive modifications followed, mostly concentrating on the aircraft's defensive capability, indeed all the subsequent major developments of the B-17 were concerned with its internal gun armament. The result was the B-17E which was the first aircraft to see service with the 8th Air Force in England.

The rear fuselage of the B-17E was extensively modified both to improve the flying characteristics and to incorporate two 0.5 in guns in a manually operated tail turret. A Bendix electrical turret was located immediately aft of the cockpit and all the guns were upgraded to 0.5in calibre. These changes gave the B-17 its familiar outline with a large tapering fin replacing the more flimsy if elegant design of its predecessors. The first major order for 512 B-17Es led to production being diversified to the Douglas and Vega companies in addition to Boeing and at last the aircraft began to emerge from the production line in substantial numbers, seven long years after it was first conceived.

Externally, the B-17F looked almost identical to the E model, but it incorporated a wide range of improvements, perhaps the best known of which was the extra fuel cells fitted in the wings known as 'Tokyo Tanks' for obvious reasons. The later model B-17s were also acquired by the RAF, but it never found favour in Bomber Command and most aircraft were used by Coastal Command where it was overshadowed by the very capable Liberator. Another interesting variation was the YB-40 variant which was designed as a flying gun-ship to escort the conventional bomber. Bristling with weapons, as many as 30 guns of various calibres were carried by some versions with a bomb bay devoted to carrying ammunition, the YB-40 was so heavy that it could not keep pace with the bomber version and the concept was soon abandoned.

The final version of the B-17 was the G model which entered service with 8th Air Force towards the end of 1943. The improvements again mainly related to the defensive armament, for by the Autumn of 1943 the Flying Fortress had by no means proved its ability to defend itself unescorted over Germany in daylight. The B-17G was also operated by Bomber Command for special operations and radio countermeasures, and although it was used in some of the mass night raids, it was usually employed as a decoy or for dropping 'Window'. Interestingly, captured versions of the B-17, known as the Dornier 200, were also used by the Luftwaffe for clandestine operations.

Boeing B-17F Flying Fortress

Engine	Cyclone R 1820-65 × 4
Max Speed	290 mph at 25,000 feet
Economical Cruise	195 mph at 20,000 feet
Service Ceiling	27,500 feet
Range	1550 miles with 8800lbs
Max Bomb Load	12,800lbs (8 × 1600lbs)
Crew	10
Number Built	12,677 (all marks)

Production of the B-17 began to run-down in 1944 as the B-29 Super Fortress came to the fore; but the latter, the most sophisticated of the piston engined bombers, never saw operational service in the European theatre and does not therefore form part of this story.

In comparison with the sleek Flying Fortress, the B-24 was an ungainly ugly duckling, but in contrast to the B-17 which was almost entirely used as a bomber, the B-24 was assuredly the most versatile of the heavy four engined aircraft developed during the war years. It served with distinction in the bomber, maritime reconnaissance and transport roles as well as in a host of less publicised duties. Winston Churchill's personal transport was a Liberator named 'Commando' which served him faithfully throughout the war. It was perhaps this very versatility which in the end resulted in this reliable workhorse being overshadowed by the more glamorous Flying Fortress.

The personal intervention of President Roosevelt following the Munich crisis in 1938 not only re-invigorated the B-17 programme, but it led to a request from the Army Air Corps for a bomber aircraft with a superior performance. The Consolidated Aircraft Company of San Diego had already carried-out some design studies for a heavy bomber aircraft and responded with the Model 32. A contract was let in March 1939 for a single prototype which had to be completed ready for flight testing within nine months, a remarkably short timescale for an aircraft which was a quantum leap forward in weight and performance. The design team led by I M Laddon concentrated

This B-17F belonged to the 25th Bombardment Group (Reconnaissance) based at Watton in Norfolk. WWE

The B-17G became the mainstay of the 8th Air Force during the last 18 months of the war.   IWM

on achieving the range of 3,000 miles required by the specification and hoped to achieve the performance by the use of the Davis high lift aerofoil. The wing was shoulder mounted providing a large uncluttered fuselage on a tricycle under-carriage which not only allowed a capacious bomb bay, but also led directly to the aircraft's appeal as a transport. However, the high aspect ratio wing and twin fin produced an aircraft that was not quite so stable or easy to fly in formation as the B-17 and led to its initial unpopularity with its crews.

The Company met the very tight schedule for the first flight in December 1939, but the aircrafts performance was at first disappointing, particularly in respect of maximum speed, although its long range and carrying capacity were a notable improvement over the B-17. The Air Corps had already ordered 43 aircraft, now officially designated the B-24, straight from the drawing board and the French Armee de l'Air another 120. The RAF soon followed suit with an order for 164. The aircraft destined for France were not ready when their war ended and

were diverted to Britain where the aircraft was given the name Liberator which was subsequently adopted by the Americans. The RAF first used the B-24 for transporting ferry crews to the USA, but it soon became a mainstay of Coastal Command. Although it saw early service as a bomber in the Middle East, it was not until the end of the War that the Liberator was used in a very limited way by Bomber Command.

In the USA the B-24 was also at first used in a variety of roles and it was not until the D model that a true bomber was finally derived. By now the Pratt and Whitney Twin Wasp radial engine had the benefit of a turbo-supercharger which pushed the maximum speed towards 300 mph and a variety of power operated turrets with 0.5in guns to replace the original meagre armament of hand held 0.3in calibre weapons. Once the decision was made to press ahead with a bomber variant, the expanded target was an almost unbelievable 2,000 heavy bombers per month of all types - the Ford Plant at Willow Run had a contract for no less than 350 B-24s a month. Like the B-17, later updates tended to concentrate on further improving the defensive armament.

The normal bomb load of the B-24D was about 5,000lbs

The B-24 had a very difficult introduction to bomber operations in Europe, but eventually proved its worth as a robust and capable heavy bomber. This is an early 'D' model.

IWM

which was similar to the later model B-17s, but it could carry this load farther than the Fortress and its optimum flight envelope was higher and faster than its counterpart. Formations composed of both types inevitably resulted in unsatisfactory operational compromises and they were normally employed separately after the B-24 eventually arrived in Europe. After a hesitant start when the aircraft was dogged by mechanical unreliability, the B-24 was never highly regarded in 8th Air Force even though it eventually provided eight groups of some 40 aircraft each. The aircraft really made its mark in the Pacific theatre, where its long range could best be exploited, and in support of the Allied Forces in North Africa and eventually in Italy.

Both the Flying Fortress and the Liberator eventually emerged amongst the foremost fighting machines of World War II although in North West Europe their reputation teetered in the balance for an agonisingly long time. In 1943, the 8th Air Force doggedly persisted in a policy of unescorted daylight bombing beyond the time when they might reasonably have admitted defeat. In the end, it was another great aircraft, the Mustang, which came to the rescue.

Consolidated B – 24D Liberator	
Engine	P and W R 1830-65 × 4
Max Speed	275 mph at 20,000 feet
Economical Cruise	200 mph at 20,000 feet
Service Ceiling	28,000 feet
Range	2040 miles with 8500lbs
Max Bomb Load	12,800lbs
Crew	10
Number Built	18,188 (all marks)

The American Medium Bombers – Mitchell, Boston, Marauder and Ventura

Although not used by 8th Air Force, the Mitchell was a very capable medium bomber in RAF service. This Mk II belongs to No 98 Squadron.   IWM

The Americans began to develop a family of light medium bombers in the late 1930s which were larger than the Blenheim, but rather smaller than the Wellington albeit of similar maximum weight. They all eventually served with the USAAF, all bar the Ventura with distinction, and were widely exported to other Allied nations including the RAF where they filled the niche vacated by the Blenheim, the limitations of which were exposed all too soon after the outbreak of war.

The Army Air Corps initiated a formal requirement for a twin engine medium bomber in 1938 which attracted wide interest amongst the aircraft manufacturers. North American Aviation, who had little experience in bomber production,

responded with a prototype designated the NA-40, a high wing monoplane with two underslung radial engines and a tricycle undercarriage, the latter a very sensible development which was becoming increasingly popular in the United States, but not adopted in Britain until much later. The NA-40 had a crew of three, pilot, navigator/bombardier and waist gunner, with fixed 0.3in guns in the wings as well as hand held guns in nose and rear fuselage. It was first flown in January 1939 and the early performance was most promising, but the second more powerful prototype was given to the Air Corps for evaluation who almost immediately lost it in a landing accident. Although this mishap did not cause the Army to lose interest, they requested major design changes. The required bomb load was doubled to 2,400lbs, the wing spar lowered to a mid position and the cockpit incorporated into the slab sided fuselage. Additional guns enhanced the defensive armament and the crew complement was increased to five. The new aircraft was ordered straight from the drawing board in September 1939 and by the following August was ready for flight testing. It was now formally designated the B-25 and soon named the Mitchell in honour of the pioneering bomber strategist, Brigadier General Billy Mitchell.

The B-25 quickly made a dramatic entrance on the world stage with the legendary raid led by Lieutenant Colonel James H Doolittle on Tokyo in April 1942 when 16 aircraft were launched from the aircraft carrier Hornet 800 miles from the Japanese coast. Tokyo and other Japanese cities were bombed, but none of the aircraft made their intended landfall in China. The physical effect of the bombing was minimal, but the psychological impact on both Japan and America was spectacular. Although the Mitchell was not used by the 8th Air Force, many were delivered to the RAF to replace the Blenheim in No 2 Group. The 23 Mk 1s delivered early in 1942 were used only for training, but the Mk II which arrived in October 1942 for No 98 Squadron was the first of 500 with an increased performance and payload as well as additional defensive

armament. The Mitchell flew its first operational mission in January 1943 against an oil refinery in Belgium. The Mitchell III, of which the RAF received 314, had a larger bomb carrying capacity, but the main improvement was in its defensive armament which now consisted of no less than 13 0.5in machine guns with provision for another five in the ground attack version. The Mitchell featured strongly in the build-up to the invasion of Europe and continued in mainstream service to the end of the war. By then it had built-up an impressive reputation and was much loved and respected by its crews for its reliability, strength and destructive power.

North American Aviation B – 25 Mitchell Mk III	
Engine	Cyclone R 2600-13 × 2
Max Speed	272 mph at 15,000 feet
Economical Cruise	180 mph at 10,000 feet
Service Ceiling	23,000 feet
Range	925 miles with max load
Max Bomb Load	3200lbs
Crew	6
Number Built	9816 (all marks)

The Boston was only briefly employed by 8th Air Force in England in 1942. This Mk III was used by the 15th Bombardment Squadron.

WWE

One of the most interesting and versatile aircraft developed by the Americans in the pre-war years was the Douglas DB-7, known eventually in the RAF as the Boston and in the USAAF as the Havoc. Although achieving few spectacular feats, it made a solid contribution to the Allied bomber war in various guises and many theatres. Unlike the B-25, the DB-7 was conceived ahead of any formal specification from the Army Air Corps and its genesis owed much to the perceived lessons of the Spanish Civil War. The DB-7B first flew at the end of 1938 and impressed immediately with its outstanding performance. A shoulder wing, single fin, twin engined aircraft with a crew of three, a top speed of over 300 mph and possessing excellent manoeuvrability combined with docile handling, it was regarded from the beginning as a 'pilot's aeroplane'. The French Armee de l'Air was the first to show contractual interest, ordering 100 aircraft in February 1939, rising eventually to nearly 1,000. The French DB-7Bs which were actually delivered saw brief action on the Western Front in May 1940 before France was overwhelmed, but a few in North Africa which initially fell into Vichy hands survived to participate in the bombing of South West France in 1944.

Before the capitulation of France in June 1940, many of the DB-7Bs on order, including some ordered by Belgium, were hurriedly transferred to the RAF where they were designated Boston Mk 1s. The RAF was initially totally bemused by this strange aircraft they had acquired in which the instruments were calibrated in metrical units and the throttles operated in the reverse sense - front to back to increase power. The first batch of 20 was used for training and of later arrivals about 100 were converted to night fighters and night intruders and re-designated Havocs. The Boston Mk III was the first variant to be used in its true role as a low level day bomber and began to replace the Blenheim towards the end of 1941 with the re-equipping of No 88 Squadron. This version could carry 2,000lbs of bombs over a thousand miles and was armed with seven 0.3in machine guns in various locations. It was in this aircraft that 'official' American aircrew first saw active service in Europe with No 226 Squadron. The Boston was now gaining a sound reputation as a durable, reliable workhorse that could fill many roles from conventional bomber to low level strafing, reconnaissance and torpedo bombing. If ever an airframe was needed to evaluate some obscure or eccentric new device, for example an aerial mine or a caterpillar track undercarriage, it was the Boston which more often than not was the vehicle used. In more familiar roles, the

The Boston Mk III was a most versatile bomber in RAF service for both low and medium level operations. This aircraft belongs to No 107 Squadron. RAFM

Mk IV and V followed in 1944 and the Boston made a major contribution during the lead-in to Operation 'Overlord', the invasion of Europe. Although the type was never used by the 8th Air Force from Britain after October 1942, the 9th used the A-20 (Havoc) in raids on mainland Europe from their bases in North Africa and the aircraft was very extensively used by the Russians.

The B-26 Marauder had a somewhat chequered career with 8th Air Force and was also used by the RAF. WWE

Douglas Boston Mk III	
Engine	Cyclone A5B × 2
Max Speed	304 mph at 13,000 feet
Economical Cruise	200 mph at 15,000 feet
Service Ceiling	24,250 feet
Range	1020 miles with max load
Max Bomb Load	2000lbs
Crew	4
Number Built	7385 (all marks)

Looking like a larger, sleeker brother of the Boston, the Martin B-26 Marauder had few of the same docile flying characteristics. It was conceived in January 1939 from a specification for a high performance, heavily armed medium bomber from which the Marauder was selected by competition and ordered immediately from the drawing board. Its design characteristics necessitated a high wing loading which resulted in very fast take-off and landing speeds, and numerous training accidents twice led to a review of the future of this potentially potent addition to the Army Air Corps. The normal bomb load of the earlier marks was 2,000lbs which was progressively increased to over 5,000lbs, and the American predilection for overcoming losses in combat by fitting ever more guns soon took the edge off its high performance. The Marauder was the first American bomber to be fitted with a power operated turret in the dorsal position and later versions had as many as 12 machine guns, equivalent in defensive power to the B-17 heavy bomber. Despite many misgivings, the USAAF retained its faith in the Marauder and after service in the Pacific and North Africa, the first Marauders arrived to join 8th Air Force in March 1943. The

somewhat apprehensive Command staff initially intended to use the aircraft only for low level bombing, but a disastrous raid on Ijmuiden on the Dutch coast on the 17th May was a grave blow to the Marauders debut in England. Low level operations abandoned, the by now 250 strong Marauder groups turned to medium level operations, heavily escorted by Spitfires. Despite its heavy armament, the Marauder was hard pressed to defend itself against enemy fighters if caught unprotected and also suffered heavily from flak when operating at around 12,000 feet. Proposals to integrate the Marauder into heavy aircraft formations came to nought and the aircraft was eventually transferred to 8th Air Support Command for interdiction and strafing missions to which it was more suited. All were transferred to 9th Air Force in November 1943. The RAF also took on board, one feels reluctantly, five squadrons of Marauders and they too were used in the European theatre on army support missions. Despite the misgivings of the crews who nicknamed the aircraft the 'Baltimore Whore', its final record was not wholly unsatisfactory. It eventually had the lowest loss rate of all the American medium bombers despite a less than

The Ventura was too cumbersome for low level missions and was increasingly employed on 'Circus' operations. This is a Mk I of No 21 Squadron. RAFM

auspicious beginning, but it was never viewed with the same affection by either its crews or the operating commands as its two revered cousins, the Mitchell and the Boston/Havoc.

The final, and unequivocally the least successful, of the quartet of American medium bombers was the Lockheed Ventura. It had sound antecedents as a derivative of the Hudson maritime patrol aircraft which itself evolved out of the successful Lockheed 14 civil airliner. The Ventura, based on the larger Lockheed 18, was instigated at the request of the British Purchasing Commission in 1940 and first flew on the 31st July 1941. It was quite well armed with nose, ventral and dorsal turrets, but this could not compensate for its slow and cumbersome performance at low level. Although 675 were ordered initially, delivery was stopped after about 300 had been accepted by the RAF. The balance of the aircraft was inherited by the USAAF who used it mainly as a trainer.

Martin B – 26 Marauder Mk II

Engine	P and W R 2800-43 × 2
Max Speed	305 mph at 15,000 feet
Economical Cruise	175 mph at 10,000 feet
Service Ceiling	28,000 feet
Range	900 miles with max load
Max Bomb Load	4000lbs (2 × 2000lbs)
Crew	7
Number Built	5157

Lockheed Ventura Mk I

Engine	Double Wasp SIA4-G × 2
Max Speed	274 mph at 14,000 feet
Economical Cruise	175 mph at 16,000 feet
Service Ceiling	25,000 feet
Range	925 miles with max load
Max Bomb Load	2500lbs
Crew	4
Number Built	About 300 for the RAF

CHAPTER THREE

The Men and the Infrastructure

The Organisation

From 1923 onwards the whole of the Metropolitan Air Force, the home based element of the RAF, had been combined, despite its concentration upon an offensive strategy, under the inaptly named Commander-in-Chief of the Air Defence of Great Britain. But as the expansion programme gathered pace, it was decided to split the constituent elements – fighter, bomber and maritime – and in July 1936 Bomber Command was formed, initially at Uxbridge, but scheduled soon to move to its new headquarters at High Wycombe in Buckinghamshire. Although on balance a sound decision at the time, the division later brought its own problems for the co-ordination of the fighters and bombers as well as leaving air support of the army and maritime reconnaissance as sadly neglected elements of air power.

The organisation of Bomber Command remained generally consistent throughout the war. Its operational formations were divided into groups with their headquarters, some located in comfortable country houses such as Bawtry Hall near Doncaster, in close proximity to the stations which they controlled. The groups were usually, but not exclusively, responsible for one type of aircraft; thus in September 1939, No 3 Group had under its control all the operational Wellington Squadrons, No 4 Group the Whitleys and No 5 Group the Hampdens. By 1943 they had been joined by Nos 1 and 6 Groups, which was formed of Royal Canadian Air Force squadrons operating a mix of Halifaxes and Wellingtons, and No 8 Group which had been introduced to provide a pathfinder force with aircraft and crews seconded from the other groups. Also by this time there were three groups specifically responsible for training, Nos 91, 92 and 93. At the end of the war, Nos 1, 3 and 5 Groups operated only Lancasters, No 4 Group Halifaxes and No 6 Group an almost equal mix of Lancasters and Halifaxes. No 8 Group had by then developed well beyond its initial pathfinding duties with 11 Mosquito squadrons, most of which were employed on independent bomber operations.

The operational bomber stations, somewhat confusingly commanded by a group captain (a group was usually commanded by an air vice marshal), contained one or two squadrons depending upon their size. In 1943 a squadron was normally established for 16 aircraft with two reserves. In practice, of course, the number actually on unit charge varied widely depending on losses and the availability of replacements. By 1945 most bomber squadrons had grown to an establishment of 20 aircraft and in many cases to 30. A squadron was commanded by a wing commander with at least two squadron leader flight commanders. The number of operational crews on each squadron varied widely, again depending on losses and the flow through the training organisation.

The organisation of the American air forces based in Europe was rather more complex, conditioned as it was by the formalisation of its gradual separation from the Army. The advocates of an independent air force in the United States, enmeshed in the isolationist policy of the Monroe Doctrine, had an even stonier path to tread than in Great Britain. A measure of independence was gained in 1926 by the formation of the Army Air Corps with representation on the General Staff, and further progress came in 1931 when, as a result of somewhat devious collaboration with the Navy, a requirement was developed for an off-shore patrol aircraft which opened the door to the eventual acquisition of a long range strategic bomber. A more significant step in 1941 was the introduction of the US Army Air Force (USAAF) which brought all bomber and fighter aircraft into one command structure, an arrangement which facilitated co-ordination between the two elements which was so often missing from RAF operations in which the fighter and bomber forces were the responsibility of two separate commands, often with a rather different view of their strategic objectives.

Tentative discussions regarding the possibility of basing American aircraft in the UK occurred even before the Japanese onslaught on Pearl Harbour in December 1941 and the first planning staffs of the USAAF arrived in England on the 20th February 1942. Led by Brigadier General Ira C Eaker, they soon moved into their own headquarters at Wycombe Abbey, previously a girls school and conveniently close to the Bomber Command Headquarters at High Wycombe. The organisation was originally known simply as the Army Air Force in Great Britain, but it acquired the identity of the 8th Air Force in April when that formations projected role in North Africa was cancelled.

The planned strength of the 8th Air Force was originally 60 combat groups totalling 3,500 aircraft of which more than half were to comprise heavy, medium or light bombers. No less than 75 airfields concentrated in eastern England were designated for American use with training, logistics and maintenance bases in the north west and in Northern Ireland. The first combat aircraft arrived on the 1st July when a B-17 of the 97th Bombardment Group landed at Prestwick in Scotland, and the first wave of 180 aircraft were all in England four weeks later. But already 11 aircraft had been lost in accidents, a grim warning of the far more difficult operating conditions to be experienced in north western Europe than that to which most of the crews had been

now for all practical purposes an independent service and Spaatz reported directly to General Arnold in the Pentagon in Washington. There were two subordinate formations under the Commander 8th Air Force – VIII Fighter Command under Brigadier General Frank O'D Hunter at Bushey Hall (no connection with Bushey Park) and VIII Bomber Command under Brigadier General Eaker which remained at Wycombe Abbey. The appellation of Bomber and Fighter Commands was not regularly used, the unit identity and loyalty always being directed towards the 8th Air Force with its winged figure eight badge. But it was actually the Commands which planned, directed and controlled the individual operations, and VIII

The first B-17E of the 97th Bombardment Group arrived at RAF Polebrook in July 1942 to form the vanguard of the 8th Air Force in England.   IWM

accustomed in the more benign climate of the southern states of America.

The 8th Air Force was formally inaugurated on the 18th June 1942 under Major General Carl Spaatz who set up his headquarters at Bushey Park in Teddington to the west of London. Although still nominally part of the Army – it did not in fact achieve formal independence until 1947 – the USAAF was

Bomber Command headquarters may be regarded as the American equivalent of the RAF's Bomber Command headquarters at High Wycombe rather than as a group.

The USAAF organisation was rather different to that of the RAF which descended from High Wycombe through group headquarters and stations to the individual squadrons. Subordinate to VIII Bomber Command were bombardment wings which, very broadly, equated to a group headquarters. There were originally four such wings, the 1st and 4th Bombardment Wings operated the B-17 Flying Fortress, the 2nd was equipped with the B-24 Liberator and the 3rd with the

B-26 Marauder. The latter was transferred in August 1943 to the 9th Air Force in North Africa and the Liberator Wing, which suffered many teething problems, was also detached to Africa in support of Operation 'Torch'. Within each wing were a number of bombardment groups, the basic combat unit, each of which was based on a single airfield, but which in organisational terms equated rather more closely to a large squadron than a RAF station. There could be any number of groups within a wing; for example in August 1943 the 1st Bombardment Wing had nine groups of B-17s, the 4th six and the 2nd only two groups of B-24s. The group was broken down into three or sometimes four squadrons which had far less autonomy than a RAF squadron, perhaps more nearly equivalent to a flight. To confuse the terminology yet further, the wings were redesignated as bombardment divisions in September 1943. The Americans were never as fastidious in their rank structure as the RAF, the Command could be the fief of either a major general or a brigadier whilst a wing and its successor a division was the responsibility variously of a major general down to a 'bird' colonel, the equivalent of a group captain. A group was nominally a colonel command, but it was by no means unusual for the post to be filled by a lieutenant colonel.

To an even greater extent than in the RAF, there was very little real experience in the ten man B-17 crews. As we have already noted the USAAF had only 23 B-17s in its inventory at the outbreak of war and thus a massive flying training programme had to be introduced within a very short period with no clearcut indication of the kind of operating environment in which the bombers might be employed. Each bombardment group was activated in the United States and the crews worked-up in the ideal flying conditions of the deep south, by no means the ideal preparation for crews who would soon be operating in the cloud, mist and rain of a European winter. When considered ready, the group support equipment was shipped to Britain whilst the crews ferried their aircraft via Labrador or Newfoundland to Scotland. After arrival in Britain, there was still a considerable amount of local indoctrination and more practice in formation flying before a group could be considered combat ready. New crews were transitioned through a Combat Crew Replacement and Training Centre, the first of which was quickly set-up at Bovingdon in Hertfordshire.

The pilots of VIII Fighter Command soon adopted the well tried methods and practices of the RAF and the fighter squadrons were integrated into RAF fighter wings until they found their feet. There was no such easy lead-in for the bomber crews, for their daylight precision bombing in close formation was a totally different concept to that which had been adopted in the RAF by the middle of 1942. It was not, therefore, surprising that a long and protracted learning curve was necessary before the VIII Bomber Command groups were ready to join Bomber Command in the assault upon the heartland of Germany in the Spring of 1943.

The Leaders

Top Left
Marshal of the RAF Sir Charles Portal (later Viscount Portal of Hungerford). A bomber squadron commander in the First World War, Portal was a protégé of Trenchard and rose rapidly through the ranks between the wars. He was appointed C-in-C Bomber Command in April 1940 and moved on to become Chief of the Air Staff in October where he remained for the rest of the war. His resilience, patience and clear thinking sustained him through many difficult encounters with Winston Churchill and he became an outstanding war leader. IWM

Below left
Air Chief Marshal Sir Edgar Ludlow-Hewitt. An outstanding fighter pilot in the First World War which he ended as a Brigadier, he was regarded by Trenchard as having one of the best intellects of the newly formed RAF. Appointed as C-in-C Bomber Command in September 1937, he quickly recognised the limitations of his force. But he was regarded as too negative, even defeatist, and lost the confidence of his masters in Whitehall. He became Inspector General of the RAF in 1941 where he served very successfully until the end of the war. IWM

Top right
Air Chief Marshal Sir Richard Peirse. Achieving his pilot's certificate in 1913, he served in the RFC and RNAS during the First World War. He rose rapidly through the ranks between the wars and was AOC in Palestine and Transjordan in 1933-36. Deputy Chief of the Air Staff at the outbreak of war, he was appointed C-in-C Bomber Command in October 1940. It was the period when the inadequate preparation for war was coming home to roost and by the end of 1941 Bomber Command was at its lowest ebb. He gave way to Sir Arthur Harris in February 1942 after an unhappy tenure and spent the rest of the war in various posts in the Far East. IWM

Below right
Air Chief Marshal (later M.R.A.F.) Sir Arthur Harris. Spent his formative years as a farmer in Rhodesia before joining the RFC in 1915. A night fighter specialist, he commanded a bomber squadron between the wars. AOC No 5 Group (Hampdens) soon after the outbreak of war, he became C-in-C Bomber Command in February 1942. An inspirational leader, he generated a new sense of confidence in his crews when the Command was facing increasing opposition in both political and military circles. He was gravely disappointed by the lack of recognition given to Bomber Command after the war and retired to South Africa. IWM

<table>
<tr><td>

The Leaders

Top left
General Henry Arnold. Entering West Point in 1903, he became an infantry officer, but soon volunteered for flying training with the Wright Brothers in Dayton, Ohio, becoming one of America's earliest aviators. On the staff in Washington during the First World War, he had a varied career subsequently, but this did not prevent him becoming Chief of the Air Corps in September 1938 when the incumbent was killed in an air crash. A strong advocate of strategic bombing, Arnold had to withstand much infighting within the Pentagon in developing an independent air arm. He succeeded in building the largest air force in the world which deservedly achieved its independence in 1947. IWM

Top right
Major General Ira Eaker. Joined the Army in 1917 as an infantry officer, but became a pilot a year later. He established a reputation as a record breaking aviator and author between the wars as well as progressing steadily through the ranks. He led the mission which was the precursor of the USAAF in England and was the commander of VIII Bomber Command before taking over the 8th Air Force in December 1942. He led the 8th through its most difficult formative years, strongly resisting attempts to change it into a night force, and suffering frequent dilutions of experience as units were transferred elsewhere. He was himself moved, unwillingly, to the Mediterranean theatre in January 1944. IWM

Below
Generals Spaatz and Doolittle
Left: General Carl Spaatz. Graduated from West Point into the infantry in 1914, but soon became a pilot and served in the Expeditionary Force to France towards the end of the First World War. He was a strong supporter of General Billy Mitchell, as a result of which he spent 15 years as a major. Promotion thereafter was rapid and he was posted as the first commander of the 8th Air Force in May 1942. In November he was transferred to North Africa for Operation 'Torch' and remained there until 1944. He returned to the UK in January 1944 to command the US Strategic Air Forces in Europe. A percipient airman, he did not let dogma restrain the use of air power.

Right: General James Doolittle. A pioneer of aviation, Doolittle joined the US Army in the First World War but did not see active service. Between the wars he established an international reputation as a record breaking aviator including winning the Schneider Cup in 1925. He left the Service in 1929 and joined Shell Oil, but remained closely immersed in the development of aviation. He rejoined the USAAF in 1940 and led the famous B-25 raid on Tokyo in April 1942. Promotion was rapid and by 1942 he commanded 12th Air Force in North Africa. When Spaatz moved to England at the end of 1943, Doolittle followed him to take command of 8th Air Force where he remained to the end of the war in Europe. IWM

</td></tr>
</table>

The Men and Women

At the start of the rearmament process in 1934, the RAF consisted of just 31,000 men of whom only some 2,400 were aircrew, mostly pilots. At the end of the war the number of men and women had grown to 1,100,000 with another 75,000 men from the Dominions. Many had died, over 55,000 in Bomber Command alone, and many more saw the end of the conflict from behind the wire of a prisoner of war camp. This massive increase in manpower placed a great strain on the infrastructure of the Service and its training resources and almost half the war had been fought before a reasonable stability was achieved.

That the RAF started with a firm foundation upon which to build in the mid 1930s was almost entirely due to one man, Marshal of the RAF Lord Trenchard. In the aftermath of the First World War, Trenchard did not fill the shop window of the new Service with flashy aeroplanes, perhaps the most obvious response to the ill concealed opposition and often derision of politicians, soldiers and sailors, even of the King (George V) who dismissed aircraft as 'noisy, smelly contrivances' and would never travel anywhere by air. Instead he invested in men, and with four vital decisions fashioned the bedrock on which the RAF was able to develop when the years of conflict approached. The first was the introduction of a cadet college at Cranwell in Lincolnshire in 1920 for the training of officers. From the outset the RAF, unlike the other two Services, generally recruited its officers from the middle classes, men often more amenable to professional and technical training and more ready to rub shoulders with its other vital component – the technical tradesmen. With even greater perception, Trenchard did not lavish the major portion of the meagre funds for building voted by Parliament on Cranwell, but on the creation of a technical training centre at Halton in Buckinghamshire which was not complete until 1926. Here he introduced boy apprentices between the ages of 15 and 18, 'brats' as they have long called themselves with immense pride, who were trained in the complexities of engines, airframes and armament, forming the core of the Senior Non Commissioned Officers in the RAF of the war years. An electrical and wireless school was also established at Flowerdown. Several of the best apprentices were allowed to transfer to Cranwell and many reached the highest levels of the Service. The third pillar of the new Service was the setting-up of the RAF Staff College. Housed in wartime brick buildings on a bleak airfield at Andover, it had little of the prestige or portentous splendour of its long-standing army and naval equivalents at Camberley and Greenwich. But its aims were similar; to enable the middle ranking officer to enhance his knowledge of his profession and above all to think logically and innovatively – in Trenchard's message to the opening ceremony on the 3rd April 1922, it was 'the cradle as I may call it of our brain'. The first class list of 20 contained names which were to bear the burden of leadership in the conflict to come including Portal, Sholto Douglas, Peirse, Baldwin and Park. Of these three great institutions, Cranwell, Halton and Andover, only the last has now disappeared to be replaced by the RAF's present Staff College at Bracknell. The final plank of Trenchard's Air

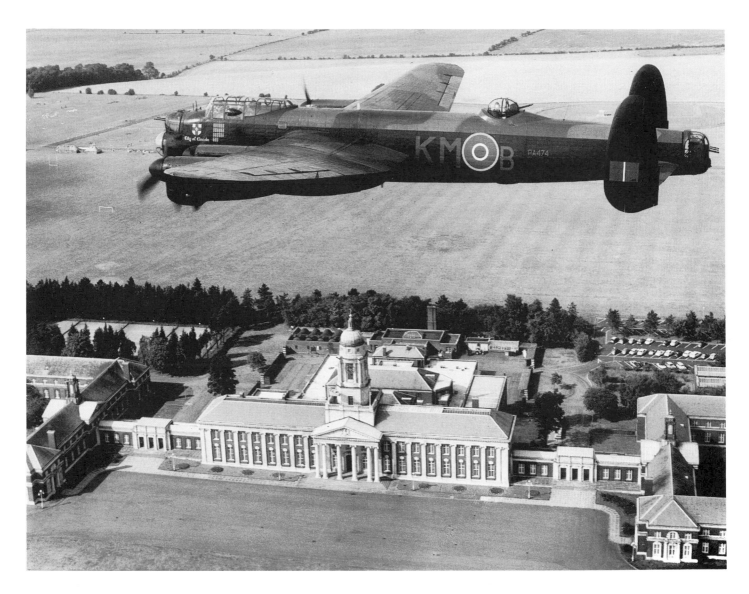

Although founded by Trenchard in 1920, the fine buildings of the RAF College at Cranwell were not completed until 1933. The College is overflown by the RAF's preserved Lancaster.

IWM

Force was the short service officer. Flying is a young man's profession and the RAF needed pilots, observers and engineers who would serve and leave before their expectations became frustrated by the tyranny of seniority and slow promotion in a peacetime service. Although often criticized in the early years as a two tier structure, the system served the RAF well, enabling the Service as a whole to retain the enthusiasm of youth whilst sustaining and nurturing a small core of experience and excellence.

This then was the shape of the RAF as the clouds darkened over Europe. It was quite sufficient for a peacetime air force, less than adequate for the expansion which slowly gathered pace in the late 1930s and became a flood in the 40s. The Auxiliary Air Force, a blue uniformed equivalent of the Territorial Army, already existed with its 'weekend gentlemen flyers' who were to play such a vital role in the Battle of Britain, but a more substantial development was the creation in 1936 of the Royal Air Force Volunteer Reserve (RAFVR). Air Commodore Arthur Tedder (then Director of Training) called it a Citizens Air Force to complement the core of regular servicemen, but

untrammelled by 'grading according to social class'. Whether a recruit was to serve as officer or airman would only be decided later when leadership qualities had been demonstrated. The scheme was more successful than expected with the initial aim of training 800 pilots a year far exceeded: by the outbreak of war the RAFVR contained well over 6,000 pilots and nearly 4,000 rear crew members. These men, from all professions and walks of life, formed the core of the officer and particularly the SNCO aircrew who were ready for the aircraft hesitantly appearing off the production lines in 1940. Airmen, 'erks' as they were affectionately dubbed, also volunteered to maintain the aircraft and their ever more sophisticated systems. Many of them came from related backgrounds, small scale engineering, the motor industry and the armament factories, often to be replaced at their work benches by their sisters or girlfriends as they were gathered-in to the regular Service. Women too increasingly played their part with the creation of the Women's Auxiliary Air Force in June 1939 with Queen Elizabeth as Commandant-in-Chief to provide encouragement and respectability. Numbering some 8,000 at the beginning of the war in a restricted number of trades, this figure had grown to over 180,000 by 1943 embracing a wide range of employments from manning operations rooms, station headquarters and signals offices to the repair and maintenance of aircraft and the preparation of weapons. Their contribution was of inestimable value and perhaps achieved far more in the struggle for equality and recognition for women than Mrs Pankhurst ever managed by chaining herself to the railings of Parliament before the earlier conflict.

One final vital source of manpower for the RAF must be mentioned, the contribution of the Dominions, the Colonies and other friendly countries. In addition to the four million men and women from the Empire who enlisted in the services of their own nation in support of the Allied cause, thousands more joined the RAF, some before the war started. In 1945, 30,000 men from the Dominions were serving in Bomber Command alone; one whole group, No 6, was Canadian and other Dominion squadrons were widely integrated into all roles. There were also men of other nations; Poles, Czechoslovaks, French, Norwegians and many others; some Americans who joined the RAF before their country entered the war elected to stay in the light blue. Of all the commands, Bomber Command grew most quickly as the war gathered pace. At the outbreak of hostilities it accounted for about ten per cent of the RAF's manpower resources, little more than 20,000 personnel of which about one tenth were officers. By May 1945, this number had grown to 219,000, one fifth of the RAF's total complement. There were a few all officer crews, many more composed of all SNCOs, but the majority were mixed. The relationship between the two, all of whom were volunteers, was remarkably casual and friendly; rank did not feature strongly in a bomber crew over Germany.

Once training was complete, a bomber crews standard tour of operations was 30 'trips' and there were precise rules as to what constituted an operational sortie. The greatest risk of not returning, as might be expected, occurred in the first few sorties followed, rather more surprisingly, by the last trip or two of an operational tour. The reasons varied, in some cases 'pressonitis' to get the ordeal over, in a few over confidence, perhaps more often excessive caution – it seemed careless to 'blow-it' at the final hurdle. An operational tour in the early years might take six months or longer because of the many days when weather interfered with flying, but towards the end of the war an operational tour could be completed in three months or less. A welcome interlude in a staff or instructional post was often followed by a second or even third tour of operations. Pathfinder crews, at the outset all of whom had already served on a conventional bombing squadron, were required to complete a double length tour to gain maximum benefit from their experience.

Perhaps the most remarkable aspect in retrospect was the

Flt Lt T. Overend – Observer

Morale on my Squadron was very high. We had a lot of confidence in the Lancaster, in the other crew members and in our training. My pilot was a flight commander, something of a martinet and a training fanatic, but we grew to have a tremendous respect for his ability and an almost blind confidence that we were somehow immune from being shot down ourselves even though we collected our share of flak. We used to complain that our captain, as a flight commander's prerogative, only chose to fly on the difficult missions – not for us the French ports, always the Ruhr, Hamburg, Berlin, but I suppose that it boosted our confidence and spirits at the time. It all sounds irrational looking back, but we certainly believed it at the time. I was a lot happier flying with my captain on an operational mission than I was later flying with some of the young pilots on the Operational Training Unit. There were times when I felt frightened, but I think we were often more afraid of showing fear than of fear itself. There was always a feeling almost of detachment when friends were killed – I feel sadder now than I did then. It was an exhilarating period.

---

incredibly high state of morale which sustained the Bomber Command crews throughout even the darkest days before 1943. Leadership, peer pressure, pride and sound training all played their part, but perhaps the greatest factor binding morale was crew empathy; so close was the co-operation between crew members that they lived, fought and often died for each other. The comparatively comfortable life style – a good bed, regular food and convivial relaxation – was a mixed blessing, there was always another mission to be contemplated on the morrow. Perhaps the most frustrating and distracting element of a bomber crew's life was the cancelled operation; sometimes crews would plan and brief a sortie day after day only to find that the fickle weather led to yet another abort, often at the last minute. It was certainly not the absence of fear which boosted morale, very few aircrew were lucky enough to avoid the cold grip of terror both before and often during the mission; comparatively few displayed their tension overtly to their colleagues. Failures of morale were surprisingly infrequent and always severely dealt with under the chilling sobriquet of 'Lack of Moral Fibre' (LMF), much to the long lasting anger of their colleagues who felt far more sympathy for their plight than those in authority who always feared, perhaps exaggeratedly, that such understandable weakness could be infectious.

Apart from wearing the brown uniform of the United States Army, the American aircrew were in many respects very similar to their RAF counterparts in background and attitude. Whilst their leaders were permanently commissioned officers of the Army Air Corps, the majority of the crew members were enlisted as war threatened from a wide variety of civilian occupations; only a few had any previous involvement with flying. One difference in the USAAF was that all the pilots were officers whilst virtually all of the rear crew members were enlisted men. Their standard tour of operations was 25 missions and a second tour was constrained by legislation, albeit sometimes circumvented. Although the American aircrew perhaps displayed emotion rather more openly, their courage, conviction and enthusiasm were as infectious as that of their colleagues in blue.

Flt Lt L. Richards – 460 Squadron

My own feelings before and after an attack surprised me. I have always been a coward and was very nervous before every operation. When an operation was scrubbed I was delighted. I dreaded, before each trip, how I would react if we got shot-up or in difficulties, and my nerves were as taut as a bowstring throughout every mission. However, when we did meet trouble, to my absolute amazement, my stomach froze but I was as calm as could be, calmer than at any time throughout my tour of operations. I worked like the devil to get us back on course with what instruments were left. When we finally arrived over an airfield in England, the calmness left me and the fear returned. I was quite terrified at the thought of a crash landing and yet I had every confidence that our pilot would manage it. There was such a strange and unreal feeling of fear and confidence.

Throughout our whole tour of operations I was pretty certain that we would be killed. All my fear and nerves were unfounded, as each operation was as uneventful as a training cross-country. But there was no comfort in that, I still died thirty deaths just down to cowardice. I suppose I simply couldn't see us surviving when others were not. Towards the end, say from about 25 operations onwards, I began to see that there was a chance that I would survive a tour. That made each operation more of a nerve wracking experience than ever. I used to calculate the days it would take to complete the remaining operations, and to say to myself if I live for just another two weeks I will live forever. Obviously I kept all this from the crew. They had great faith in my ability as a navigator and thought that this and the skill of our pilot would help get us through the tour. I think it was just luck, but the leadership of our pilot throughout was a tremendous example to each member of the crew.

Training

When war came in 1939, not only was Bomber Command poorly equipped with aircraft to carry out its assigned tasks, but its crews were less than adequately trained. For this there were three main reasons. The Air Ministry, preoccupied with the re-equipment programme, simply gave insufficient attention or resources to the equally important task of training the crews. Secondly, the RAF had always regarded the pilot as pre-eminent in the crew structure and was deplorably slow to recognise that the successful operation of a bomber aircraft required the intimate co-operation of several crew members, each with his own specialised role. Finally, scant attention was given to the tactics of bomber operations before the war and thus the training was stereotyped and ill directed.

In 1934, the training organisation, mainly based in Britain but with one flying training school at Abu Sueir in Egypt, turned out some 300 pilots a year. The first rearmament programme in 1934 (Scheme 'A') already required an additional 1,000 pilots and each succeeding scheme increased the demand. The solution was sought in the expansion of civil air training schools for the provision of elementary flying training before the successful students progressed to the Service run schools for more advanced and type training. However, there was a shortage of both aircraft and instructors within the RAF, and to maintain a throughput of trained pilots the course length for advanced flying training was only six months rather than the nine considered necessary. There was invariably, therefore, a backlog of training when a pilot eventually reached his operational squadron.

The inadequate training of rear crew members was even more significant. It only gradually became apparent that a single pilot could not be expected to perform adequately all the diverse tasks expected of him, particularly the ability to navigate accurately over long distances. The answer at first seemed to lie in the provision of a second pilot who would concentrate upon the navigation, with the added bonus of a gentle lead-in to the responsibilities of becoming an aircraft captain. But this involved additional training costs and in any case some of the new aircraft such as the Hampden were provided only with a single pilot position. The traditional Royal Flying Corps trade of Observer was therefore resurrected, and as before he was expected to be a 'jack of all trades', doubling-up as necessary as bomb aimer, wireless operator and even air gunner. It was not until 1941 that the position of navigator was finally recognised as an essential full time member of the crew.

The standard of training provided was also conditioned by the equipment and facilities available in the pre-war years. The lack of navigation aids and techniques led to most training flights being conducted in good weather in daylight in the immediate vicinity of the airfield where familiar land marks could be readily recognised. It is not surprising in the circumstances that squadron commanders were reluctant to launch their inexperienced crews on extended flights at night. In any case, the conditions for night flying with a myriad of ground lights pinpointing cities and towns would be very different to that over a hostile territory subjected to blackout. Thus very little night flying training was undertaken in Bomber Command in the years leading up to the war; in 1938 only 14,000 hours compared with nearly 150,000 day training hours. There had, therefore, to be radical and rapid changes in training if Bomber Command was to be expanded and sustained in a war environment.

Most RAF bomber pilots at home and overseas were trained on the Avro Anson or the very similar Airspeed Oxford. This is an Anson Mk I. IWM

With the outbreak of war the need for trained aircrew escalated rapidly and there was simply insufficient space within the United Kingdom to contain all the necessary training schools. The vast open airspaces of the British Empire and the Dominions were an obvious alternative and tentative approaches to the latter were made before 1939. Not all, however, were enthusiastic towards the idea of training aircrews for the mother country with Canada and South Africa in particular evading the question until hostilities were actually underway. Thereafter their help was unstinting and the agreement for the formation of the Empire Training Scheme

was signed in December 1939 with the first training school opening its doors the following April. At their peak in 1943, the majority of RAF aircrew was trained in no less than 175 flying schools across the globe, over half of which were in Canada. In all, some 205,900 aircrew were trained under this scheme by 1945.

The training of the rear crew members remained unsatisfactory until well into the war and both the Bombing and Gunnery Schools for a long time continued to be the poor relations of the training organisation with a shortage of aircraft, equipment and instructors. Gunnery training was perhaps the most neglected with obsolete weapons, aircraft without turrets and instructors who themselves had come straight from training. Not surprisingly the Groups complained of the end product and in December 1941 the course length was doubled to six weeks. Bombing training was almost as basic and specific training in night bombing was not started until the end of 1942, a ludicrous state of affairs for a Command which had been virtually committed to night bombing for almost three years.

In Bomber Command, the practice of crews going straight from the advanced training schools to the operational squadrons was considered impracticable even before the outbreak of war. Group pool squadrons were formed in January 1939, normally two for each group, to train crews to an operational standard and to provide a reserve to top-up squadrons as required. Each pilot received about 55 hours training and the pool squadrons inevitably grew to an unmanageable size as the flow of pilots increased: in January 1940, for example, 70 Wellingtons and the same number of Whitleys were employed in this role in their respective groups. It was soon recognised that this was an inadequate arrangement and in April 1940 a special group was formed, No 6, to provide all Bomber Command training by means of Operational Training Units (OTUs). A typical Wellington OTU comprised a Conversion Flight and an Armament Flight with eight Wellingtons each and a Navigation Flight of eight Ansons. After completing their conversion and bombing training, the crews were formed-up and proceeded to the Operational Flight, also with eight Wellingtons. Although streamlining the training system, the OTU course was only six weeks in length and the crews still had a steep learning curve when they reached their operational squadrons.

By May 1940, as the flow of aircraft rapidly expanded, each operational squadron was estimated to need eight new crews every month, and this took no account of the deficit of 258 crews within Bomber Command at that time. To redress the shortfall and to provide for the future, it was decided to disband squadrons already forming and replace them by two new OTUs. It was also decreed that no new squadrons would form unless there was sufficient OTU capacity to provide the crews. This

The pre-war system of 'Pool Squadrons' soon had to give way to a more efficient training system. This line-up of Wellingtons is at No 30 Operational Training Unit, Hixon. IWM

investment in training was vital for the future even if, as was inevitable, the build-up of operational squadrons was slower than expected. In July 1940 another training group, No 7, was formed under Air Commodore R A Cochrane, later to become the distinguished AOC of No 5 Group.

These intensive developments paid dividends in terms of numbers and by the end of 1941 the flow of crews to the squadrons was generally satisfactory although the AOCs were not always very happy with the quality, in particular complaining of the inadequate practice in night flying. The emphasis was now adjusted, therefore, to concentrate rather more on quality than quantity with an inevitable increase in course lengths, in one case to as long as 17 weeks. Each pilot was now receiving about 80 hours flying at the OTU and the number of OTUs further expanded. Another change which was to have a major impact upon the whole training system was the decision in March 1942 to dispense with the second pilot in medium and heavy bombers with the flight engineer being trained as a 'pilot's mate' who could take over the flying of the aircraft in an emergency, at the very least for long enough for the other crew members to bale-out. A final change in May 1942 was the renumbering of Nos 6 and 7 Groups as Nos 91 and 92 with the addition in June 1942 of No 93 Group. Together, they eventually administered 27 OTUs. When the heavy bombers first arrived to replace the Whitleys and Wellingtons, they were given to the experienced operational squadrons and conversion training was initially undertaken on the squadron. Later, this practice was superseded by the introduction of Heavy Conversion Units at separate airfields, each with about 32 aircraft.

By the end of 1942 the training structure was largely in place for the rest of the war and the flow of crews remained more or less in balance until 1945. Nevertheless, it had taken a long time to recognise the validity of Lord Trenchard's much earlier dictum that training was 'that on which the whole future of the Royal Air Force depends'. But as we shall see as we look at the other elements of the infrastructure with which Bomber Command fought its war, it was to take the same periods of time, sometimes longer, before the Command was really in the condition necessary to mount and sustain an effective strategic bombing offensive. The pressures of war are a powerful incentive to development, but that it took so long is a powerful condemnation of the lassitude which had infected the years leading-up to the conflict.

Airfields

A wartime Bomber Command pilot returning after a time warp of some 50 years to one of the mainstream bomber airfields like Scampton in Lincolnshire would find much that was familiar. The buildings will look a little more weathered, the trees more mature, but the stations built in the last years of the 1930s have proved remarkably resilient to the needs of the modern RAF.

It had not only been the RAF's aircraft establishment which declined so dramatically after the First World War, there was also a massive reduction in the number of aerodromes, as they were then called, from over 300 to just 27. A sizeable proportion of the money allocated to the rearmament programme in the 1930s had perforce therefore to be spent on building new airfields to accommodate the increase in aircraft. In 1934, the Aerodromes Board within the Air Ministry Works Department was formed under two retired senior officers to scour the country in a search for new landing grounds. Opposition from influential local bodies and individuals was often strong, albeit not perhaps so strident as it would be today, but where necessary recourse was had to legislation and the programme gradually gathered momentum. Before 1934, priority had been given to air defence airfields which had to be sited far enough back from the coast to allow time for the fighters to get aloft after the raids had been plotted. The bomber airfields were located even further inland behind this defensive ring which placed them a long way from their potential targets and would have necessitated refuelling on the coast or in France. Henceforth, however, the bomber airfields tended to be located in East Anglia, Lincolnshire and Yorkshire with the fighters mainly concentrated in the south east of the country. By 1939 the number of active airfields had expanded to 116 and the building rate increased still faster to reach a peak in 1942.

The early aerodromes did not have hard surface runways although both Fighter and Bomber Command began to press for these from 1937 onwards. In the end, a parsimonious but short sighted Treasury reluctantly authorised runways to be built on selected airfields in April 1939. The standard airfield layout was for three runways forming an isosceles triangle with a minimum runway length initially of 1,000 yards, but by 1941 the main runway was normally 2,000 yards with the two subsidiary strips 1,400 yards in length. Runways were either of concrete or tarmac surface and a network of taxiways and hardstandings, of even stronger construction than the runway, were built round the periphery of the field to allow aircraft to be dispersed. Many main bomber airfields had one or two satellite airfields with rudimentary facilities, usually within five to 15 miles. The only further significant development was the building of three strips on the East Coast at Manston, Carnaby and Woodbridge for disabled aircraft which were 3,000 yards long and 250 yards wide. Late in the war, a few airfields were built for very heavy bomber operations with a 3,000 yard main runway.

Air traffic control as we know it today did not exist before the war and even by 1945 had only reached a comparatively rudimentary stage of development. Known originally in the UK

**Bomber Command Airfields
Autumn 1944**

KEY
GROUP HEADQUARTERS

1 Group	◆
3 Group	○
4 Group	□
5 Group	▲
6 Group (RCAF)	△
8 Group (PFF)	✳
91 Group (OTU)	✚
92 Group (OTU)	■
93 Group (OTU)	●
100 Group	✕

△ Middleton
St George

Croft △

△ Leeming
Skipton-on-Swale △   △ Wombleton
Topcliffe ▲
Dishforth △   △ Tholthorpe
Linton-on Ouse △   △ East Moor   □ Driffield
ALLERTON △   □ Full   □ Lisset
Sutton
Marston □   YORK □
Moor   Rufforth □   □ Pocklington
Elvington □   □ Leconfield
Riccall □   □ Melbourne
Burn □   □ Holme
□ Snaith   Breighton
Elsham   ◆ North
Sandtoft ◆   Wolds   Killingholme
Lindholme ◆   ◆ Kirmington
Finningley △
Blyton ◆   ◆ Grimsby
Bircotes ◆   ◆ BAWTRY   Binbrook ◆
Hemswell ◆   ◆ Kelstern
Worksop ◆   Faldingworth ◆   ◆ Ludford Magna
Scampton ▲   ◆ Wickenby
Gamston ○   ▲ Dunholme Lodge
Skellingthorpe ▲   ▲ Fiskerton   ▲ East Kirby
Wigsley ▲   ▲ Bardney
Ossington ●   ▲ Waddington   ▲ Woodhall Spa
▲ SWINDERBY
Winthorpe   ▲ Coningsby
Syerston ▲   ✕ North Creake
Church   Little ✕
Broughton   ▲ Langar   Snoring   ✕ Oulton
● EGGINGTON   Gt Massingham ✕   ✕ Foulsham
Hixon ●   ✕ Swannington
Seighford ●   ● Castle Donnington   West Raynham ✕
Peplow ●   ● Wymeswold   Downham Market ○   ✕ BYLAUGH HALL
Lichfield ●
○ Methwold
Bruntingthorpe ■   ○ Feltwell
Market ■   Upwood ✳
Bitteswell ■   Harborough ■   Warboys ✳   Mepal ○   ○ Mildenhall
Desborough ■   ✳ Wyton   Witchford ○
Husbands ■   Waterbeach ○   ○ Tuddenham
Bosworth   HUNTINGTON ✳   ○ EXNING
✳ Graveley
Little Staughton ✳   ✳ Oakington   ○ Chedburgh
Wellesbourne   ✳ Bourn
Mountford ✚   Gaydon ✚   Tempsford ○   ○ Stradishall
Long Marston ✚   ■ Chipping Warden   ✳ Gransden
Honeybourne ✚   ✚ Stratford   Lodge   ○ Wratting
Edgehill ■   ■ Silverstone   Common
Moreton ✚   ■ Turweston
in the Marsh   ■ Little Harwood
Barford ■   ■ WINSLOW
Upper Heyford ■   St John   ■ Wing
■ Westcott
Stanton ✚   Enstone   ■ Oakley
Harcourt ✚   ✚ ABINGDON   ⊕ HIGH
WYCOMBE
HQ Bomber
Command

LONDON

✚ Lossiemouth
✚ Milltown
✚ Kinloss
Forras ✚   ✚ Elgin
SCOTLAND

RAF Snetterton Heath was a standard triangular runway airfield developed in the early 1940s. This was the home of the USAAF's 96th Bombardment Group from June 1943.   RAFM

as a watch office or watch tower (control tower is American terminology), this squat two storey building was a prominent feature of the airfield landscape and many still exist today, either developed for some alternative use or standing derelict and forlorn on a long disused airfield. The watch office was responsible for logging aircraft in and out, looking after the airfield and its lighting and controlling aircraft on the ground and in the immediate vicinity of the airfield. When the weather was good, control was exercised by means of light signals to avoid providing a gratuitous homing device for enemy bombers. Radio telephony (RT) was, however, increasingly used as the intensity of traffic built-up, particularly by the 8th Air Force.

The main approach aid to an airfield at the beginning of the war was radio direction finding (DF) operated from the watch office. The pilot was homed to overhead the airfield and then directed to descend along a safety lane. Turning back towards the airfield at a suitable height, the pilot continued to descend with assistance from DF until in sight of the airfield. The procedure was known as Controlled Descent Through Cloud and a good controller could handle up to five aircraft at the same time. This basic procedure is still in use at some training airfields today.

A more sophisticated approach aid introduced into Bomber Command in 1941 was the Standard Beam Approach (SBA), a system designed by Lorenz in Germany and in use at civil airfields in Britain before the war. It was also incidentally the basis of the 'Knickebein' system for guiding enemy bombers over England in 1940. SBA comprised a radio beam aligned along the direction of the runway with radio marker beacons on the approach indicating the distance from the threshold. If the pilot was to the left of the beam he received a series of dots in his headphones and if to the right a series of dashes. The aircraft was in line with the runway when the dots and dashes intermeshed into a continuous tone. Although it allowed aircraft to land in cloud bases as low as 50 feet, the SBA approach was difficult to fly accurately and the Americans introduced a more developed system called the Instrument Landing System (ILS). Like the SBA, it consisted of a radio beam called the localiser to indicate the alignment of the runway, but also introduced a second beam known as the glide slope to indicate a continuous descent path to the runway threshold. Rather than through his headphones, the pilot interpreted the aid by means of a dial on his instrument panel consisting of a pair of intersecting needles, the vertical needle indicating the relationship of the aircraft to the runway heading and the horizontal one its position above or below the glidepath, normally set at a three degree angle above the ground. Late in the war, a system called the Beam Approach Beacon System (BABS) was introduced in which a radio beacon in the aircraft interrogated a ground responder with the resulting information displayed on a cathode ray tube in the cockpit.

Airfield lighting was also very rudimentary at the outbreak of war. At first airfields tended to devise their own system, but the layout designed for the fighter airfield at Drem near Edinburgh was soon adopted as the standard pattern. This system contained hooded runway lights, angle of approach indicators, a 'V' shaped funnel of approach lights on poles and an outer circle of lights 2,000 yards from the centre of the airfield feeding into the approach funnel. The whole system could be switched on and off and aligned to the runway in use from a panel in the watch office. The lights were switched off whenever enemy aircraft were suspected in the vicinity and many a late returning bomber pilot was embarrassed by the lights being extinguished at a critical stage of the approach.

Many bombers were lost in the early years of the war because the airfields were shrouded in fog on their return from operations and one final aspect of airfield operation to be briefly mentioned is 'Fido' (Fog Investigation Disposal Operation). The intention of 'Fido' was to create sufficient heat in the vicinity of the runway to burn off the fog. Petrol feed pipes were laid either side of the runway and into the approach funnel with burners which were ignited about 15 minutes before the aircraft was due to land. When the initial smoke cleared, forward visibility could be enhanced from a few yards to as much as four miles. Greeted with considerable scepticism within Bomber Command, the first trial installation was laid at Graveley near Cambridge by January 1943 and tested by Air Commodore Bennett, AOC 8 Gp (Pathfinders), one of the few early enthusiasts for the system. 'Fido' was first used in anger in November 1943 when four Halifaxes returning from the Ruhr found the whole of eastern England covered by dense radiation fog: all landed safely. Thereafter 'Fido' became a regular feature of Bomber Command operations and it was estimated that some 2,500 aircraft had used the system by the end of the war.

The most prominent buildings on a permanent RAF station were the hangars, but within Bomber Command it was the practice to disperse aircraft over as wide an area as possible and the hangars were used only for long term rectification. There were several standard designs and pre-war hangars were of quite substantial brick and steel construction, but many of those built on the east coast bases designated for Bomber Command were unfortunately limited to aircraft of less than 100 feet wingspan

A typical 1930s pattern Watch Tower at RAF Waddington in Lincolnshire. IWM

which proved, as we have seen, a significant constraint on aircraft design. Simpler, corrugated steel hangars soon proliferated, many still in use for agricultural storage and the sole remaining indication of the site of a wartime airfield.

The expansion in the 1930s required the development of many new airfields and the opportunity was taken to provide a very high standard of permanent buildings. Elegant neo-Georgian style brick structures were designed for messes, barrack blocks, station headquarters and stores; and a standard pattern officers' mess, with either two or three storeys, still graces most modern RAF stations. Not surprisingly, the standard could not be maintained as the claims upon scarce resources intensified and a proliferation of temporary structures soon disfigured the basic layout. The best known, of course, was the ubiquitous Nissen hut, a resurrection of a First World War design. Nissen huts were used for domestic accommodation, crew rooms, stores, even operation and briefing rooms, and some of the satellite airfields were constructed entirely of Bellman corrugated steel hangars and prefabricated huts.

Airfield defence was nominally the responsibility of the Army in the early years and there was particular concern in 1940 that airfields could be used by enemy paratroops or airborne forces. To supplement the meagre protection provided by the Army, the RAF formed its own ground defence sections armed with machine guns and rifles. Concrete pill-boxes were

scattered over and around airfields and several aircraft succumbed to a badly sited but all too solid obstruction. Bofors anti-aircraft guns provided some protection against attack from the air. The RAF Regiment was formed in February 1942 to relieve the Army of its responsibility for airfield defence and soon became a professional and highly motivated force. To camouflage an airfield successfully was always difficult, but many experiments were conducted in toning down runways and taxiways and breaking-up the outlines of large buildings. Dummy airfields were constructed with considerable ingenuity but doubtful utility. The decoy airfield was perhaps the most successful measure against night attack with Drem lighting installations laid enticingly across open fields, a device not always appreciated by the local farmer. As the threat of invasion and aerial bombardment diminished, the ground defences were gradually run-down or dismantled after 1944 and many RAF Regiment personnel were transferred to the Army.

When the 8th Air Force arrived in England in 1942, they took over some existing RAF airfields until additional capacity could be provided. Perhaps inevitably, they generally acquired the newer prefabricated stations, but in December 1942 no less than 70 airfields were designated for eventual use by the USAAF. American Engineer Aviation Battalions brought much needed assistance to the hard pressed civilian contractors and the 8th Air Force airfields soon possessed their own distinctive

character. Considering that 125 new airfields were brought into use in 1942 alone, the scale of airfield building during this period was quite remarkable, fully justifying an American description of Britain as 'just one giant aircraft carrier'.

Navigation and Bomb Aiming

In order to successfully complete its mission, the bomber had to find its way to and identify the target, drop its bombs accurately and defend itself against any opposition that might be ranged against it. None of these proved as easy in practice as the pre-war proponents of strategic bombing had expected and it was not until the latter stages of the war that most difficulties were successfully overcome.

The Royal Flying Corps, and subsequently the RAF, were surprisingly slow to embrace the science of aerial navigation. In the First World War it was the Royal Naval Air Service which led the way in developing navigation equipments and techniques to support their longer range bombing sorties into Germany. In contrast the RFC crews in close support of the Army depended more upon map reading and ground observation than compass and stop watch to determine their position. Apart from a few notable long distance flights between the wars, the designated roles of the RAF which depended upon day visual conditions inevitably led to a certain apathy towards

8th Air Force Airfields
1944

Key

● Heavy Bombardment Airfields

✚ Headquarters Formations

precision blind navigation techniques which persisted well into the 1930s.

A report in November 1937 by Air Chief Marshal Sir Edgar Ludlow-Hewitt, newly appointed C-in-C Bomber Command, highlighted this 'amateur approach to navigation' which lagged far behind the standards already commonplace within civil aviation. It was a matter of attitude as well as lack of equipment, and the little expertise that existed in the RAF tended to be concentrated in the overseas squadrons and Coastal Command. It was not until 1938 that a ten week navigation course was introduced for pilots and observers; but even in August 1939, Ludlow-Hewitt was still able to say that 'over 40 per cent of his bombers were unable to find a target in a friendly city in broad daylight'.

Aerial navigation in 1940 was generally dependent upon dead reckoning and astro techniques. In the former, the pilot was required to fly accurately on compass and air speed indicator to maintain a previously calculated track over the ground: by applying a factor for forecast wind, the drift could be added or subtracted to the aircrafts heading to maintain the given track. But the forecast and the actual wind could be significantly different, and so the dead reckoning calculation over even a short flight could be dramatically wrong unless updates were applied in flight. If the ground or water was visible, primitive drift sights were used to measure the actual drift so that adjustments could be made to the aircrafts track, and the introduction of the Air Mileage Unit which measured True Air Speed (TAS) was a crucial development in maintaining an air plot. If the stars were visible from the aircraft, the astro sextant was used to provide a fix over the ground, but this equipment required considerable expertise and experience in a bomber wallowing at height in turbulent conditions. Navigation in the early years of the war was, therefore, a rather crude technique which could easily go sadly awry as was demonstrated by a raid against the pocket battleship Deutschland in the Norwegian Sea in November 1939 when 48 Hampdens not only failed to find their target, but almost missed the British Isles on their return, landing on nearly dry tanks in the far north of Scotland.

The first specialist navigation aid to be provided for Bomber

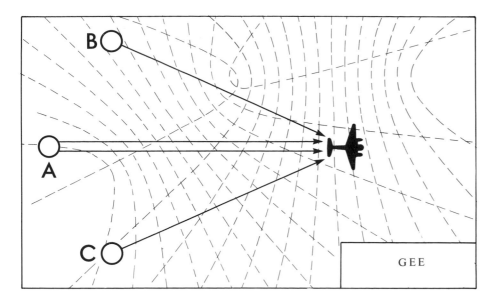

Gee. The system comprised a master station (A) and two slaves (B) and (C). The time difference between a pulse received in the aircraft from A and B was compared with one from A and C and plotted on a lattice grid to determine the aircraft's position.

Oboe. The aircraft flew along a line of constant radius from the 'Cat' station determined by the elapsed time of a pulse from that station and its reponse from the aircraft. A signal from the 'Mouse' station indicated the point at which the bombs were released.

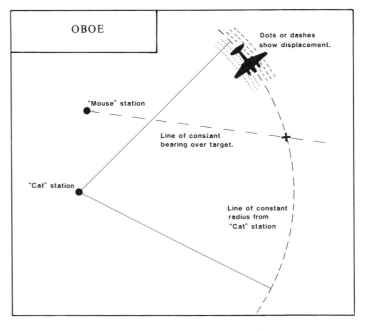

Command was Gee, a radio direction device invented in 1937 by R J Dippy. It was not, however, seriously developed until 1940 and introduced into operational service in a raid against Essen on the 8th March 1942. A Gee chain consisted of three stations, one master and two slaves, with transmission aerials on 120 foot towers from which pulses were displayed on a cathode ray tube at the navigator's position in the aircraft. The time interval between the pulses from one master and one slave provided a position along a line of constant radial which could be compared with the pulses from the master and the other slave and plotted on a special chart bearing a lattice like grid. The equipment was dependent on a line of sight between the transmission aerial and the aircraft and thus had an operational radius of little more than 300 miles which just covered the Ruhr. It was hoped to use Gee for blind bombing, but results were disappointingly inaccurate. However, the main limitation of Gee was a susceptibility to jamming which was achieved, as predicted, about six months after its introduction into use over Germany. Thereafter Gee was regularly jammed, but continued to provide a useful navigational aid, particularly on the return flight when the greater relative strength of the pulses overcame the jamming. Gee remained the standard RAF navigation aid to the end of the war.

A more sophisticated radar device called Oboe was introduced in December 1942 which depended upon a responding signal from the aircraft. Oboe required two ground stations, a tracking station known as the 'cat' and a releasing station called the 'mouse'. The range of the aircraft from the tracking station was measured by the time interval between the transmitted and the received signal. The principle of operation was that the pilot flew a predetermined radial course of constant range from the 'cat' which passed over the target. If he deviated from that radial, he received in his headphones a signal, either dots or dashes, which indicated whether he needed to turn left or right to regain the track. A signal generated from the 'mouse' marked the target at the point where the two beams intersected. Oboe was a far more accurate aid than Gee, but again depended upon line of sight and was also susceptible to jamming. Individual Oboe ground stations could be interpreted only by a single aircraft at a time, thus restricting its use to one aircraft every 15 minutes or so.

Two more advanced equipments were introduced before the end of the war. G-H, a development of Oboe, transmitted a signal from the aircraft which was radiated back from responders on the ground from which the navigator calculated the aircraft's position on a chart similar to that used for Gee. It was accurate and could be used by far more aircraft simultaneously than Oboe. Loran was an American equipment similar in concept to Gee, but usable over a much longer range.

As a result of the limitations of Gee and Oboe, effort was also devoted to producing a navigation device which was self contained within the aircraft. The answer was sought from an adaptation of the Air to Surface Vessel (ASV) Radar recently introduced into Coastal Command, using a small rotating aerial

fitted in a radome below the lower fuselage which transmitted a pulse towards the ground. The surface texture – land, water or buildings – radiated different strength pulses which when displayed on a cathode ray tube delineated topographic patterns which could be compared with a specially prepared chart. The device was originally given the code designation 'Home Sweet Home', later amended at Lord Cherwell's suggestion to H2S. The first ASV systems were powered by a klystron valve which transmitted a wide 10cm pulse giving a somewhat woolly response, but the introduction of the magnetron and a 2cm pulse provided far better definition. H2S proved very useful against coastal targets or those situated adjacent to lakes or rivers as the definition between land and water was most pronounced. It was not so useful against large cities which tended to flood the display, but small towns could be more readily identified.

The introduction of H2S into operational service was by no means straight forward. As so often happened with promising new inventions, a battle ensued between the Air Ministry and the Admiralty for the small supply of magnetrons, and the latter was able to exploit concern that in using H2S over Germany,

the secrets of the magnetron might fall into enemy hands. The prestige generated by the 1,000 bomber raid, with some support from the very influential Lord Cherwell, tilted the argument in favour of Bomber Command and the magnetron H2S system was installed in the Lancaster. The one operational disadvantage of H2S was that the transmitter could equally well be detected and pinpointed by ground stations or night fighters, thus disclosing the bomber's exact position. H2S never quite fulfilled its designer's expectations, but in the right conditions it was a valuable blind bombing aid. The Americans used a development of H2S called H2X.

Not all bombing was of course dependent on blind techniques and we must conclude this section by briefly looking at visual bomb sights. There were two basic types, the Course-Setting Bombsight (C.S.B.S.) and the Tachometric Bombsight. In the former certain basic criteria – height, speed, wind vectors and the ballistic performance of the bomb – were manually or automatically fed into the bombsight which then computed and displayed the release point. The Mark XIV Stabilised Vector Sight was the most widely used and successful of the C.S.B.S.

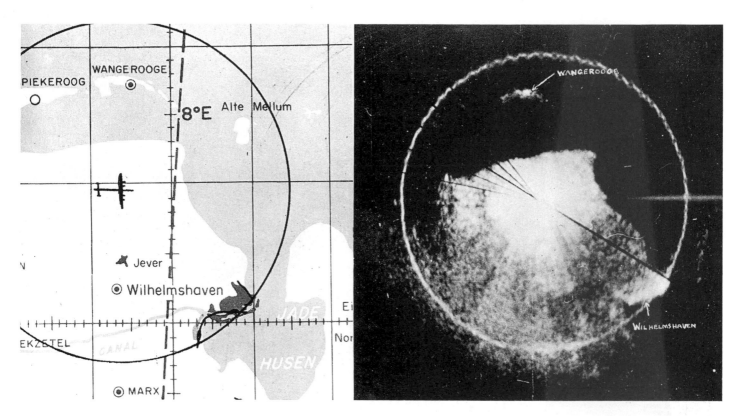

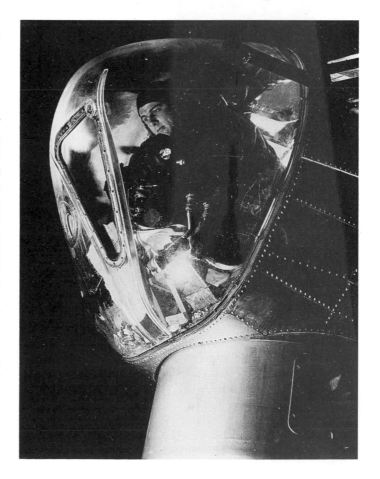

Top: This photograph clearly shows how well a coastal target could be identified on a H2S display. Inland and city areas were far harder to interpret. IWM

Left: A navigator operating a H2S set used for blind bombing from 1943 onwards. IWM

Right: A USAAF Bombardier using a Norden gyroscopic bomb sight. This equipment was well in advance of anything available to Bomber Command in the early war years. IWM

type, but still required the insertion of an accurate wind vector which was always a very problematical calculation. The American Norden Bombsight was a more advanced and accurate gyroscopic equipment which was well ahead of its early British counterparts. To overcome the limitation of the C.S.B.S., the Tachometric Bombsight was introduced which involved the observation of the target relative to the vertical and azimuth displacement of the aircraft. The Mk II Stabilised Automatic Bombsight (S.A.B.S.) was already in advanced development in 1939, but it was not until 1942 that it was fitted to the Lancaster for operational trials. It required considerable expertise and experience in operational use, but specialist squadrons like No 617 used it successfully for the development of precision bombing.

By 1944 the efforts of the scientists had revolutionised navigation and bomb aiming techniques. In 1941 it was calculated that, in difficult areas like the Ruhr, less than ten per cent of bombs fell within five miles of the target. By 1945, photographic reconnaissance proved that over 95 per cent were falling within two to three miles. But not only does the bomber have to find the target, its weapons must also be effective, and there were difficulties in this area as well.

Weapons

No matter how efficient the bomber aircraft, its destructive power is only as effective as the bombs it conveys and the accuracy with which it can dispense them. Whilst glaringly self evident, many air forces throughout the brief history of air power until recent years have in fact consistently devoted resources to putting aircraft into the 'shop window' at the expense of providing efficient weapons in sufficient numbers. Such was the situation which faced Bomber Command in the early years of the war; indeed, the attitude and the morale of the crews would have been seriously jeopardised if they had known just how many of the bombs they so assiduously carried to the heart of Germany actually failed to explode.

Excluding air laid sea mines which will be considered later (Page 124), the weapons carried by Bomber Command may be conveniently divided into three categories: high explosive bombs, incendiaries and target indicators. Producing an effective iron bomb was not quite so simple as might be imagined. A careful compromise had to be drawn between the weight of the explosive charge and the strength, and thus the weight, of the casing. If the casing is too thin as a consequence of trying to obtain a high charge to weight ratio, the ballistic properties of the bomb may become erratic, the penetration power reduced and the likelihood of the case breaking-up on impact increased. The standard weapon in use at the beginning of the war was the General Purpose (GP) bomb with a relatively low charge/weight ratio of 27 per cent compared with the much more efficient 50 per cent of the equivalent German bomb. They were made in sizes varying from 20 to 1,000lbs in 1940 and up to 4,000lbs by 1943, but by far the largest number of GP bombs dropped in the war were only of 500lbs capacity. Given the low charge/weight ratio, the GP bomb was never a very effective weapon, but because the bomb was produced in vast quantities, they continued in general use until 1944.

The GP bomb was increasingly superseded in later years by the Medium Capacity (MC) bomb with a charge/weight ratio of about 40 per cent. These bombs were initially even less effective than their predecessors with inferior explosives, faulty detonators and a tendency to break-up on impact. Nevertheless, the quality improved as did the size of the weapon, and the best known bombs of the war fell into this category; the 4,000lb 'Cookie', which was mainly carried by the Mosquito, and the 10,000lb 'Tallboy' and the massive 22,000lb 'Grand Slam' which were restricted to the Lancaster.

The final category of bomb was the High Capacity (HC) with an 80 per cent or greater charge/weight ratio. Up to 12,000lbs capacity and known as 'Block Busters', they were used where the requirement for blast effect was paramount. They were originally provided with parachutes to reduce their terminal velocity, but this so degraded accuracy that tail fins were quickly

A 22,000lb 'Grand Slam' being removed from a bomb dump for loading onto a Lancaster. IWM

A 'Grand Slam' being dropped from a Lancaster onto a viaduct at Arnsberg in 1945. IWM

substituted. In essence, the development of bombs paralleled the development of the bomber aircraft and it was fortuitous that the Lancaster and the most effective weapons increasingly came together from 1943 onwards.

The increasing realisation that high explosive bombs were relatively ineffective led to the early introduction of the incendiary which depended upon the latent self destructive propensity of densely built urban areas. The Great Fire of London of 1666 was a potent reminder of how rapidly fire can consume a city, and many of the German towns with close knit medieval timbered dwellings were not unlike the London of the seventeenth century.

The standard incendiary was the 4lb magnesium bomb which was dropped in clusters, initially in free fall from a box called a Small Bomb Container. This was, however, both a wasteful and a dangerous procedure, for not only were the incendiaries widely scattered, but they often peppered another bomber unseen in the darkness below. The solution, only hesitantly embraced, was to drop the container which could be provided with better ballistic qualities and dispense the incendiaries in a concentrated pattern closer to the ground. As the war progressed, larger incendiary devices were developed up to 40lbs in weight, but their use was abandoned when it was recognised that presenting the enemy with 35lbs of good quality steel for 5lbs of magnesium was not necessarily a beneficial exchange. Liquid filled incendiaries of which the 'J' bomb of 30lbs was the most widely used were less effective and the 4lb magnesium bomb was the preferred weapon to the end of the war.

The early method of indicating the target was to illuminate it with flares, but not only were the flares inefficient, the technique was often impractical because of cloud or smoke. Incendiaries were also a useful indicator of the target and a dedicated marker bomb was developed containing benzol, rubber and phosphorus. These grew in size from the 250lb version to the 4,000lb 'Pink Pansy'. The advent of the Pathfinder Force led quickly to the provision of the dedicated target marker of which 40 different versions were used between January 1943 and the end of the war. Although all contained pyrotechnic candles, they were basically of two types; air burst and ground markers. The former were released at a predetermined height by a barometric device and clusters of candles floated down on miniature parachutes. Drifting in the wind, they were inevitably less accurate than ground markers which formed a circle of coloured fire on the ground of about 200 yards diameter. Explosive candles were inserted in the cluster to deter fire fighting and many different predetermined colours were employed both to differentiate between good and bad marking and to make it more difficult for the Germans to ignite credible decoys. Coloured smoke generators were also developed for daylight use, but were generally ineffective because of the smoke and dust engendered by the bomb bursts.

The development of iron bombs in the United States followed similar lines and initially suffered the same inadequacies; but unlike the RAF, the 8th Air Force never had an

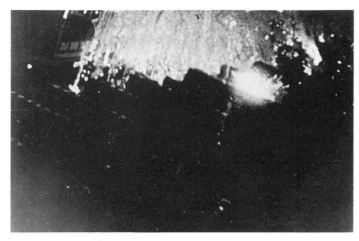

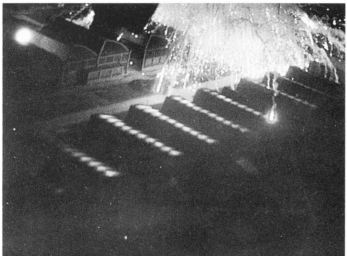

Target Indicators. These were dropped by Wg Cdr Cheshire from a Lancaster on the Gnome-Rhone aero-engine works at Limoges on the 8th February 1944. IWM

aircraft which could carry an outsize weapon like the 'Tallboy'. Typical bomb loads were also much smaller than became commonplace in Bomber Command, particularly with the Lancaster, often no more than 5,000lbs.

Defensive Armament

Although there was a period when it had been thought that the high performance bomber might be able to elude or out-run any opposition, the advent of the fast, manoeuvrable monoplane fighter soon put paid to any such fleeting optimism. If the bomber was to survive, it had to defeat the fighter in the air or seek the cloak of darkness. After a brief flirtation with the former, Bomber Command elected to concentrate its operations at night where it enjoyed about two years of near immunity to fighter opposition before it too had to fight for survival. The 8th Air Force on the other hand decided from the outset to confront the enemy in the air in daylight. To them the defensive armament of the bomber was of paramount importance.

In the First World War the air gunner was accommodated in an open compartment around the lip of which was a circular track called a Scarff Ring upon which was mounted one or two rifle calibre machine guns. The main problem was rotating the guns against the slipstream which became ever more difficult as aircraft speeds increased. It was recognised by the early 1930s that the answer was a power operated turret in which man, guns and sighting equipment all rotated over as wide a horizontal and vertical arc as was practicable given the location of the turret on the aircraft structure. Nevertheless, the technical complexities inhibited development for many years and many succumbed to the theory that it could prove counter productive to fit defensive armament which increased weight and thereby decreased performance.

There were two fundamental problems with turret design which to a great extent persisted throughout the war. Turrets were perennially criticized for their cramped and uncomfortable design, of which perhaps the ball gunner position in the B-17 was the worst example. But it was the tail gunner who usually complained the loudest: he was almost invariably frozen despite electrically insulated suits and often suffered frost bitten extremities. He also felt isolated from the rest of the crew and if the intercom should fail, as it often did, could even be unaware that the rest of the crew had abandoned a stricken aircraft. Many tail gunners were lost in this way and some even survived the crash of an otherwise empty aeroplane. The other more significant problem was that small calibre machine guns, although their high rate of fire was lethal at short distances, were invariably outranged by the canon equipped German fighter. The latter could therefore destroy a bomber without coming within reach of its defensive armament. This inexorably led to deception and evasion becoming the main defensive tactic of the British bomber and the provision of fighter escort the only viable method of operating in daylight.

Development of the power turret in the United States lagged far behind even that of Europe. It is, nevertheless, surprising that an air force which had so championed the long range self defending strategic bomber should in 1939 have no aircraft with more than 0.3in calibre hand held machine guns. The Army Air Corps contemplated building British turrets under licence, but eventually decided to produce their own design. They also made

The Nash and Thompson tail turret of a Whitley with four 0.3in Browning machine guns. IWM

The chin turret on the B-17G was developed to counter head-on attacks used by experienced Fw 190 pilots. IWM

an early and eminently sensible decision to standardise on the 0.5in machine gun rather than the 0.3in in standard use in the RAF. Sperry was selected to design and build gun turrets for the B-17 and by 1940 was ready to produce a power operated upper turret and a remotely controlled dorsal turret. Whilst the former was relatively successful, the latter was soon abandoned in favour of a self contained hydraulically operated ball turret which became standard on the B-17 until the end of its life. Although the early B-17s were under gunned, once the green light was given to development and procurement, the American industrial machine burst into life and progress was remarkably rapid. The B-17G was equipped not only with the ball turret, but also with a power operated computer sighted upper turret and a nose turret, all provided with 0.5in machine guns. The distinctive nose, often called the chin turret, was developed after the Luftwaffe began to employ a head-on attack profile against which the early B-17s were particularly vulnerable. The defensive armament was completed with two machine guns in a manually controlled tail turret and three hand held guns firing belted ammunition through slots in the fuselage sides. Development of powered turrets on the Liberator was rather more protracted and it ended the war with four turrets – upper, ball, nose and tail – from four different manufacturers, the last of which was never truly satisfactory. The medium bombers also became increasingly heavily armed, the B-25 eventually bristling with as much firepower as an early B-17.

Even so, despite the valiant efforts of gunners in both the RAF and the USAAF, the heavy bomber throughout the war was always hard pressed to defend itself, even within the protective envelope of a close formation, against a determined and experienced fighter pilot who not only had the benefit of speed and agility, but far more importantly the hitting power of a fixed forward firing cannon. The bomber aircraft, therefore, became increasingly dependent upon electronic countermeasures for its survival in a hostile sky.

Electronic Warfare

Electronic warfare was conceived at the beginning of the Second World War and although it took rather a long time to gather momentum, it developed rapidly thereafter and has remained one of the most important features of aerial warfare ever since. The story has been admirably recounted in Alfred Price's 'Instruments of Darkness', but here it is only possible to describe briefly the equipments which were developed for Bomber Command by the Telecommunications Research Establishment (TRE), originally located at Swanage in Dorset and later moved in the Spring of 1942 to the relatively safer haven of Malvern College.

Electronic warfare followed-on inevitably from the development of radar, for beams which could be radiated from the ground or an aircraft could also be interfered with from the same sources, this latter activity becoming known as jamming. Similarly, voice communications from ground to air which were needed to exploit the benefits of ground based radars could also

British paratroopers carried out a daring raid on the German radar unit at Bruneval in February 1942 to steal a Wurzburg radar.

IWM

be distorted or jammed. For reasons which in retrospect seem rather obscure, the British believed in the early years that they had a significant lead in radar development, but it soon became apparent as the strategic offensive got underway that the Luftwaffe had quite an effective radar screen of its own. Somewhat hesitant attempts to employ jamming transmitters had been tried by the Germans as early as the Battle of Britain, but it was not until they had used the technique to conceal the highly embarrassing dash down the Channel of the *Scharnhorst* and the *Gneisenau* in February 1942 that the British elected join the jamming war in earnest. The famous Bruneval raid of the same month in which British paratroopers removed key elements of a Wurzburg radar only emphasised the urgency of producing countermeasures.

The first such device, codenamed 'Moonshine', was directed not at the Wurzburg, but at the longer range Freya radar operating on a lower frequency. The concept was to receive the radar pulses and radiate them back at a much higher amplitude, creating the impression on the radar display of a large formation of aircraft which in fact emanated from only a single source. The device was mounted in obsolete Defiant fighters of No 515 Squadron and was designed to attract German fighters away from a real bomber formation. It was not a jammer in the strict sense, more of a spoofing device which could only be used effectively in daylight because at night the bombers at this stage of the war operated relatively independently. It was used with mixed success throughout the Summer of 1942.

A more useful device called 'Mandrel', which could be used at night, was introduced in December 1942 to jam the Freya radars. It was a crude noise jammer designed to flood the radar display with interference and was complemented by a similar device, codenamed 'Tinsel', which was mounted in an engine compartment to drown the voice communications of the fighter controllers. First employed in a raid against Mannheim, the

This Ju 88 G-I landed accidentally at Woodbridge in Suffolk in July 1944, bringing with it invaluable information on the latest developments in German air interception devices.   IWM

technique was initially very successful, but as invariably happened in electronic warfare, the opposition soon devised a remedy. By operating the Freya radar at random over a wider frequency range, the skilled operator was soon able again to differentiate between real returns and noise. Furthermore, it was quickly realised that an enemy fighter could itself home on to a 'Mandrel' transmitter and it was decided therefore that it could only be employed intermittently, further reducing its effectiveness.

Whilst 'Mandrel' was useful for a while against the Freya early warning radar, jamming the high frequency Wurzburg sets which were actually used for the ground controlled interception was a rather more complicated affair, albeit not technically difficult. The best technique was quite straightforward and both the Germans and the British were well aware of its existence. It consisted of dropping metallic strips of a complementary wave length to the radar frequency which reflected the beam in exactly the same way as a real aircraft. If dispensed regularly in sufficient quantities, it proved very difficult for the controller to differentiate the one from the other, for the strips would take up to 20 minutes to drift slowly out of the radar beam. The only certain information now detectable on the radar was the head of the bomber stream; how many aircraft were actually involved and where the stream ended were impossible to determine. The main difficulty was not technical, indeed rather the reverse, the idea was so simple that it could be readily adopted by the enemy as well. Indeed, it was demonstrated at a very early stage that it had a devastating effect on the RAF's night fighter Airborne Interception (AI) radar. It is not surprising, therefore, that a controversy soon raged between the bomber and fighter champions as to when this simple device should be introduced into service. Fighter Command, supported by the very influential Lord Cherwell, won the early rounds; but Harris, strongly backed eventually by Sir Charles Portal, argued that

the use of this measure could reduce bomber losses by as much as a third. It was a telling argument, for by this time the new A1 Mark X radar which would be largely impervious to this form of jamming was scheduled to enter service in August 1943. Known now by its familiar designation of 'Window', it was first used in July 1943 in Operation 'Gomorrah' – the devastating attack on Hamburg which left the town gutted by fire. The strips were 30 cms long by 1.5 cm wide and dropped through the flare chute in bundles of 2,000 at regular intervals of about a minute. Automatic dispensers were developed later. The effect was outstandingly successful and 'Window' continued to be used throughout the war. It is still in use today although now called 'Chaff'.

Despite the interference of 'Window' and 'Mandrel', it was of course still quite possible for an enemy fighter to locate a bomber, and usually the first intimation of its presence was the clatter of shells raking the fuselage or wings. To give some warning to the crew that a fighter was in their immediate vicinity, a rearward looking radar called 'Monica' was fitted which scanned an area out to about 1,000 yards over a 45 degree cone. Whilst it might still not help the rear gunner to pick-up a black painted aircraft on a dark night, it enabled the pilot to initiate evasive action such as the 'barrel corkscrew' manoeuvre perfected in the Lancaster. Unfortunately, it proved to be a double edged sword as the Germans soon invented a device called 'Flensburg' which could home onto the 'Monica' transmission. When this device was discovered in July 1944 after a Ju 88 night fighter had accidentally landed at Woodbridge in Suffolk, 'Monica' was soon withdrawn from operational use. A passive device called 'Boozer' which recognised when either 'Wurzburg' or airborne 'Lichtenstein' radiations were illuminating the aircraft did not suffer from this failing; but its warning of 'Wurzburg' radars, which generated an orange light on the pilot's instrument panel, were too frequent to be of practical value. The red light which identified a 'Lichtenstein' set was also of limited value if the night fighter pilot had switched-off his radar when in visual contact which, with the help of the exhaust glow from the engines, could be quite some distance behind the bomber. Both 'Monica' and 'Boozer' were of limited practical value, but are good examples of how the ebb and flow of countermeasures marked the fast moving development of electronic warfare.

'Tinsel' and its successor 'Special Tinsel' voice communications jammers initially proved successful, but again the Germans managed to circumvent its most damaging effects by frequency agility and increased transmission power. To counteract this, a new jammer called 'Airborne – or A.B.C. – Cigar' was invented at TRE which was manually tuned to the frequency actually in use by the nightfighters. It required a special operator and had to be fitted to a dedicated jamming aircraft. 'Airborne Cigar' was used on all major bombing raids after October 1943. One totally different tactic, codenamed 'Corona', was not to jam the radio frequency at all, but instead to actually make use of it by broadcasting in fluent German misleading instructions to the pilot. For example, a broadcast might be put out that fog was developing at a fighter base airfield in the hope that the pilots would break-off their sortie and make a dash for home. An attempt by the Germans to counteract this by using female controllers or local slang was rapidly countered by the ingenious operators at Kingsdown in Kent; but although a most entertaining game, its effects were usually limited. The Germans even resorted to issuing directions in morse or by broadcasting music as a coarse code system to direct the fighters to a predetermined area. These too were soon countered by high powered jamming transmitters called 'Drumstick' and 'Dartboard' respectively.

By mid 1944 electronic warfare had become such big business that a special organisation, No 100 Group, was formed using a variety of aircraft including Flying Fortresses, Stirlings and even Mosquito night fighters to exploit the ultimate range of jamming and other electronic devices in a single airframe. Although less dependent than the British on electronic deception, some of these devices were fitted into the American bombers as well. The climax in communications jamming was provided by 'Jostle IV'. Looking rather like a giant dustbin weighing over a quarter of a ton, it was able to jam a whole range of frequencies simultaneously, a considerable advance on the fixed or selectively tuneable sets of previous years.

'Jostle IV' was the last of the major advances in electronic warfare during the war, but its increasingly sophisticated and far more costly successors continue to flourish to this day. It was a fascinating period of innovation and countermeasure, testing the skill and ingenuity of the most dedicated scientists on both sides of the North Sea as well as that of the aircrew and fighter controllers who devised equally ingenious tactical plans to circumvent the latest development in electronic wizardry.

Target Selection

We have traced the development of the bomber force's organisation, aircraft, equipment and techniques, and it might, perhaps, be thought that the selection of appropriate targets was the least difficult aspect of maximising the effectiveness of their striking power. In fact, no other aspect of the strategic force's effort was to be more racked with controversy or lead to so much recrimination between its leaders, ultimately to the diminution of the contribution they would make to the outcome of the war. There were several areas of difficulty influencing the selection of targets of which the most fundamental was the strategic role to be fulfilled. Should it be purely offensive in character, striking at the very heart of Germany's capacity to continue the war, or should it be defensive in the sense of attempting to curtail a particular enemy initiative or restricting her ability to sustain an offensive action? The differences, indeed, could become easily blurred, but a general onslaught against the enemy's industrial capacity and the morale of its people was undoubtedly offensive in character whereas an attack against targets such as U-boat bases was defensive in the sense that it was intended to curtail Germany's ability to wage the Battle of the Atlantic. On the other hand, an attack directed against the aircraft industry might readily be classified in either category depending upon the circumstances at the time. Targets could also be tactical in character, for example those attacked directly in support of the land forces or to forestall an enemy counter-thrust. These distinctions might be thought somewhat esoteric, but because of the endemic shortfall of resources, they lay at the heart of divisions over the employment of the bomber forces throughout the war. Sir Arthur Harris at one end of the scale envisaged Bomber Command as the means to win the war on their own, whilst in contrast General Eisenhower saw the bomber forces as just one of the supporting elements of a massive land operation. It was all a far cry from the simple and straight forward philosophy of the pre-war pundits of strategic bombing. Only the mechanics of target selection will be discussed here, what actually happened will frequently appear in the succeeding chapters.

Even when the strategic aim was clearly defined at the highest level, which was not always the case, most of the parties involved in its implementation believed that they should have a major if not overriding influence upon the selection of the target system, even sometimes the actual target itself. There was also often a potential conflict between the ideal objective defined from a theoretical strategic viewpoint and the practical ability of the bomber forces to deal effectively with that type of target; synthetic oil plants were a very good example of this dilemma during the early war years. Having selected and attacked a target, there was then the problem of accurately assessing the damage, not only against the target itself which was difficult enough, but upon the overall German war capability. Only when such an analysis was complete could it be determined whether it was necessary or desirable to pursue a particular course of action. There were many other factors to be weighed, not least the risk assessment – did the importance of the objective justify the likely casualty rate? And finally there was the unpredictable weather which was often the overriding determinant at the final stage in the selection process.

That it was necessary to have access to comprehensive intelligence on a potential enemy's economic capacity for war had long been recognised and the machinery for this purpose had been in place since 1929. The Industrial Intelligence Committee comprising civil servants from the Board of Trade

The Operations Room at Bomber Command Headquarters High Wycombe with ACM Sir Richard Peirse and AVM Robert Saundby, the Senior Air Staff Officer. IWM

and other Government departments was provided in 1936 with an Air Targets Sub-Committee which was to focus specifically upon the strategic offensive against Germany. From this embryo organisation, the Economic Intelligence Department was formed within the powerful Ministry of Economic Warfare (MEW) on the outbreak of war with the specific task of advising the Air Ministry on suitable economic targets. The Committee of Imperial Defence, however, was very alive to the rivalry and jealousy which had plagued the many intelligence agencies in the First World War, and thus interfaced between itself and all other departments a Joint Intelligence Committee (JIC) composed of the Directors of Intelligence of the three Services whose role was to provide an agreed appreciation to the Chiefs of Staff and the Defence Committee. But the JIC had its own intelligence staffs and sources upon which they tended to rely and thus the other agencies, including the Economic Intelligence Department, were only consulted at their discretion. That this potentially disjointed system was gradually persuaded to pull together was largely the result of the co-ordinating influence of the Cabinet Secretariat and the

development of close personal relations between the individual sections. But there were inevitably misunderstandings and differences of opinion as the war progressed, notably whenever Sir Arthur Harris was directly involved.

Representatives of the MEW were eventually incorporated within the JIC and also sat upon the Bomb Targets Information Committee within the Air Ministry. Their expertise on most economic and industrial matters was gradually recognised, but there was one very important area in which there was still conflicting lines of advice. Recognising its criticality, the Government appointed a Special Committee in 1939 under Lord Hankey to oversee the vital task of restricting the flow of oil to Germany. This Committee had many sources of information which often disagreed with that provided by the MEW, and thus yet more committees were established to resolve the conflict. To crown the potential for

The last stage in the planning of a bomber operation was the mass crew briefing when the 'target for tonight' was finally revealed.   IWM

misunderstanding, Mr Churchill had his own sources of information co-ordinated by Lord Cherwell.

The MEW and the other intelligence agencies over a period of time collected a mass of detailed material on individual targets, their construction, layout and economic importance, supplemented by maps and, where available, reconnaissance photographs. These were disseminated in a simplified form in target books known as the Bomber's Baedeker, first issued in January 1943. Bomber Command maintained a comprehensive record of its own of all potential targets including their searchlight and flak defences. This information was maintained by the Wing Commander Targets and updated from intelligence reports and debriefs from previous raids.

By 1942 the pattern was fairly well established. The strategic direction of the bomber offensive was decided at the highest level within the Defence Committee of the Cabinet who had to take note not only of strategic imperatives, but also of political realities. Following the Cabinet decision, the Air Ministry then prepared a directive for Bomber Command which not only included objectives and target systems, but sometimes even nominated individual targets. It also laid down the relative priorities and occasionally the conditions under which individual targets should be attacked. It was thus in danger of impinging upon the tactical rather than purely strategic considerations, thereby opening-up a potential source of disagreement between the Air Ministry and the Command. Indeed, the Commander-in-Chief was often able to use these detailed limitations to his own advantage. For example, if the Bomber Directive stated that a particular target was to be attacked 'only when conditions were particularly favourable', it was not hard for the Command, if they disapproved of the target, to have difficulty in recognising when such conditions existed!

When the 8th Air Force arrived in Britain in 1942, it at first made use of the target material provided by the MEW, but gradually the United States began to formulate its own estimates of the German economy. A Board of Economic Warfare in Washington mirrored the activities of the MEW in London and the two organisations worked closely together. In London, the 8th Air Force had its own Target Intelligence Unit which also maintained close links with the MEW. The United States, almost from the outset, outlined its strategic aim rather more positively and distinctively than was usually done in the UK where, often for good reasons, a more pragmatic and short term view prevailed. The USAAF, it was decreed, would 'concentrate its effort upon the systematic destruction of vital elements of the German military and industrial machine through precision bombing in daylight' – in other words, the destruction of 'panacea' targets rather than the area bombing strategy adopted by the RAF. To translate this strategy into actual targets, General Arnold set-up in December 1942 a Committee of Operations Analysts. Their reports, which still depended heavily on detailed information from the MEW, laid the foundation of the Combined Bomber Offensive of 1943-45.

Within Bomber Command, detailed target selection was carried-out on a day to day basis throughout the war. Sir Arthur Harris almost invariably held his planning conference in the Operations Room at High Wycombe starting at 9.0 am and attended by most of his senior subordinates, a myriad of more junior staff officers and a senior representative of the 8th Air Force. After a brief review of the previous nights operations, the Senior Met Officer provided the all important weather brief. It was not easy to predict the weather over Europe, few actual observations of course emanated from occupied countries and forecasting was not the science it has become today with the aid of live pictures transmitted from satellites. Not only was the weather picture required over central Europe for a time some 12 to 18 hours hence, but take-off and landing forecasts were vital, in particular the likelihood of fog when the aircraft returned in the early hours of the morning. In the circumstances, the forecast was often surprisingly accurate.

Following the weather forecast, the C-in-C was briefed by the 8th Air Force representative on their plans for the day. Sometimes, but not often, these were correlated in advance under the terms of the Combined Bomber Offensive, but the 'combination' was rather more a political than a practical appellation. Briefings completed, there usually followed a long silence whilst Sir Arthur Harris pondered his options. The first consideration was whether a major operation would be mounted at all, a decision dependent as much as anything on the weather and the moonlight conditions. If the decision was positive, Harris would then announce the 'target for tonight'. After a brief discussion on the size of the raid, major tactical considerations and routeing, the C-in-C would leave and his deputy – for most of the war Air Marshal Sir Robert Saundby – tasked the assembled junior staff officers with the detailed planning. The target was then flashed to the groups which were to participate who would in turn brief their station commanders and inform them of the scale of their participation. Quite often this would be summed-up quite simply in the words 'maximum effort'.

The Rebirth of the Luftwaffe

The aircraft and men of Bomber Command and the USAAF are of course only half of the story of the Allied Bomber War, for they were opposed throughout by the air defence organisation of the German Air Force. It is thus appropriate at this stage to have a first look at the Luftwaffe, the air force which in theory should not have existed at all following the Treaty of Versailles of 1919.

In fact, the German air arm did not totally disappear after 1919. Under the Treaty of Versailles Germany was allowed a 100,000 man army for self defence, but among many other stringent restrictions was forbidden to maintain either land based or naval air forces: in theory the Imperial German Flying Service had been liquidated. But General Hans Von Seeckt, the far sighted and pragmatic creator of the Reichseer insisted that 180 of the 4,000 officers that were allowed under the Treaty were selected from the former air service. A secret agreement was reached with the Russians to create a flying school at Lipetsk, 300 miles south east of Moscow, and the clandestine General Staff, known somewhat misleadingly as the Troop Office, contained a small air organisation which kept alive, however tenuously, an embryo air arm for the future. Thus when Hitler came to power in 1933, there were already a number of pseudo military aviation units masquerading as sports clubs and commercial flying schools as well as the national airline Deutches Luft Hansa which was also not entirely what it seemed under the direction of Erhard Milch. Nevertheless, although often cited as of vital importance in the resurgence of German power, this clandestine air force did not in truth amount to much at the birth of the Third Reich.

Thereafter, however, the scene began to change quite rapidly. On 1st January 1934 the 'Rhineland Programme' was initiated in great secrecy to create an air force of more than 4,000 aircraft in less than two years. Its primary role was to be strategic bombing, intended mainly as a deterrent, and the initial plan contained only 250 fighters. On the 10th March 1935 Hitler announced to a largely incredulous world that the Luftwaffe had officially come into existence and a week later repudiated the military provisions of the Treaty of Versailles. Although the number of aircraft produced for the resurgent Luftwaffe was impressive, its rapid growth was not without its problems. The command structure under its titular head Hermann Goering became increasingly disjointed and fractious as its arrogant and ambitious leaders jockeyed for power. Furthermore, its original concept of the strategic bomber, the 'Ural Bomber' as it was called because it was designed to reach into Russia's industrial heartland, was abandoned mainly because its development at that time was beyond Germany's technological and economic resources and its main advocate, Lieutenant General Walter Wever, was killed in an air crash. After this the main thrust turned towards the air support of the Army with the creation of a force of twin engine medium bombers and the infamous Stuka dive bomber. It was a crucial decision which constrained the effectiveness of the Luftwaffe throughout the war, but it need concern us no more in this narrative as our main interest lies in the development of the air defence of the Reich.

The three elements of the air defence system were the fighter aircraft, anti-aircraft artillery and an early warning/detection system. The experience of the Condor Legion in the Spanish Civil War had considerable influence on the development of the Luftwaffe with the introduction of the Bf 109 giving many of the eventual fighter aces valuable combat experience. Tactics such as the open finger four battle formation were devised which gave pilots far more effective mutual protection than the close formation adopted hitherto in both Britain and Germany. On the other hand, the success of anti-aircraft artillery in that conflict against slow low flying aircraft gave an enhanced prominence to this form of defence which was found to be misplaced, at least initially, when directed against higher flying aircraft at night. Furthermore, whilst the Luftwaffe had foreseen the probability of night raids, they had no designated

The Spanish Civil War provided invaluable experience for Luftwaffe aircrew. These Condor Legion pilots are briefing in front of their Bf 109DS.   IWM

The Luftwaffe Organisation

The basic fighting unit of the Luftwaffe was the 'Gruppe' which equates to an RAF Station or a USAAF Group. It comprised three or four 'Staffeln' – squadrons – of between nine and twelve aircraft each. Three to four 'gruppen' were combined into a 'Geschwader', the equivalent of an American 'Wing', but with no direct RAF equivalent other than perhaps a Group which was usually larger. Geschwader were given a distinguishing prefix – Jagdgeschwader (JG), day fighters; Nachtjagdgeschwader (NJG), night fighters and Zerstorergeschwader (ZG), heavy fighters. The designation of individual units was complex:

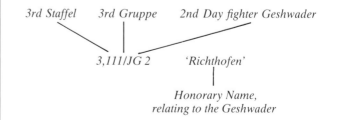

3rd Staffel   3rd Gruppe   2nd Day fighter Geshwader

3,111/JG 2   'Richthofen'

Honorary Name, relating to the Geshwader

Although ill suited for its intended Zerstorer role, the Bf 110 became a formidable nightfighter. This G-4 model seen at Farnborough was captured by the RAF. IWM

night fighters at the outbreak of war. Indeed, the Luftwaffe placed a low priority on fighter defence; they had no equivalent of Fighter Command and their structural organisation was horizontal rather than vertical with all roles subsumed into each Luflotten, itself designed to provide integrated and flexible support for the Army.

In the early years of the war, the Luftwaffe fighter defences were entirely dependent on two aircraft built by Professor Willy Messerschmitt's Bayerische Flugzeugwerke (BFW), a company not hitherto renowned for the production of fighter aircraft. The Bf 109 was conceived from a requirement of 1933 to provide Germany with a modern agile monoplane fighter. Four companies vied for this potentially lucrative contract of which BFW, already in financial difficulties, was included more for political than practical reasons. Nevertheless, the BFW entrant, powered by a Rolls Royce Kestrel engine, handsomely defeated its rivals in a 'fly-off' at Travemunde in October 1935. As the clear winner of the competition, the Bf 109 was now united with the Junkers Jumo engine and entered squadron service with the celebrated Jagdgeschwader 2 'Richthofen' in the Spring of 1937. Despite initial mishaps, it soon established itself as a formidable rival to the Hurricane and Spitfire which were also coming into service in the same era. The Bf 109 passed quickly through the 'B', 'C' and 'D' variants to the 'E' model with which the Luftwaffe was largely equipped at the outbreak of war. Now powered by a Daimler Benz engine, the most significant development was the introduction of two 20mm canon in the wings. These could outrange the 0.3in or 0.5in machine guns of the bombers, which along with its speed and agility, gave the 109 a very real advantage in air combat. At the outbreak of hostilities the Luftwaffe had over 1,000 Bf 109s in service and it remained in use throughout the war. Albeit subsequently outclassed by the later Allied fighters, over 33,000 were built in all, a total exceeded only by the Russian IL2. In spite of its limitations, some of which such as the narrow fragile undercarriage persisted throughout its long life, it remains one of the classic fighter aircraft of the period.

The most serious limitation of the BF 109 was its very limited radius of action – little over 125 miles – and the Luftwaffe required a larger twin engine fighter both to escort its bombers and to intercept intruders at a greater range. This niche was filled by another of Messerschmitt's designs, the Bf 110. The prototype made its first flight in May 1936 and showed initial promise reaching a speed of 316 mph, comparing favourably with the Hurricane which had flown a few months earlier. But the 110 was dogged by engine problems with both Jumo and Daimler Benz power plants being tried before the choice settled on the latter. As a result, production was delayed and only 159 of the 'C' models were available at the outbreak of war. The Zerstorergeshwader units were provided with elite crews on the direct orders of Goering and the Bf 110 played a major role in the invasions of both Poland and Norway. Although no match for the RAF's single engine fighters, it proved itself quite capable of dealing with the Wellingtons and Hampdens which made the early daylight sorties into German coastal waters at the end of 1939. Like the Bf 109, the 110 also remained in service until the end of the war, but although undoubtedly failing in the Zerstorer role for which it was designed, it made a very real contribution as a night fighter and we shall frequently encounter this aircraft again as the narrative develops.

The Luftwaffe, however, did not really depend on its fighter aircraft to defend the Reich against air attack in 1939; this was entrusted to the Fliegerabwehrkanone – the flak units. These were regarded as an elite body, totalling over 100,000 men and equipped with 2,600 heavy and 6,700 medium and light guns as well as 3,000 searchlights. Operational control was vested in the regional Luflottens under the overall direction of General Alfred Haubold, the Inspector of Flak Artillery. The light and medium guns were generally ineffective other than for the point defence of targets against low flying aircraft, but the much more formidable 88mm could reach, with diminishing accuracy, to above 30,000 feet. The majority of the guns were deployed in the Western Defence Zone which extended in 245 reinforced bastions for 375 miles along the Rhine from Holland to Switzerland, varying in depth from 12 miles to as much as 60 where it encompassed important cities close to the border. Searchlight batteries were interspersed within the line to illuminate targets and, in theory, every intruding aircraft would be subjected to five minutes of continuous fire from at least three gun batteries. In addition, many of the more important cities such as Berlin, Hamburg and Bremen had their own discrete searchlight and flak defences.

The anti-aircraft defences, however, suffered from serious shortcomings in the early stages of the war. They were not initially radar directed and thus almost useless in bad weather, and at night the searchlights in the Western Defence Zone were easily evaded by the bomber crews. Furthermore, the accuracy of the guns fell away quite markedly with height and it was estimated in the early years that on average some 3,400 shells were required to destroy a single bomber. Radar was the answer to the detection problem, but at this stage the Germans had only eight Freya radar stations capable of detecting aircraft in ideal conditions out to 93 miles. But even if the radar could detect incoming aircraft, the means did not exist to target the guns which still depended upon visual laying. Although the point defence of the more important locations could be concentrated more effectively, the flak units of the Western Defence Zone had little impact on the early night raids into Germany. In the first two years or so of the war, therefore, although the German air defences had successfully thwarted the daylight raids, they had almost negligible success against intrusions at night.

At the outbreak of war the Germans depended primarily on their anti-aircraft guns for air defence. The 88mm gun eventually became a very effective weapon which took a high toll of Allied bombers.

IWM

============ CHAPTER FOUR ============

Years of Disappointment — 1939-41

The Demise of Daylight Bombing

At 5 am on the morning of the 1st September 1939 German aircraft initiated the bombing of Polish airfields, to be followed less than an hour later by the onset of the 'Blitzkrieg' which was to destroy that oft ravished country in little more than a month. Two days later, a sombre Neville Chamberlain announced to an apprehensive population that Britain was at war with Germany. Bomber Command had been at readiness for two days and in less than an hour a Blenheim of No 139 Squadron was on its way to carry-out a reconnaissance of German north sea ports. It was the onset of six years of unrelenting effort, acts of almost inconceivable bravery, many disappointments and, ultimately, fulfilment of its mission.

It will be recalled from Chapter One that Bomber Command had emerged from the traumatic years of rearmament with its counter offensive strategy in tatters, committed mainly to conserving its forces until the heavy bombers emerged from the aircraft factories in 1941. The two roles with which it would occupy itself in the meantime being the attack on naval targets and the dropping of propaganda leaflets. Any raid against an overland target which might invite retaliation in kind was strictly forbidden. Its order of battle was not impressive. With the obsolete Battles already dispatched to France, it could offer only 25 squadrons for operational service consisting of some 350 aircraft. Nevertheless, this insubstantial force was soon in action in support of both its two new objectives.

Until the advent of the Whitley, all the bomber aircraft contained within the rearmament programme were intended for daylight operations. The early months of the war were to lead to a drastic reappraisal of this concept, for many of the tactical doctrines formed in the interwar years were shown to be invalid. The advent of radar, better communications, concentrated anti-aircraft defences and, above all, a fast, agile day fighter added a new dimension to aerial warfare.

The Blenheim figured prominently in early raids against German naval targets. These 3 Mk IVs are from No 139 Squadron which had the distinction of mounting the first operational sortie of the war. IWM

NORWAY
Bergen
OSLO
Stavanger
SWEDEN
Lossiemouth
NORTH
SEA
600 Miles
400 Miles
200 Miles
DENMARK
Prestwick
Flensburg
Kiel
Warnemunde
Peenemunde
Brunsbuttel
Rostock
Lubeck
Wilhelmshaven
Hamburg
Stettin
Lincoln
Bremerhaven
Emden
Bremen
UNITED
KINGDOM
Gt Yarmouth
BERLIN
Hanover
HOLLAND
Osnabruck
Brunswick
Magdeburg
High
Wycombe
LONDON
Rotterdam
Bielefeld
Eindhoven
Leuna
Leipzig
Ostend
Dunkirk
Calais
Antwerp
Kassel
Dresden
Cologne
Boulogne
BELGIUM
Chemnitz
Lille
Aachen
GERMANY
Arras
Bruex
Abbeville
Albert
Gembloux
Koblenz
Hanau
Cherbourg
Amiens
Bruneval
Trier
Mainz
Frankfurt
Billancourt
Darmstadt
Nuremberg
Brest
PARIS
Mannheim
Saarbrucken
Regensburg
Karlsruhe
Villacoublay
Stuttgart
Lorient
Augsburg
Munich
St Nazaire
FRANCE
AUSTRI
BERNE
BAY
of
BISCAY
La Pallice
La Rochelle
SWITZERLAND
Milan
Turin
Bordeaux
ITALY

The impact of these developments, however, was but dimly perceived when the first daylight attacks were mounted in the opening days of the new conflict. In theory there were three methods by which daylight raids could be safely pursued. The first was to fly at a height and/or speed which would provide immunity from enemy defences; this option was clearly not available in 1939 and would not be until the advent of the Mosquito. Secondly, the bombers could be escorted by long range fighters, but again this option, although used ineffectively by the Luftwaffe against Britain in 1940, was not available to the Allies until much later. The only practical course at this time, therefore, was to concentrate bombers in tight tactical formations, relying on collective fire power to beat-off enemy fighters. On the other hand, these tight formations were more vulnerable to flak, either directly or by breaking-up the formation to enable the fighters to pick-off the stragglers.

The first daylight raid of the war was an early portent of the difficulties involved. Fifteen Blenheims and 14 Wellingtons departed in the late afternoon of the 4th September to attack respectively German ships at Wilhelmshaven and at the mouth of the Kiel Canal. The first problem was the weather; dense cloud made both navigation and formation keeping difficult and No 139 Squadron's five Benheims returned without reaching the target area. The Wattisham wing led by Flight Lieutenant Ken Doran of No 110 Squadron seemed to have achieved a degree of surprise, but anti-aircraft fire nevertheless claimed five overall, four from the second wave from No 107 Squadron. Five of the Wellingtons were also defeated by the weather and although the remainder found targets, they were engaged by Bf 109 fighters and two failed to return. At the time, both were thought to have fallen to the anti-aircraft defences rather than the fighters. The returning crews reported that the 109s did not press home their attacks and that their shooting was wild. Although two hits were scored by the Blenheims on the 'pocket' battleship *Admiral Scheer*, both 500lb bombs failed to explode, forewarning of a problem which was to frustrate the crews for a long time. The ensueing debate concluded that the principle of the defensive formation was correct and the importance of disciplined station keeping was re-emphasised. Nevertheless, a loss rate of nearly 25 per cent was hardly in keeping with the policy of conserving resources.

There were few opportunities for assessing the tactical doctrine again until December because of indifferent weather and the difficulty of locating the German Fleet. However, three raids in that month by No 3 Group were of outstanding significance for future bomber operations by the RAF throughout the war. On the morning of the 3rd December, 24 Wellingtons from Marham and Mildenhall were launched to attack ships in the Heligoland Bight, about 25 miles north of the Freisian Islands. The raiders met no fighters as they approached the target at 8,000 feet and some hits and near misses were reported, although as we now know no damage was caused: two aircraft were hit by flak but managed to return safely. Shortly thereafter the bombers were engaged by both Bf 109 and 110 fighters, but again they generally attacked from astern and did

The Wellington suffered serious losses in the early daylight raids against German naval targets. These Mk IAs are from No 9 Squadron.
IWM

One of the attributes of the Wellington was its ability to absorb considerable damage and still keep flying. The geodetic structure of the aircraft is well shown in this picture.
IWM

not approach too closely: one that closed to 350 yards was at least damaged. All aircraft returned and the only disturbing factor was that the close formation again appeared to break-up too readily in the face of flak. Not surprisingly, this operation was well received and the Command eagerly awaited another opportunity to seek out the German Fleet.

It came on the 14th December and was an altogether different story. The weather was very poor and only 12 Wellingtons from Newmarket led by Wg Cdr J.F. Griffiths participated in a raid against the cruisers *Nurnberg* and *Leipzig* in the Jade estuary. The formation was driven down by low cloud until it was flying at only 200 feet as it approached the target area. Although not authorised to bomb below 2,000 feet, Griffiths pressed on with great courage albeit less prudence and in the target area the formation was intercepted despite the weather by a mixed force of 109s and 110s. The Luftwaffe claimed, probably correctly, that the fighters shot down five aircraft over the target (one more crashed at Newmarket on landing), but the RAF's appreciation was that all again fell victim to the anti-aircraft defences. It was generally agreed that it had been rash to press-on and, it was alleged, loiter in the target area in conditions which in any case were unsuitable for bombing. Confidence was dented but not destroyed.

The final nail in the coffin of daylight bombing was not long delayed. Four days later on the 18th December, 24 Wellingtons, led by Wg Cdr R Kellett who had been responsible for the successful raid on the 3rd December, were dispatched to seek targets of opportunity in the same area. They were sensibly ordered not to attack below 10,000 feet as most of the losses sustained so far were thought to be from flak at low level: the threat from the fighters was almost discounted. The sky was

cloudless and visibility 30 miles, very different from the conditions encountered on the two previous sorties. Forewarned by radar, Bf 109s intercepted the Wellingtons south of Heligoland and attacks persisted until what remained of the formation was well on the way home. Joined later by Bf 110s, the fighters pressed home their attacks much more vigorously than previously and although some were again from astern, quarter attacks from the beam proved far more lethal. From this angle each aircraft was dependent for its survival on its neighbours, and this would only be possible if formation discipline had been preserved. The greater lethality of 20 mm canon compared with the Wellington's 0.3in Brownings was another crucial factor. In all, 12 Wellingtons failed to return, and this time there could be no doubt that they were the victims of the fighters rather than the anti-aircraft guns.

The subsequent post mortem still did not at first reach the obvious conclusion. Morale remained buoyant despite the 50 per cent casualty rate and the crews claimed that 12 fighters had been shot down (a sixfold exaggeration): it could thus be asserted, and was, that the bombers had given as good as they received. The losses were attributed to indisciplined formation keeping and some credence was given to this view by the fact that Wg Cdr Kellett's leading section of nine aircraft only suffered one casualty. But sections towards the rear of a formation are usually more vulnerable and the difficulties of maintaining tight order whilst under intense attack were quite clearly not fully appreciated. Some of the deficiencies of the Wellington also became very apparent of which the lack of self sealing petrol tanks and a dorsal turret for beam defence were the most obvious.

Although the debate continued for some months, these two disastrous raids in December 1939 had a marked influence on Bomber Command operations thereafter. Although the light bombers continued to operate by day and the medium bombers regularly participated in such daylight operations as 'Circuses', the heavy bomber force due to enter service in 1941 was, special operations apart, now regarded as a night force right through to the last year of the war. It was left to the United States Army Air Force to resurrect daylight bombing as a mainstream policy in 1942.

It was not, however, only the experience of the December raids that caused the switch to night operations, for during this same period the Whitleys had been ranging widely over Germany at night dropping leaflets with almost complete immunity from attack. There, apparently, lay the answer to the unexpected setbacks of 1939: time would show that it was to be at least another three years before Bomber Command could find and destroy a target at night with any consistent degree of precision.

The Paper War – Leaflet Raids Over Germany

The Commander-in-Chief Bomber Command, Air Marshal Sir Edgar Ludlow-Hewitt, first suggested as early as the 19th September 1938 in a letter to the Air Ministry that his aircraft might best be employed in dropping propaganda leaflets. Although at the time this was regarded as a somewhat defeatist attitude, in the light of Prime Minister Chamberlain's ban on the bombing of mainland Germany, Bomber Command had little option but to employ its Whitleys of No 4 Group, a dedicated night bomber, in this way.

In fact, this apparently innocuous practice, soon known as 'Nickelling', proved to be quite valuable in a number of ways. It provided reasonable training and despite the difficulties which soon became apparent, was on the whole beneficial to the morale of the crews. During the next six months the Whitleys, occasionally joined by No 5 Group's Hampdens, ranged far and wide over Europe to the Ruhr, Stuttgart, Vienna, Berlin, Prague, even Warsaw. Few towns of any size did not receive their share of paper, enough said Harris 'to supply the Continent's requirements of toilet paper for the five long years of war'.

The leaflet raids did not get off to an auspicious start. Ten Whitleys of Nos 51 and 58 Squadrons were tasked on the first night of the war to drop leaflets on the Ruhr, Bremen and Hamburg and although successfully accomplished with no sign of any opposition, three aircraft had to make emergency landings in France as a result of engine trouble – a persistent problem with the Whitley at this time.

At first the leaflets were somewhat naive and crude, designed to show that the Allies had no quarrel with the German people, only with their vindictive and corrupt masters. Churchill commented, somewhat doubtfully, that they were intended 'to move the Germans to a higher morality'. They exaggerated Allied operations and successes to an extent that was barely credible to a nation which was only too well aware that at this stage their armed forces were sweeping all before them. Their impact on the morale of the recipients was probably negligible, except perhaps in the thought that if the bombers were able to penetrate so far into Germany with leaflets, then they could doubtless do the same with a more lethal load. Even so, it was considered a serious offence in Germany to be found in possession of a leaflet and even more incongruously, for a long time the content of the leaflets remained classified at home. They became increasingly more sophisticated as new and more imaginative minds were drawn into their creation.

So what were the benefits of the leaflet raids apart from keeping the crews occupied? In most respects they were of a negative kind, highlighting some of the difficulties of operating over Germany at night at an early enough stage to enable remedial action to be sought before the strategic offensive began in earnest. Compared with the daylight raids, the most obvious difference was the absence of opposition from German fighters and the ineffectiveness of their anti-aircraft defences, the latter compounded by the poor quality of the searchlights.

*This Whitley Mk V is taking-off just before dusk on a leaflet dropping
raid over Germany.* IWM

Leaflets being dispatched through the flare chute of a Whitley. IWM

Although the Luftwaffe had detailed some Bf 109 squadrons to
operate at night, the task for a single crew aircraft without radar
was quite hopeless and they suffered heavy attrition through
accidents.

Of far greater significance than the opposition was the
weather. The Whitley suffered badly from icing and it was not
unusual for engines to seize and layers of ice inches thick to
settle on the flying surfaces, breaking-off from time to time and
crashing against other parts of the aeroplane with a clap of
thunder. Aircraft frequently lost thousands of feet as the pilots
struggled to regain control of a machine whose flying
characteristics more resembled a brick than an aerofoil. Almost
as bad were the conditions inside the aeroplane, particularly for
the air gunner isolated in his lonely compartment in the tail,
often cut-off from the rest of the crew by the failure of the
intercom. On the 27th October, a 51 Squadron rear gunner
survived a crash with bruises and minor burns after the rest of
the crew had, without his knowledge, abandoned the aircraft
which had suffered a double engine failure. The inadequacies of
the de-icing equipment, cockpit heating and oxygen supplies
were all problems that could be tackled quickly, although
remedial action was not always effective.

Of greater significance were the problems of navigation. The
Whitley was equipped only with a rather ineffectual radio
compass and a sextant for astro navigation, both requiring
training and experience for accurate results, qualifications
which were often lacking in the winter of 1939/40. More often
than not the crew was dependent upon a glimpse of the ground
for updating their position, and even when this was possible

through the cloud, it was only too easy to misidentify topographical features at night, either natural or man made. Visual observation was the only means of identifying the target and this was virtually impossible on moonless nights at high altitude. In this respect there was undoubtedly greater optimism in the crew reports than was really justified – after all leaflets floating on the wind left no tell tale marks on the ground to indicate whether the target had been found or not. Deliberate efforts were made to identify which topographical features were of most use for navigation purposes, and areas of water and, more surprisingly, railway lines glinting in the moonlight often provided valuable clues. Nevertheless, the higher the aircraft the more difficult the navigation and about 10,000 feet was recognised as the maximum feasible height. The value of a timed run from a clearly identified feature was already recognised as one means of reaching a target not otherwise seen, and the need for a target illuminating flare was another conclusion drawn from these early sorties over Germany. But even though valuable experience was gained, it was generally recognised that accurate navigation and target acquisition was a rather hit and miss affair.

Leaflet raids continued with some longish breaks due to weather until April 1940 and were never entirely abandoned. In this first phase 65 million leaflets were scattered over Europe, and although several aircraft were lost due to mechanical failure or extreme weather, not a single Whitley succumbed to enemy action. This was the most telling feature of this phase of Bomber Command's apprenticeship, and in combination with the denial of daylight bombing was to set the pattern for the next five years of night operations, a concept which all the theorising between the wars had never seriously envisaged.

Ground support for the BEF in France was largely provided by Battles and Blenheims. This is a Blenheim Mk I of No 107 Squadron with 2 Battles of No 226 Squadron. RAFM

Interlude in France

Other than at sea where there had already been some sharp encounters, the 'Phoney War' had proved strangely frustrating to the Government, the armed forces and the general public alike. Much attention in ministerial circles had been given to Norway, but nothing was actually done until after Hitler's bold and well executed invasion on the 9th April 1940. Bomber Command was involved in the margins of the campaign in Norway as potential targets could only be reached with a worthwhile bomb load from airfields in Scotland. Nevertheless, Wellingtons and Blenheims were detached to Kinloss and Lossiemouth from where they attacked Norwegian and Danish airfields taken over in strength by the Luftwaffe. The attack by three Wellingtons of No 115 Squadron at dusk on the 11th April on the airfield at Stavanger marked the first Allied mainland bombing operation of the war. Later in the month the Whitleys of No 4 Group joined-in, but very few of the raids caused any worthwhile damage. Perhaps the most significant achievement during this disastrous campaign was the sinking of the cruiser *Konigsberg* at Bergen by Fleet Air Arm Skuas, the highlight of an otherwise undistinguished career for this obsolete dive bomber.

In France, the British Expeditionary Force (BEF) and the seemingly more powerful French Army waited expectantly for the blow to fall. The BEF had commenced its build-up in September 1939 and comprised ten divisions by the Spring of 1940. In support, ten Fairey Battle squadrons of No 1 Group had actually moved to France on the 2nd September before war was declared to form the Advanced Air Striking Force (AASF) where they were regarded, somewhat optimistically, as the forward arm of Bomber Command's strategic offensive force. In the event, the policy of restricting bombing to naval targets gave them a brief respite from the horrors that awaited them, although a high level reconnaissance sortie on the 30th

September in which four of a flight of six aircraft of No 150 Squadron were destroyed by Bf 109s was an ominous portent of what was in store. Including those aircraft of the BEF Air Component, the Battles had been reinforced by six Blenheim squadrons and some Hurricanes when the blow actually fell on the 10th May.

Perhaps the aspect most readily recalled today of the RAFs air war at this time was Dowding's grim and determined struggle to prevent Fighter Command's most valuable assets being dissipated in the hostile skies of France and the Low Countries. That he was largely successful in this quest is now an indelible part of the history of that great air battle over the Channel which followed, but it is not part of our story. We are concerned with the less glorious, indeed the tragic fate of the Battles and Blenheims based in France and those of No 2 Group, Bomber Command, which tried to stem the relentless tide of Panzers streaming through the Ardennes and the Low Countries.

That the Fairey Battles of the AASF were no longer regarded as a strategic force was confirmed in January 1940 when Air Marshal Sir Arthur Barratt was charged with setting-up the British Air Force in France Command (BAFF) with specific responsibilities to Lord Gort commanding the BEF. The Army's estimate of the air support required, totally unrealistic in the circumstances, was some 100 squadrons. Barratt actually had 14 light bomber squadrons comprising some 200 serviceable

aircraft. In addition, there were five Blenheim squadrons of No 2 Group based in East Anglia which were committed to bombing operations in France. The French Air Force bomber squadrons, equipped with aircraft even more ineffectual than the Battle, took little part in the campaign although their fighters mounted a spirited, if hopeless, defence.

The Battles were thrown into the fray at noon on the first day of the invasion when four flights of eight aircraft each were tasked with the tactical bombing of German columns approaching through Luxembourg. Already convinced of the need to operate at low level following their experience of the previous September, they now encountered the formidable light anti-aircraft guns which could seemingly keep pace with even the fastest moving advance. Almost every aircraft on the first operation was damaged and 13 destroyed for no obvious return. Ten more were lost in a similar operation later in the afternoon. Another constraint was also immediately apparent: intelligence was so poor that locating any target, let alone that for which they had been tasked, was often well nigh impossible. Of eight more Battles dispatched to the same area on the following day, only one badly damaged aircraft returned. An added misfortune was

MRAF Lord Trenchard talking to No 12 Squadron crews in France who suffered heavy losses in a desperate attempt to stem the tide of German tanks in May 1940. RAFM

the loss of almost all the Blenheims of No 114 Squadron on the ground at Conde-Vraux. At this point Barratt was enjoined by the Air Ministry to conserve his forces for the decisive moment. With 1,500 tanks now rolling nose to tail through the Ardennes, he could be forgiven for thinking that this event had already arrived.

On the 12th, seven of nine Blenheims of No 139 (Jamaica) Squadron were lost attacking armoured columns near Maastricht and a Belgian Air Force Battle squadron had been virtually eliminated in a fruitless attempt to destroy bridges on the Albert Canal near the same town. No 12 (Battle) Squadron – the 'Dirty Dozen' – were now asked to make another attempt on the same targets. They could muster only six aircraft, one of which failed to get airborne because of radio failure. The second section led by Flying Officer D Garland succeeded in damaging the bridge at Veldwezelt in a suicidal low level attack; all died in the attempt, but Garland and his navigator Sergeant Gray were awarded the RAFs first Victoria Crosses of the War. They could with equal justice have gone to almost any of the Battle crews during these fateful first few days of the Battle of France. Out of 15 more Battles launched later that day against General Rundstedt's columns at Sedan, only nine survived. Barratt's bomber force had already been halved. Even worse was to follow in yet another raid against pontoon bridges at Sedan on the 14th – of 70 bombers launched, no less than 40 were lost (35 Battles and the rest Blenheims). It was the highest loss rate suffered in any major bombing operation of the war.

The slaughter could not continue, the remaining Battles were withdrawn from daylight operation, to be used with almost total ineffect at night. Even so another 33 were lost bringing the overall total to 137 before the final withdrawal of the AASF on the 15th June. It was a pathetic loss of so many valuable young lives in an aircraft which, by 1940, should never have been sent to war against a fighter of the calibre of the Bf 109. But it was a tragedy steeped in glory which has rarely received due recognition. Never before had the courage, fortitude and grim perseverance of the RAF's aircrews been so cruelly exposed. It was an example which would be repeated many times in the next five years.

If the name Sedan will for ever be embedded in the memories of the Battle crews in France, Gembloux is as similarly poignant for those of No 82 Squadron based at RAF Watton in Norfolk. By the 17th May, the Panzer columns were across the Meuse and heading for Mons through the Gembloux Gap, a few miles to the north west of Namur. Led by Sqn Ldr Paddy Delap, two boxes of six Blenheims each were orbiting Tangmere at 0530 hours waiting for their promised escort of Hurricanes. Thanks to a mix-up in timing the Hurricanes did not appear and the Blenheims headed-off alone across the Channel to Le Touquet where they turned east for Lille and their target, tank columns in the valley between Namur and Gembloux. One of the notable features of the German advance already remarked upon was the efficiency with which their anti-aircraft artillery kept pace with the fast moving columns, and 82 Squadron ran directly into one such battery. The tight formations broke-up in the hail of fire,

but only one aircraft appeared to have succumbed and the rest pressed-on. But within a very short time after the barrage ceased, the still dispersed formation was set-upon by about 15 Bf 109s which simply picked-off each defenceless aircraft in turn: only one escaped the melee, badly damaged, to return to Watton. A whole squadron destroyed in half a dozen dramatic minutes of a beautiful Spring morning.

This was the most disastrous of the many raids on France by the five Blenheim squadrons of No 2 Group during these six weeks of the Battle of France, but it epitomised the problems they faced. The Blenheims were usually armed with twenty 40lb anti-personnel bombs and two 250lb bombs which could not be dropped below 1,000 feet above the ground because of the blast effect on the aircraft, thus making it alarmingly vulnerable to anti-aircraft fire during the target run. The available intelligence on the movement of enemy formations was in any case very poor, but by the time it had percolated back to the No 2 Group stations in East Anglia it was all but useless. In consequence, squadrons more often than not had to dissipate their efforts on targets of opportunity. The arrangements for co-ordinating a fighter escort were primitive, and as happened in the Gembloux raid, sometimes broke down completely. But most dangerous of all was the inability of the Blenheims to match the speed, manoeuvrability and above all striking power of the cannon armed Bf 109. Once forced out of its tight box formation, the Blenheim was defenceless and rarely survived an encounter with a fighter.

Nevertheless, No 2 Group aircraft valiantly continued to support the BEF, attacking bridges, railway lines, roads, villages and above all concentrations of tanks and vehicles. Led by men of the calibre of Wg Cdr Basil Embry and Wg Cdr the Earl of Bandon, the crews went back day after day into the fray: Embry himself was shot down on the 27th of May, but on the 2nd August after a string of adventures returned to Wattisham as anxious as ever to resume the fight. By the 14th June when No 2 Groups participation in the Battle of France ended, the five squadrons had flown 1,441 sorties for the loss of 97 aircraft and 234 aircrew killed, wounded or missing. Fortunately, many of the missing in the confused situation pertaining in France at that time managed to evade the enemy, and with the help of the Army and local civilians were able to return home.

Bomber Commands first attempts at tactical bombing, along with the even more disastrous experiences of the BAFF gave more food for thought. Tactics, fighter co-ordination and above all equipment had to be improved if the bomber war was to be pursued successfully in a hostile air environment in or close to the battle zone. There was little reason for satisfaction in mid 1940: driven out of the skies in daylight, humiliated in France, and until May confined to dropping paper on Germany. A review of the policy for the employment of Bomber Command was clearly opportune.

Searching for a Policy – 1940/41

Although daylight bombing as a primary policy was now generally discarded for the time being, the leaflet raids had shown that night attacks on Germany were feasible, at least in terms of an acceptable casualty rate. The precision bombing of individual targets was also still a live issue even though the difficulties of night navigation and target acquisition were beginning to be recognised, if not as clearly as they would be a year later. There had already been a minor skirmish on the 16th March when German bombs intended for ships in Scapa Flow had landed on the island of Hoy and, in retaliation, Bomber Command attacked a seaplane base on the island of Sylt three nights later. The results were not encouraging; 41 crews claimed to have bombed the target, but subsequent reconnaissance disclosed no signs of damage. Ludlow-Hewitt's policy for the conservation of crews to await the arrival of the heavy bombers was by now generally accepted, although this realistic approach had cost him his job. He was considered too cautious and pessimistic for the more aggressive minds in London: the truth is not always palatable in war. In any event, the bombing of land targets in mainland Germany was still not to be initiated until the enemy had struck the first blow.

The lull did not last long, for within four days of the German invasion of the Low Countries the Luftwaffe had mounted a heavy and indiscriminate raid on Rotterdam causing 900 civilian casualties, although the figure was grossly exaggerated at the time. For Bomber Command the gloves were off at last. On the 15th May, 99 Wellingtons, Whitleys and Hampdens set out to attack oil and railway targets in the Ruhr; the strategic bombing offensive which was to last for five long years and which eventually was to help bring Germany to its knees was at last underway.

The outbreak of the strategic offensive brought with it the first of many 'panacea' targets – an individual target system, the destruction of which it was believed would in itself cripple the German war effort and bring hostilities to an end. There was to be a continuing controversy throughout the war as to the validity of such 'panacea' targets, but none were ever pursued with sufficient dedication for long enough to determine the issue one way or the other. Nevertheless, the very first in 1940 – oil – was in fact also the last in 1944, and in the final year of the war there is at last evidence to justify the effectiveness of the concept.

Unfortunately, there was considerable difficulty in identifying oil targets at night and the new Commander-in-Chief, Air Marshal Charles Portal, soon sought authority to attack other targets, particularly in the aircraft industry, when weather or other reasons made it impracticable to strike at oil. But other considerations were already arising. The tide in France was swinging alarmingly against the Allies and there were frantic demands from the French, who had no credible bomber force of their own, to attack communications leading to the forward battle areas. Thus within the first month of the real war, the factor which eventually was to haunt Sir Arthur Harris, dispersion of effort, was already very evident. The strategic

In retaliation for bombs which fell on the Orkneys during a raid on Scapa Flow, Bomber Command attacked the seaplane base at Hornum on the island of Sylt which lies off the Danish coast.   IWM

offensive, severely restricted by Bomber Command's limited assets, was further weakened by the imposition of a defensive strategy of attacking railway junctions and marshalling yards in France and the Low Countries.

After the fall of France, another defensive strategy soon arose to take its place. As the Luftwaffe marshalled its forces to confront Britain directly, the need to constrain its potential destructive power became paramount. In June 1940 the Command was directed to attack aircraft factories and storage depots, thus further reducing the effort which could be directed against the 'panacea' target – oil. To add to the diversification, the Hampdens of No 5 Group were now increasingly employed in sea mining operations, which as we shall see was quite a profitable pursuit throughout the war. As the threat of invasion intensified, yet a further change of direction ensued in July when the highest priority was given to attacking German ports, shipping and invasion barges whilst maintaining as much effort as possible against the other objectives formulated earlier. Quite clearly Bomber Command with its limited range of resources could not hope to make any real impact on this multiplicity of target priorities and this diversification of effort has been subsequently criticized. But in the late summer of 1940, with disasters following one upon another and the homeland under very real threat of invasion, it was inevitable that the policy changed as rapidly as the threat: to paraphrase Mark Twain, 'it is difficult to remember when you are up to your ears in alligators that your intention was to drain the swamp'.

Portal only remained at Bomber Command for six months before his elevation to Chief of the Air Staff, but it was an important period because it marked the first stage of the transition towards an area bombing policy, and with it the strategy of striking directly at the morale of the civilian population. The first indirect shots had already been fired by Portal in July 1940 when he drew the Air Ministrys attention to the fact that many primary targets are 'isolated and in sparsely inhabited districts, the very high percentage of bombs which inevitably miss the actual target will hit nothing else of importance and do no damage, and the minimum amount of dislocation and disturbance will be caused by the operations as a whole.' Even Portal at this stage was unaware of just how many bombs were ineffectually blasting the countryside, or indeed how many were not actually exploding at all.

The Air Ministry remained largely unimpressed by these subtle suggestions, for whilst recognising the morale effect, they considered it, in line with Trenchard's dictum, essentially a by-product of the strategic objective of industrial destruction. The first Luftwaffe bombs on London in August (accidental, they were intended for an aircraft factory at Rochester) reopened the subject and Winston Churchill was undoubtedly reflecting the public mood when he authorised a retaliatory attack on Berlin on the 25th August. Furthermore, he suggested to Portal that Bomber Command should henceforth spread its bombs as widely as possible over the cities of Germany. But Berlin was the most significant objective in this context, for although the actual targets were industrial, the raid was essentially directed against the morale of the inhabitants. The Air Ministry continued to insist that any benefits accruing against morale were a bonus, but Portal now openly declared that the 'by-product' should become the 'end product'. The debate on the morality of area bombing – or terror bombing as it was later described by its antagonists – was now joined. Sir Arthur Harris is widely thought to have been the initiator of this new form of warfare, but the record clearly shows that its real instigator was Portal, soon to be encouraged more openly by the Prime Minister himself.

With Portal as CAS and Air Marshal Sir Richard Peirse translated to Bomber Command, it might have been expected that as the threat of invasion receded, the transition towards area bombing would be rapid. In fact, over the next six months the official policy moved strongly back towards the attack on oil targets. An influential economic report to the War Cabinet at the end of 1940 stressed again the criticality of oil supplies to Germany's ability to continue the war and suggested that 17 major synthetic oil plants were key targets. Whilst other objectives were not totally discarded, Bomber Command made several determined but largely futile raids against oil targets in the first three months of 1941. But yet another factor appeared in March. The U boat campaign and the economic blockade were becoming increasingly menacing, and thus the primary objective was changed again to submarine and long range aircraft activities: as described by Portal, 'a very high proportion of bomber effort will inevitably be required to pull the Admiralty out of the mess they have got into'. Ships in harbour were added to the list and several abortive attempts were made to bomb the *Hipper*, *Scharnhorst* and *Gneisenau* at anchor in Brest.

Albeit with some hesitation, however, there was increasing recognition that bombing accuracy was inadequate for pinpoint targets like synthetic oil plants and ships in harbour. The effort wasted in planting hundreds of tons of bombs in open fields was particularly galling to those who believed with Portal that the effort should be applied against German cities. Lord Trenchard joined in the debate from retirement suggesting, with little supporting evidence, that the Germans were particularly vulnerable to this form of attack. But to lay waste the major urban centres across Germany would require a force of 4,000 heavy bombers and nothing approaching these numbers was available. It was decided instead to select another 'panacea' target – transport – some features of which such as railway marshalling yards at least stood a reasonable chance of being hit with the added bonus that most stray bombs would fall in an urban area with the consequential impact on morale. The transport directive was issued on the 9th July 1941 although attacks against anti-blockade naval targets were to continue, and indeed did so with various levels of intensity for the rest of the war.

By the end of 1941, therefore, Bomber Command had been directed to concentrate against a bewildering array of selective targets – oil plants, communications, aircraft factories and storage depots, ships and communications to name but the most prominent. Furthermore, the concept of area bombing was already coming to the fore, if not yet fully endorsed. It is now appropriate to review in more detail how effective Bomber Command had proved during this formative period of the strategic offensive.

Precision Bombing – 1940

The Blenheims of No 2 Group excepted, Bomber Command spent most of 1940 exploring the possibility of hitting a precise target at night. Single factories, bridges, even on one occasion a road junction, were nominated as individual targets for aircraft operating at medium levels. In the light of the already known capabilities of the Wellingtons, Hampdens and Whitleys involved and the experience gained from the leaflet raids, it is surprising in retrospect that this demanding task was ever thought feasible, and even more so that senior commanders believed for a long time that it was actually succeeding. We have already looked at the bewildering range of target priorities which were decreed during these months of 1940, and study of the nightly operational reports indicates that a great variety of targets were attacked by small groups or even single aircraft on each night that bombing was possible. So much so that it is difficult to discern the priorities laid down by the Air Staff from a review of what actually occurred. After the 10th June when Italy entered the war, the target list was extended to embrace

Flt Sgt G. Dove CGM, DFM – 10 Squadron

We were at RAF Leeming in 1941 with Whitley Vs and were briefed that if our primary or secondary targets could not be found, any target of opportunity could be bombed. Despite the good met forecast, we found ourselves in 10/10ths cloud and any hope of finding either target was soon dashed. After sniffing around for an hour looking for a break, the skipper called up and said 'that's it, we'll head North West over Holland and home'.

The thick cloud persisted until we were well over Holland when it suddenly cleared and there, right ahead of us, was an airfield fully lit-up, with aircraft circling with nav lights on. The navigator said it was Schipol and it was the Luftwaffe doing circuits and bumps. It was at this point that our pilot, who was a pre-war regular and very much a press-on type, decided to switch on our nav lights and join the circuit. Picture a Whitley in the circuit with assorted Luftwaffe aircraft over a German airfield. We must have arrived towards the end of the night's exercise because one by one the aircraft landed until we were the only one left in the circuit. The runway controller was flashing us a persistent green to come in. The pilot called on the intercom 'I am going to do a long downwind leg, then come back over the hangars low and fast. Navigator drop the bombs on the hangars and rear gunner spray the airfield as we pass'. As we sped out to sea, I gave a running commentary on what was happening. All the lights went out at once, bursts of flak, searchlights and red flares – all too late, we were well on our way home.

It is easy to imagine a 'Mossie' getting away with it, but a WHITLEY?

industrial objectives in Turin, Genoa and Milan and other cities as far south as Naples. As we have already seen, aircraft regularly went to Berlin after the first raid on the 25th August.

It was of course appreciated from the experience of 'Nickelling' that some targets would be hard to find. Self illuminating targets such as factories with blast furnaces were easy to find whereas those which were dispersed in the rural areas were particularly difficult. Factories implanted in towns which themselves could be readily identified, such as Hamburg straddling a prominent river, were also generally easier to locate than those in heavily built-up conurbations such as the Ruhr which was invariably shrouded in haze and the glare of searchlights. Unfortunately, the synthetic oil plants, which always hovered around the highest priority, were particularly difficult to identify. The second critical factor after identification was bombing accuracy. AOC No 4 Group, Air Marshal Coningham, whose Whitley crews at this stage had the widest experience estimated somewhat optimistically that accuracy at night should be little different from daylight, and calculated that in moonlight conditions the average bombing error should not exceed 300 yards.

The first reports were encouraging. AOCs 4 and 5 Groups

(Hampdens) believed that crews using a combination of dead reckoning, DF bearings and map reading had achieved a high standard of navigation. AOC 3 Group (Wellingtons) sounded a note of caution, expressing concern that dazzle from searchlights and parachute flares made map reading extremely difficult in the critical run-in to the target itself. That some aircraft became hopelessly lost was not denied, but this was put down to inexperienced crews still finding their feet. Crew reports were certainly optimistic; during a moonlight raid on the oil plant at Gelsenkirchen on the 19th July 1940, all but one of the 19 Hampdens dispatched claimed to have bombed the target. Even on moonless nights, for example on the 2nd July when 16 Whitleys went to the marshalling yards at Hamm, ten claimed to have attacked the target. If these reports were indeed accurate, then Bomber Command had made remarkable progress during the year in improving long range navigation techniques and performance.

The invasion barges assembling in the North Sea and Channel ports were much easier to find, and often moored together in sizeable batches, should have been easier to hit. There were some notable successes and Bomber Command raids certainly alarmed those responsible for preparing the invasion. But even despite a constant battering in a period of over two months from July onwards, German figures indicate that only 12 per cent were destroyed or damaged, hardly in itself sufficient to cause the postponement of Operation 'Sea Lion'.

Even at this early stage of the war, enterprising special operations were mounted from time to time. One such was a low level raid on the 12th August by five Hampdens against an aqueduct on the Dortmund-Ems canal near Munster. The first four aircraft failed to reach the target in the face of dense flak, but the fifth piloted by Flight Lieutenant R Learoyd severely damaged the structure with his 1000lb bombs – the first time they were used operationally. Despite immense damage, Learoyd staggered back to Scampton: he was awarded the Victoria Cross for his efforts. Most sorties were, however, less dramatic and the results more problematical.

At this time there were only two methods of confirming the validity of the crew's reports: intelligence from covert sources within Germany itself and photographs taken from the bombers over the target. Intelligence reports were encouraging; a direct hit was reported on the oil plant at Gelsenkirchen on the 3rd July and serious traffic jams in the Ruhr four days later. More general intelligence indicated the apparent ease with which pilots were finding their objectives, and in October a 'reliable source' suggested that 25 per cent of the industrial capacity of Germany had been affected by the bombing. Only a small number of bombers carried cameras which were intended to confirm the accuracy of the navigation in the target area; even as late as January 1941 only 22 cameras were actually available. The resulting photographs were difficult to decipher and there was undoubtedly a tendency to seize upon those which apparently showed a positive result and to disregard the vast majority which were described as 'inconclusive'.

Assuming, however, that the bomber identified the target,

how much damage were the bombs actually causing? There was little hard evidence from objective experiments, and that which was available from before the war was not encouraging. In such circumstances, there was inevitably a resort to theorising and an expert was employed by Bomber Command in late 1940 to provide a view. Mr D Dewdney, the Commander-in-Chiefs' oil adviser calculated that 260 five hundred pound bombs would be required to destroy a square target with sides of 100 yards, but only 530 for one of about 700 yards square. The former, theoretically, would require only about 65 aircraft sorties if all found and attacked the target with an average bombing error of 300 yards. The theoretical analysis, the pilot's own reports, and the intelligence coming out of Germany all encouraged an optimistic view, the only shaft of doubt arose from the 'inconclusive' photographs from the bombers themselves. Unfortunately, the latter was the only objective method of measuring the actual performance and the need for better photographs was readily accepted.

But there were other signs that the picture was not perhaps as rosy as that painted. Detailed analysis of the reports made by crews attacking the same target threw up disconcerting inconsistencies. One wave would report the presence of

Flt Lt R. Learoyd was awarded the Victoria Cross for leading a flight of 5 Hampdens against an aqueduct on the Dortmund-Ems Canal.
IWM

The advent of the high flying Spitfire photo reconnaissance aircraft provided proof that bombing results were not up to expectations. This is the first recce version – a Mk IV.
IWM

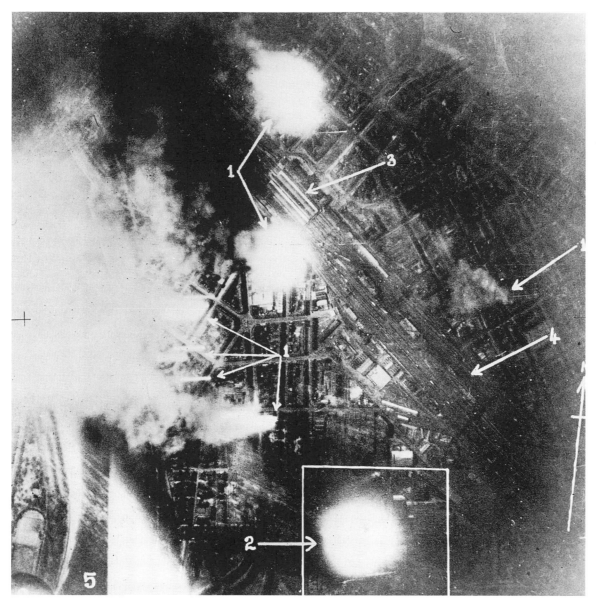

A photograph taken during the raid on Mannheim on the 16th December 1940. Photo reconnaissance by a Spitfire the following day disclosed very little damage to the target area. IWM

extensive fires in the target area whilst the next arriving a few minutes later would report that all was dark – could they really be looking at the same place? There was also increasing recognition that crews were bombing fires rather than precisely identified targets – all very well if it was actually the target on fire, but a complete waste of effort if in fact it was an adjacent wood which was ablaze. Better evidence was clearly needed.

It was provided at the end of 1940 by the new Spitfire photographic reconnaissance unit which, unarmed, could fly sufficiently high in daylight to avoid interception and on a clear day provide good quality photographs. Such pictures were available following an attack on Mannheim on the 16th December. It was a clear moonlight night, the target area in the centre of the town was readily discernable and it was attacked by a large mixed force of 134 aircraft of which 102 claimed to have bombed the target. Despite the ideal conditions, the resulting photographs showed that although there was some damage, it

was scattered over a wide area, far more than the 300 yards average bombing error still held to be accurate. More disconcerting evidence soon followed: the heavily raided synthetic oil plant at Gelsenkirchen was photographed by a Spitfire on the 24th December; there was little sign of damage or recent repairs, just a few scattered bomb craters at some distance from the plant.

Two disturbing conclusions had to be drawn: firstly, that many crews who claimed to have identified and bombed the target were in fact mistaken and secondly that the average bombing error was significantly greater than 300 yards. There is no evidence that crews deliberately misrepresented the truth in their post flight reports: most genuinely believed they had attacked the right target and it is hardly surprising after a long gruelling flight that they wanted to regard the result optimistically. The intelligence officers who debriefed the crews were also inexperienced and undoubtedly wished to join-in the aura of optimism that all this effort was productive. But the first concrete evidence from the Spitfires of the damage actually caused showed conclusively that all concerned, the commanders as well as the crews, had been grossly over optimistic in their assessment of the effectiveness of most of the raids mounted so far. Some attacks had been successful, but the damage caused was disproportionate to the effort expended. Furthermore, losses were steadily increasing although not yet excessive. The German night fighter had not so far posed the threat which was to emerge in the future, but light anti-aircraft guns were now disturbingly accurate and too many aircraft were lost in accidents. And the heavy bombers for which the crews were theoretically being conserved had not yet arrived.

Although severely denting the confidence of the Air Staff and Bomber Command, the Spitfire reconnaissance photographs by no means destroyed the myth of night precision bombing at the end of 1940. Certainly at this stage there was acceptance of the need for better navigation equipment, more effective target illuminating flares, and the first recognition of the need for a pathfinder force of the most experienced crews. But even more damaging evidence of the limitations of precision bombing was to be provided before the need for a change of policy towards area bombing was totally accepted.

The Demise of Precision Bombing

The concept of daylight bombing had been destroyed in just four dark days in December 1939, the policy of precision bombing by night, despite equally clear pointers, took rather longer to die. Despite the revelations of the Spitfire photographs, the next target system to be selected for Bomber Command as 1941 dawned was a return to the first 'panacea' – oil plants. This was a surprising decision in the circumstances, but even more incredible was the belief of the Group Commanders that such pinpoint targets could be successfully attacked even in moonless periods. Fortunately, this doctrinaire anachronism did not survive long, or Bomber Command's prestige would have sunk even lower than it actually did in 1941. Despite the laid down priority, this same three month period saw sizeable raids on German cities similar to that on Mannheim of the 16th December. Targets were selected in major city centres which inevitably resulted in the random destruction of surrounding houses and office buildings – this was in practice area bombing in which widespread disruption of the economic life and the morale of the people were the inevitable if unspecified targets.

A Stirling crew being debriefed after a raid on Berlin in 1941.   **IWM**

The ill-fated Manchester entered operational service in February 1941. This is a No 207 Squadron aircraft. IWM

This period also saw the first hesitant introduction of the heavy bombers, the Stirling and the Manchester in February and the Halifax in March. For some time yet, however, the main load continued to be born by the older Whitleys, Hampdens and, particularly, the Wellington. The weight of raids was also growing steadily, on the 8th May 360 aircraft were dispatched to just two locations, Hamburg and Bremen. But there was little co-ordination between stations or even squadrons, bombers still tended to operate as individual units or in small groups and crews often flew to Germany and back without seeing another aircraft.

The grave crisis of the Battle of the Atlantic which erupted in March 1941 dictated yet another shift in priorities. The need to reverse the tide of U boat successes required that the primary effort should now be directed against naval targets, destined to prove one of the least successful of the many target systems imposed upon Bomber Command in the war. Unsuccessful attempts were made to bomb battleships in harbour, particularly at Kiel, Brest and La Pallice, but the instruction to bomb towns which contained naval installations such as Kiel, Wilhelmshaven and Bremen was of greater significance. Whilst the selection of pinpoint targets was not totally abandoned, there was now formal acknowledgement of the disruptive effect of the bombs which missed their target but fell in a built-up area. The Command continued to attack industrial objectives when conditions were unsuited to the naval strategy, but here too the emphasis moved more formally towards targets in urban areas which would enhance the 'by-product' effect on morale. An Air Ministry paper of April 1941 actually recognised that on moonless nights 'it is only possible to obtain satisfactory results by the 'Blitz' attack of large working class and industrial areas in the towns'.

This formal recognition of an inevitable change of direction

had arisen from yet more damning evidence of the inaccuracy of the navigation and bombing techniques practised in 1941. On a perfect moonlit night, 54 Wellingtons were directed on the 12th March to bomb the Focke-Wulf factory at Bremen: 33 aircraft, each carrying four bombs plus incendiaries, claimed to have attacked the target. The factory was quite large measuring some 800 yards by 500 yards, but photographic reconnaissance disclosed that only 12 bombs hit the target, with the rest scattered over a wide area – far greater than the theoretical average bombing error. It was also of concern that over one third of the force even failed to find the target at all. Indeed, following Mr Dewdney's calculations in respect of oil plants, a target of this size should have required only about five hundred 500 pound bombs for its complete destruction. Based on the success rate disclosed by the photographs, destruction of this single factory would have required no less than 2,300 Wellington sorties alone. The reconnaissance camera was once again undermining the whole principle of the strategic bombing offensive. By now the average bombing error had been arbitrarily increased to 600 yards: further evidence would show that this was still wildly optimistic.

Doubts regarding the bombing strategy now extended beyond the RAF. Lord Cherwell, the influential confidant and adviser of the Prime Minister had persuaded the War Cabinet to commission Mr Butt of the Secretariat to compile a report on bombing effectiveness. From examination of 600 photographs taken by the bomber's own cameras, he concluded that only one third of those crews that claimed to have attacked the target had actually penetrated as close as five miles. In difficult areas like the Ruhr, this figure dropped to below one tenth where, it

A 51 Squadron Pilot – Whitleys 1940

I shall not forget my first operational sortie. I was a sergeant pilot, but I had been flying since 1936 and had about 1000 hours experience – a lot more than my flying officer captain. He immediately sent me down to the bomb aimer's position to help with the map reading – not the happiest position in a Whitley on take-off, but we eventually staggered off the ground and wallowed up to about 3000 feet when he called me back and said it wouldn't climb any higher. I raised the flaps for him and then resumed my position in the nose – my confidence was not increasing at this stage. It was cloudy all the way out to the target (Bremen) and there was nothing to see, but eventually after about the right time by dead reckoning, we saw some searchlights well off to the left. We turned towards the lights, but it was still hazy and we couldn't identify the target, and so in accordance with our instructions in those days we didn't bomb and turned for home.

After a short time, the captain called me back to the cockpit to give him a break. I settled down in the seat, but soon realised that although the gyro showed us heading west, as we should have been, the master compass had been set-up 180 degrees out (red on black as it was called) and we were actually heading east. I reset the compass and gyro correctly and turned back onto west. But I then began to wonder just how long the compass had been synchronised incorrectly and a long and increasingly heated conversation ensued within the crew. It eventually appeared to me that the captain had not reset the compass since take-off – so every heading actually taken had been the reciprocal of the one intended. By my estimation this now put us somewhere out over the Atlantic rather than the North Sea. Fortunately my experience prevailed over the captain's seniority and we turned back towards the east and the long drag back towards land. But where were the searchlights that we had clearly seen when we thought we were over Bremen? We settled for Dublin, but I think we calculated later that they must have been Sligo. We let down below the cloud, still over the sea, but fortunately I recognised the Irish coast when we reached it and eventually landed at Aldegrove (Belfast) some 10 hours or so after take-off. I don't think we were the only crew to make this mistake.

was calculated, only seven out of every 100 aircraft actually bombed an area of 75 square miles around the aiming point. This startlingly damaging report was not unnaturally at least partly repudiated by the Air Staff and Mr Butt himself acknowledged the inevitable imprecision of his analysis. But no amount of wriggling could disguise the fact that the general thrust of the report was accurate and it had a powerful influence on the Prime Minister and the Cabinet. It also had some very positive and beneficial effects upon Bomber Command itself. The urgent need for precision navigation aids, the provision of an elite pathfinding force and the necessity for more accurate analysis of bombing results all received a resounding boost from the Butt report which was of inestimable value in years to come when the effectiveness, and prestige, of Bomber Command was on a much sounder footing.

The old calculations of bombing accuracy had now been discredited and were abandoned. Instead a survey was carried-out of the effectiveness of the Luftwaffe bombing of British cities, in particular London, Liverpool and Coventry. The raid on the latter on the 14th November 1940 was subjected to detailed analysis, and the study concentrated not only upon the material damage, but also upon the psychological impact – clear recognition of the morale factor as an 'end product' of bombing policy. The study concluded that two thirds of industrial activity had ceased on the day after the raid and that recovery had taken 35 days. If repeated on the same scale, after six raids Coventry would have been 'beyond all hope of recovery'. That these estimates were also wildly pessimistic was only fully recognised when detailed analysis of the effect of the far more intensive bombing of Germany was carried out after the war.

Nevertheless, the study was helpful in determining tactics for area bombing which were different to those required for precision targets. It was concluded that greater damage was caused by incendiaries than by high explosive and that if an intensive fire storm was created early in the raid cycle, subsequent high explosive and incendiaries would be more effective. The Air Staff recommended that a minimum of some 25,000 incendiary bombs should be included in each raid and that the majority of these should be concentrated in the opening phase. The main significance, however, of all these projections was that any pretence of attacking selected pinpoint targets was now abandoned. In future, the potentially awesome power of Bomber Command was to be unleashed against the larger cities and towns with the intention of creating the maximum disruption. Whether this disruption was of industrial production or of the morale of the people was now, if not irrelevant, at least of secondary importance. The era of area bombing had arrived.

Mr Churchill was still, however, not overly impressed with the new strategy. Bomber Command was the only asset in his inventory which could actually carry the war to Germany, and the now well proven inability of the bombers to make any serious impression upon her capacity to wage war had been a grave blow to his confidence. He was reluctant to sanction the vast increase in heavy bombers demanded by the Air Ministry to wage the area war, casting faint praise upon the impact of bombing so far, the effects of which were 'greatly exaggerated'. Any future campaign he hoped would be 'a seriously increasing annoyance'. Certainly, if the Prime Minister ever had any lingering belief that the bombing strategy might win the war on its own, this had been dispelled by the end of 1941.

Yet another factor concentrated the minds of the War Cabinet and the Air Ministry at this period: the aircraft losses on night raids against Germany were still increasing. Over 100 bombers were lost during the first three weeks in August, a casualty rate which the leaflet dropping Whitleys, ranging widely over Germany just a year earlier, had never had to face. But worse was to come, for on the 7th November over 400 aircraft participated in raids ranging from Berlin to Boulogne with the loss of 37 aircraft. This high loss rate was exacerbated by the bad weather and some of the crews who went to the more distant targets such as Berlin had gruelling and often fruitless sorties which long remained in the memory. Some raids suffered a disproportionately high casualty rate, 12.5 per cent against Berlin and a staggering 21 per cent against targets in the Ruhr. On the other hand, 133 aircraft which went to Cologne, Ostend and Boulogne suffered no losses at all. Although not designated as such, this large raid was in essence seen as a trial of the Command's capability after a year of heated controversy over the effectiveness of the strategic bombing policy. As such it was a dismal failure. The casualty rate could not be sustained, crews were being frittered away in small scale raids in the obsolescent medium bombers – at this rate there would be few experienced crews left to man the heavy bombers when they arrived in strength in 1942. A reappraisal of the strategy was clearly needed – and a new Commander-in-Chief – for Sir Richard Peirse was the final casualty of the disastrous night of 7th November.

A line-up of Bleinheim Mk IVs of No 2 Group on the ground at RAF Watton in Norfolk. WWE

The 'Cinderella Group'

We have moved ahead with the night bombing campaign, but one of Bomber Command's groups, No 2, did not fit easily into the same mould by nature of its equipment and role which were fundamentally suited only for daylight operation even though several attempts were made to make it conform to the developing pattern. No 2 Group had passed through a torrid time in defence of France, but its surviving crews were battle hardened, determined and still full of confidence.

If Coastal Command, with some justification, saw itself as the 'Cinderella' command of the Royal Air Force, No 2 Group in 1940 could certainly regard itself in the same light within Bomber Command. Equipped only with the Blenheim for which the high expectations held in 1936 had already been dissipated even before the carnage in France, it was not easy to foresee a role for No 2 Group in the latter half of 1940 and beyond. Its role in France had been tactical bombing in support of ground operations, but there was no longer an Allied army to support within Europe other than perhaps in defence of an invasion of the homeland. Some planning was conducted to this end by which links were established to the Army Regional Command Headquarters, two squadrons dispatched to Lossiemouth in Scotland and 48 Hawker Audax and 54 Ansons

earmarked to reinforce the Group. To pit these obsolete machines against the German fighters really would have been a last ditch effort, for it had been shown conclusively in France that the Blenheim itself was no real match for the Bf 110 let alone the far faster and more agile 109.

Nevertheless, in those dark days of 1940, a productive role had to be found for the Blenheim and intruder attacks against recently occupied airfields in France fulfilled a real need. These commenced on the 15th June when Nos XV, 18 and 82 Squadrons raided Boos, setting a pattern which was to continue almost to the end of the war. The Blenheims could be escorted by Hurricanes when they were available to airfields in the Pas de Calais, but this was not feasible when the allotted targets were more distant. Although losses at this stage were not high, the potential risk was only too apparent. Night attacks had been tried, but the Blenheim was generally unsuitable in this role unless good weather conditions and moonlight facilitated map reading.

No 2 Group had also been tasked when weather conditions were suitable with small scale intruder raids against oil plants and railway marshalling yards as far afield as Hamburg and Hanover. The intention was to supplement the strategic bomber offensive at night, but the Blenheim's meagre carrying capacity of 250lb bombs was unlikely to cause much more than irritation to the industrial economy. Furthermore, the right weather conditions existed only when there was sufficient cloud to hide from enemy fighters, but not too much to interfere with navigation and bomb aiming. Such ideal conditions prevailed only rarely, and of 88 sorties dispatched in June, only 22 penetrated to their target area: this success rate was considerably less than that against airfields. As the build-up of invasion barges became apparent in the Low Countries, these too became a regular objective for the Blenheim squadrons which by August numbered 13 including the two in Scotland, all equipped with the Mk IV version of the aircraft.

Although danger was always present for an inferior aircraft operating in a hostile environment without fighter escort, occasional raids proved disastrous. Such a day was the 13th August when No 82 Squadron from Watton was tasked to attack the airfield at Aalborg in the northern tip of Denmark. This was at the limit of the aircraft's range and involved a long sea crossing requiring DR navigation. Twelve aircraft led by Wing Commander E de Virac Lart took-off just before 0900 hours and headed across the North Sea at 20,000 feet. Their planned route should have brought a landfall just to the west of Aalborg, but in fact they crossed the coast some 30 miles to the south at Sondervig leaving a 50 mile land crossing where they ran into heavy opposition. Only one aircraft survived, returning early due to a shortage of fuel, the rest were left scattered in the estuaries surrounding their intended target. Twenty of the 33 crew members died. No 82 Squadron was of course that involved in the disastrous attack on Gembloux in May: the squadron had been destroyed twice within three months.

As Autumn faded into Winter, the immediate risk of invasion began to diminish and correspondingly No 2 Group's

Blenheims of No 2 Group were used in strikes against shipping during 1941. This picture of a merchant ship after bombing was taken by the mid-upper gunner.   WWE

tasks took-on ever more variety. Night raids in support of the strategic bombing force assumed a more prominent role, but attacks against airfields, also often at night, were still a regular part of the pattern. As with the rest of Bomber Command, Winter brought its own tribulations in the form of low cloud, icing and acute crew discomfort. The aim of the airfield attacks where possible was to catch the enemy bombers either taking-off or landing and profit thereby from the flare path lights as an aid to bombing. Some more adventurous pilots fired verey lights of the German colours of the day to deceive the gunners and even switched on their navigation lights and joined the circuit pattern. After the bombs had gone, the difficulties and dangers were by no means over, for finding base on the return flight often depended upon a DF homing which the Germans uncharitably emulated by broadcasting false bearings of their own. On the night of 3rd December, of nine aircraft dispatched by the unfortunate No 82 Squadron, only one claimed to have found the target and five crashed due to bad weather. At the turn of the year, strategic objectives – oil plants, factories and railways – were more often than not the order of the day with targets further afield such as Bremen. Despite occasional successes, nobody could claim that the Blenheim was a night bomber. It could only operate safely on clear moonlight sights – few and far between in Winter – and was vulnerable to flak at the low levels it was forced to fly. Even if it found and hit a target, its bomb load was too small to provide a real return.

The Spring of 1941 was a period when shipping losses were becoming acute and Bomber Command as a whole was directed towards the war at sea. No 2 Group's role in this new strategy was to attack German surface shipping over an area as diverse as the Brest Peninsula to the Norwegian fiords. This was not only

No 2 Group had the somewhat doubtful distinction of introducing the Flying Fortress into RAF service with No 90 Squadron. **RAFM**

difficult but hazardous work. Aircraft had to patrol at very low level to avoid radar detection, and when they stumbled across a convoy, to strike while they still enjoyed surprise and relative freedom from the lethal fire of the accompanying flak ships. Even if all this had been achieved, actually hitting the chosen ship was far from straightforward even from 50 feet, particularly in a beam attack. To draw-off enemy fighters, some aircraft were employed as decoys on so called 'fringe' attacks, an even more dangerous tactic. It was satisfying work, despite the hazards, for when a hit was achieved the results were often spectacularly apparent, and although claims were exaggerated, post war evaluation revealed that only about 30 German ships were lost during this period. It was, however, a very expensive strategy with loss rates regularly exceeding ten per cent.

Although anti-shipping strikes formed the major and most spectacular part of No 2 Group's task throughout the Summer of 1941, the squadrons had also been involved in the less obviously attractive pastime of acting as bait to lure the German fighters into the air over France. One other event must be briefly noted, for No 2 Group, rather strangely for a light bomber formation, was given the somewhat dubious honour in May 1941 of forming

the first of the RAF's B-17 squadrons – No 90. The experiment was not a success. Although the high altitude performance was notable, the aircraft was dogged with technical and crew problems. The RAF never took the Flying Fortress to their hearts and by September No 2 Group had willingly passed on its 'Gentleman's aircraft' to No 8 Group to try their hand with them at night (not the far more distinguished Pathfinder Force which was not formed until 1943). What the Group really needed though was better aircraft, and these were on their way from across the Atlantic.

'Circuses'

In the Summer of 1940, Goering had confidently boasted that his Luftwaffe could single handedly bring Britain to her knees and end the war in the West. It would do so by engaging and defeating the RAF in the skies over the Channel and south eastern England. The bombers would strike and destroy the fighter airfields and their support facilities whilst the escorting fighters would oppose the supposedly meagre number of Spitfires and Hurricanes of Fighter Command and achieve absolute superiority in the air. After this annihilation of the RAF, little more than a policing action would be needed to complete the conquest. Such was the plan – the result is well known!

Fighter Command, nevertheless, had not forgotten the tactics employed by the Luftwaffe in the Battle of Britain. Following the victory of 1940 the Command had sought to carry the battle to the enemy by introducing massive fighter sweeps called 'Rhubarbs' over occupied France. But they suffered from two disadvantages; the fighters on their own could cause only a limited amount of damage and if the German fighters did not want to play, they could not be forced into the air on unfavourable terms. The answer, it was concluded, was to cause sufficient damage on the ground to ensure the Luftwaffe reacted and to do this would require the help of Bomber Command. The latter was not entirely averse to this tactic initially although the crews themselves were not ecstatic at the idea of being used as bait. The Blenheims of No 2 Group were not proving very suitable for night bombing and following the disastrous raid on Gembloux of the 12th May it was recognised that they could only operate regularly with reasonable safety in daylight if provided with a fighter escort. Bomber Command had another reason for supporting combined operations. With the dawning recognition of the limitations of night bombing it still hankered to operate in daylight, but to achieve this in reasonable safety, the Luftwaffe had to be driven from the skies. To force the Luftwaffe to fight, therefore, the bombers would have to attack targets which the Germans could not afford to ignore.

The problem was that the fighters did not have sufficient range to reach Germany and were thus confined to operations over France, and quite apart from the natural reluctance to bomb erstwhile allies, there were few targets in France which could be considered critical to the Germans. Nevertheless, the combined operations were introduced and eventually became known as 'Circuses'.

No 2 Group was directed on the 23rd January 1941 to prepare for daylight attacks on Boulogne, Calais, Dunkirk and Cherbourg in co-operation with the fighters of No 11 Group, but it was not until June that operations were actually underway. The early results were mildly encouraging, but it soon became evident that although the enemy was inferior in numbers, the Spitfires were not going to have it all their own way. The German Freya radar system was now functioning quite effectively and the Bf 109F was marginally superior to the Spitfire V. Furthermore, the serious handicap suffered by the 109 over southern England in 1940 of operating at the limit of its range was now transferred to the Spitfire over France. Given adequate warning, the 109s could climb to height and position themselves in their own time to obtain the maximum tactical advantage for combat. The Spitfires on the other hand had little petrol to spare for an extended dogfight and even if they were gaining the upper hand, the 109s had only to dive towards the

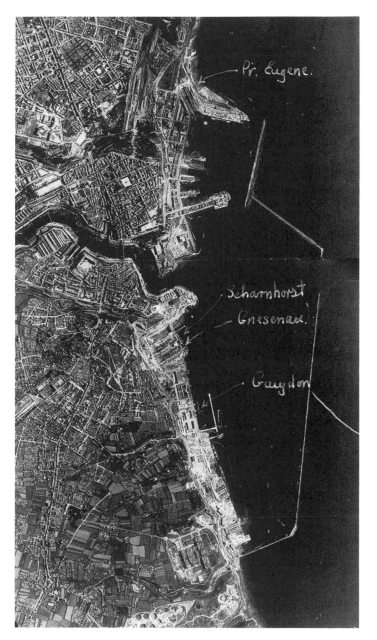

The presence of German capital ships at Brest in northern France persuaded Bomber Command to reintroduce daylight bombing in July 1941. It was not successful.   IWM

south to escape their clutches. Furthermore, the Luftwaffe soon transferred its fighters to bases beyond the Spitfires maximum radius of operation and were thus able to operate with immunity from air attack themselves.

Despite these difficulties, impressive results were claimed by Air Vice-Marshal Leigh-Mallory of No 11 Group for the first three months of 'Circus' operations; 437 German fighters destroyed and 182 probably destroyed for the loss of 194 fighter pilots and only 14 bombers. Unfortunately these figures grossly exaggerated the real losses – it transpired after the war that only 128 German fighters were in fact destroyed. Furthermore, the weight of the bomber attack, despite the occasional use of

Hampdens and Stirlings, was insufficient to compel the 109s to concentrate upon the bombers during which time they would be more vulnerable to the Spitfires. Instead they could concentrate on the latter when conditions were most favourable to themselves.

By the Autumn, Bomber Command was decidedly luke warm about 'Circus' operations and although the effort involved was comparatively small, each bomb used against France was looked upon as a bomb wasted and a distraction from the true metier of the bomber – the strategic offensive against Germany. The problem was the inadequate range of the Spitfire. What was needed was a long range fighter which could escort the bombers into the heartland of Germany and still have sufficient fuel to fight a combat action. But there was a view, strongly endorsed by Sir Charles Portal, that range could be achieved only at the expense of performance and manoeuvrability and certainly the Luftwaffe's twin engine long range fighter, the Bf 110, was no match for the Spitfire. In 1941 Portal was undoubtedly right, long range escort had to await the advent of the Mustang, still nearly three years away from its triumphant emergence as the supreme long range fighter of the war.

It was at this time that Bomber Command decided to have another look at re-introducing daylight high level bombing for the main force with a concentrated attack against the battleships *Scharnhorst* and *Gneisenau* at Brest. There were too many bombers to provide a close escort, but five squadrons of Spitfires with extra tanks were to patrol Brest which was just within range. Unfortunately, the *Scharnhorst* was moved shortly before the attack on the 24th July 1941 to La Pallice, a port much farther south and well outside the range of the fighters. Fifteen Halifaxes were sent to La Pallice of which five were shot down and none escaped damage. As some recompense, however, five hits were scored on the *Scharnhorst*. Of the 99 aircraft which went to Brest, 13 were lost. This new venture in daylight bombing against fringe targets in France could hardly be regarded as a success and unescorted daylight bombing, other than at low level, was again put into cold storage.

Although 'Circus' operations in 1941 were by no means an

The Ventura, this is a Mk II version, was heavily employed on 'Circus' operations after 1941. IWM

unqualified success, they could not be ignored completely by the Germans and tied down a good proportion of the Luftwaffe's fighter forces in northern France, including the most modern Focker-Wolfe 190s. Although there is no firm evidence that they drew fighters away from the hard pressed Eastern front, it was certainly sufficient to prevent those in France being deployed elsewhere. It was decided, therefore, to continue with 'Circus' operations in 1942, with much the same results as the previous year. But as more RAF fighters could be devoted to these operations, they slowly but surely built-up an air superiority in the area which was never to be lost. On four occasions, 24 Bostons of No 2 Group were escorted by no less than 38 squadrons of Spitfires. This air superiority was essential for the re-invasion of Europe, originally planned for 1943, and this is perhaps in the long run the greatest achievement of the 'Circus' operations.

The Years of Disappointment

At the end of 1941 Bomber Command had reached the nadir of its fortunes, its strategy and tactics discredited, its prestige at its lowest ebb. The pre-war years of parsimony, lack of foresight and lethargy had taken their toll and the very existence of a strategic bombing policy was now at stake. Although the courage and endurance of the crews was undoubted, there were questions regarding their level of skill, the efficiency and durability of their equipment and, above all, their direction and leadership.

In retrospect, it can be more readily seen now that Christmas 1941 was in fact the turning point in the fortunes of the Command. Although the build-up in aircraft was disappointingly slow – it was still difficult to raise more than 300 aircraft for a night operation – the first Mosquitos had arrived on a squadron in November and the Lancaster a month later. A new navigation aid, Gee, was fast approaching operational service and the training schools across the Empire settling down into the pattern which was to sustain the flow of crews for the rest of the war. There were many dark days of uncertainty and disappointment yet to come, but the tide was turning, and with it a new man to channel it towards an instrument of power and, rather more belatedly, precision that seemed inconceivable in December 1941. On the 22nd February 1942, Air Marshal Arthur Harris was appointed Commander-in-Chief Bomber Command.

CHAPTER FIVE

Laying a New Foundation – 1942

A Year of Controversy – 1942

The two dramatic events which were to decide the outcome of the war had both occurred in 1941. On the 22nd June Hitler launched Operation 'Barbarossa', the invasion of Russia, which brought the dormant but mighty power of that revolution scarred nation into the Allied camp. Of more immediate significance for Britain was the Japanese attack on Pearl Harbour on the 7th December which at last brought the massive resources of the United States into the war with Germany. But although these two momentous interventions changed the whole course of the conflict, the situation at the end of the year looked far from encouraging. Apart from no longer carrying the burden alone, there was little cheer for the British people as they contemplated the third year of war. The campaign against the U boats was still going badly, a resounding blow to the Royal Navy's prestige had been struck when the Repulse and the Prince of Wales were sunk off Malaya, the fortress of Singapore was threatened and Hitler was now growling at the gates of Moscow.

Bomber Command, the sole means of taking the war to the enemy, was in deep depression, its strategy and tactics in disarray, its commander removed. The policy of the conservation of resources which had been instituted over the Winter period was hardly likely to strike fear into the enemy or to inspire the frustrated air and ground crews. Nobody could deny that a reappraisal of policy was needed. In its defence, the Command could justifiably argue that many of the resources which it needed to do its job had been switched to meet other pressing requirements, for example the transfer of bombers to the Mediterranean, and that it had regularly been diverted from its true role of the strategic offensive to support the Army or the Navy in the Battles of France and the Atlantic. But this could not disguise the fact that it had signally failed to find or hit its strategic targets in Germany with any regularity or precision. 1942 had to be a decisive year if it was to regain self respect and justify the resources devoted to it. It had been agreed at the Washington War Conference at the turn of the year, not without some discussion, that the Allies' effort would be concentrated initially upon Germany, and prominent amongst the priorities was the wearing down of the German war effort by strategic bombing. But how should it be applied?

The introduction of Gee, a precise radio navigation aid which would greatly improve the track keeping accuracy at least as far into Germany as the Ruhr provided the main glimmer of hope although its utility was expected to last only about six months before the Germans could produce an effective jammer. There was thus good reason to make the best use of this window of opportunity by renewing the offensive as soon as possible. A new bombing directive was issued in February which stated that the strategic objective 'should now be focused on the morale of the enemy civil population and in particular, of the industrial workers'. The primary targets, therefore, lay within the range of Gee in the industrial Ruhr with coastal towns, Bremen, Emden and Wilhelmshaven as alternative objectives. Secondary targets included Berlin, which was to be 'harassed' whenever conditions were particularly favourable, and some were selective in the sense that the towns specified contained critical industries like Schweinfurt with its ball bearing factories. A few, for example Lubeck, appeared not because they were industrially important but because they were particularly vulnerable. The directive, in fact, gave Sir Arthur Harris considerable room for manoeuvre in tactical selection which he was to exploit to the full, leading to several altercations with the Chief of Air Staff in later years.

The first serious controversy of the year started in the Admiralty who wanted the major thrust of the bomber force directed toward naval targets, not only in the Atlantic but also in the Indian Ocean: 'if we lose the war at sea, we lose the war' minuted the First Sea Lord with impressive solemnity. Nobody doubted the gravity of the naval war, but could Bomber Command really help? The Air Staff thought not; the bombers were not equipped with the radar necessary to find submarines at sea and hitting stationary let alone moving ships was proving to be extraordinarily difficult. They claimed that, vitally important though the sea war was, greater long term benefit would accrue from attacking industrial targets in Germany which would seize the initiative from the enemy and bring indirect support to the hard pressed Russians, both politically persuasive arguments. The debate, widened to question the whole future of the strategic bombing offensive, entered the public arena when it was aired in the House of Commons in February. The decisive intervention was probably made by Lord Cherwell with a minute to the Prime Minister on the 30th

March. Despite manifest statements like 'Investigation seems to show that having one's house demolished is most damaging to morale', the minute strongly supported the attack upon German towns as a vehicle to 'break the spirit of the people'. Sir Henry Tizard, who rarely missed an opportunity to quarrel with Lord Cherwell, attacked the mathematical basis of the argument with some justification, but the latter was always closer to Mr Churchill's ear. For the time being the strategic offensive was intact.

It was also fortunate that Bomber Command at this stage scored some notable successes, particularly the highly publicised 1,000 bomber raid on Cologne in May. Sir Arthur Harris was already proving a more robust and outspoken protagonist than his predecessor and became a regular guest at Chequers, the Prime Minister's country home. Mr Churchill himself called for an expansion of the existing 32 squadrons to 50 by the end of the year and although this was not achieved, it augured well for 1943.

Attention now switched back to the target systems which would most benefit the strategic aim. Sir Arthur Harris had not always unswervingly supported area bombing, indeed as AOC No 5 Group he had once boasted of 'the accuracy with which our aircraft hit military objectives as opposed to merely browning the towns'. Nevertheless, area bombing had been adopted 'force majeure' in 1941 because of the inability to hit a precise target rather than for its own intrinsic value. It was not surprising therefore that Bomber Command's successes in early 1942 re-opened the door to consideration of 'panacea' targets. Oil plants, which were still recognised as Germany's Achilles' heel, were quickly discarded, but should the weight of attack be spread widely and inevitably thinly across German towns, or should it be concentrated against those like Schweinfurt which were specifically associated with key industries? The issue was not resolved.

The arrival of the United States Army Air Force in Britain brought another factor to bear. They were committed to daylight operations, itself a source of argument which will be discussed later, but the subdueing of the Luftwaffe, vital for the Americans, would also be beneficial to Bomber Command and thus the destruction of the aircraft production industry became the final 'panacea' target of 1942. Harris was now moving steadily towards the universal area concept, the massive destruction of the major cities of Germany with a view to the greatest disruption of industrial life and the spirit of the people. But it would require a substantial increase in the Command's resources as well as the full co-operation of the Americans to achieve this aim.

The first of the heavy bombers, the Stirling played an increasing role in night operations in 1942, but soon began to suffer comparatively high losses. This is a Mk III.　　　　　　　　　　　IWM

This leads us directly into the final major controversy of the year which concerned the grand strategy for winning the war. The Americans had supported the strategic bombing offensive at the Washington Conference and were now themselves committed to it with the 8th Air Force based in England. But was it to be an end in itself in that Germany would be so weakened that any invasion force would simply have to walk in through the front door, or would it merely be a softening-up process which would facilitate the vital land invasion? The prize, of course, was to be the major share of the Alliance's productive resources in the coming years. The British Chiefs of Staff, somewhat unexpectedly, at first endorsed the Air Staff view that resources should be concentrated on the bomber force, but the Prime Minister remained unconvinced and was subsequently supported by the other two Chiefs who soon revised their views. In August 1942 Churchill had promised Stalin that a second front would be opened in Europe in 1943 and the Americans, although tied-in at present to the Mediterranean theatre, were also anxious to invade France direct rather than approach though the soft underbelly of Europe. The Americans, as Mr Churchill was only too well aware, if not handled carefully could renege on their commitment to Europe and turn their eyes towards the Pacific. It would have been a colossal gamble to stake all on a successful strategic bombing offensive even if Portal and Harris' estimation of what could be done was correct – and the failures of 1941 were not all that far in the past. These then were the issues facing the President and the Prime Minister when they assembled with their military advisers at Casablanca in North Africa in January 1943 for the conference which was to decide the strategy for winning the war. But first we should examine how Bomber Command responded to the challenge.

Restoring Confidence – Spring 1942

The new bombing directive of the 14th February 1942 which replaced the policy of conservation of resources was already a week old when Sir Arthur Harris settled into his new headquarters at High Wycombe. He could, therefore, set about right away to restore the confidence of his bomber crews after the depressing end to their campaign of the previous year. He had a mixed force of some 600 aircraft in 49 squadrons, but of these five were Blenheim squadrons of limited value to the strategic offensive and six were non operational. He could on average count upon about 350 aircraft for a night operation against Germany, but the majority were still the twin engine medium bombers although the Stirlings and Halifaxes were beginning to make an increasing contribution.

Despite the policy of conservation, Bomber Command had not been inactive during the three months to February with generally small scale raids on Germany on 43 nights, but results were no more encouraging than had been the case throughout the previous year. Perhaps the most notable event was the failure, in poor weather conditions, to impede the dash through the Channel of the *Scharnhorst* and the *Gneisenau* on the 12th February. What was most needed was a new tactical doctrine based on Gee which was now almost ready for service. But not all aircraft were equipped with Gee and thus tactics had to be devised by which those with the equipment could help those without. A technique was evolved by which the force attacking a

The Halifax entered operational service soon after the Stirling over which it had the edge in performance. These aircraft are preparing to take off in July 1943. IWM

Lubeck was built 'like a firelighter' and suffered severe damage in the raid of 28th March 1942.   RAFM

single target was split into three sections, the illuminators, the target markers and the followers. The illuminators were Gee equipped Wellingtons, normally 20, carrying a mix of target flares and high explosives. The flares were dropped in bundles of three upwind of the target over a six mile corridor to lead in the next wave, also equipped with Gee, which would drop a maximum load of incendiaries. The followers, which were not Gee equipped carried high explosives, aiming for the fires started by the preceding waves. Trials over England had suggested that Gee was sufficiently accurate for the bombs to be dropped blind if necessary when the target could not be identified in haze or smoke. The new tactics also placed much greater emphasis on time on target, for if the benefit of the illumination and the target marking was not to be dissipated, the maximum number of aircraft had to be concentrated over the target in as short a time as possible.

The precise timing required was first tested in a raid on the Renault factory at Billancourt near Paris on the 3rd March, a location not within Gee coverage. The force contained 235 aircraft with experienced crews in the lead at low level (up to 4,000 feet) to identify and mark the target with flares and high explosives. The main force followed immediately with each aircraft dropping flares to illuminate the target for its successor. The whole force completed its bombing run within two hours of zero hour, for that time a remarkable concentration over the target of an aircraft every 30 seconds. Only one Wellington was lost in the operation and the subsequent photographic reconnaissance showed that the factory had been devastated. Subsequent intelligence confirmed that a high proportion of the machine tools, design drawings and vehicles in the plant had been destroyed. Admittedly conditions were ideal and the target was lightly defended, but it was a great fillip for morale.

The next major raid was a sterner test. Using Gee for the first time, bombers were tasked to attack the Ruhr with Essen as the main target on four successive nights starting on the 8th March. None of the first three were a conspicuous success. Crews had difficulty operating Gee and the haze, searchlights and flak all proved to be serious distractions leading to a dispersion of the flares and incendiary fires. The followers therefore had difficulty identifying the correct target and bombs were widely scattered. On the second night, a disabled Stirling jettisoned its flares over Hamborn which was promptly set upon by a large number of the followers. Although useful damage was done, none of the crews hit the designated target, the Krupp works at Essen. The third night was a complete failure with many aircraft bombing decoy fires started by the Germans near Rheinberg. The final attack in the series against Cologne was more successful, with the illuminators instructed to release their flares blind on Gee and the target markers to bomb visually if possible: about half the aircraft actually hit the designated target. It was, however, clear that still greater accuracy was required from the second wave target markers and the time over the target had to be compressed yet further if the benefit of the illumination was not to be lost. Gee had not proved an unqualified success by any means, but the result was nevertheless mildly encouraging.

The Spring campaign was concluded by attacks against Lubeck and Rostock in late March and April. Lubeck was one of the fringe targets in the February directive, not of great industrial importance, but densely inhabited and in the words of Harris 'built more like a fire-lighter than a human habitation'. Although outside of the range of Gee, the town was on the coast and easily identifiable. On the night of 28th March, 234 aircraft were dispatched in near perfect conditions of full moon and good weather. In view of the closely packed wooden buildings in the medieval town, almost half of the bomb load consisted of incendiaries. Again the bombing was concentrated into as short a span as possible, just over two hours, and the illuminators were mixed-in with the target markers. Photographic evidence showed that some 200 acres of the city had been consumed by fire with heavy damage in the suburbs as well.

At Rostock a month later, a more distant coastal target similar in many respects to Lubeck was subjected to four incendiary attacks on successive nights. In addition to area targets for the majority of the attackers, some crews were given the precise target of the Heinkel factory in the southern suburbs. The raids were smaller, the largest only 128 aircraft on the third night. The first two achieved little of note, the third was more encouraging, but the last was a spectacular success. Ninety two aircraft claimed to have attacked with 52 carrying cameras, all of which displayed the target area when the bombs were released. The daylight reconnaissance confirmed that substantial damage had been caused to the town with an estimated 100,000 people homeless. Only 12 aircraft failed to return over the four nights of sustained operations.

There were of course other raids on Germany during this period, the results of which showed considerably more damage to the target areas than that achieved in the previous year. The results began to attract attention in the highest quarters of the German hierarchy as is shown by comments in Goebbel's diary – 'Conditions in parts of Lubeck are chaotic', and five days later 'The damage is really enormous … it is horrible. One can well imagine how such an awful bombardment affects the population'. The attack upon morale was beginning to bite. Post war analysis showed that the impact was not perhaps as great as believed at the time, for both cities made a remarkable recovery with production in the factories nearly back to normal in a

---

Flt Lt I.H. Davies – 51 Squadron

On the 23rd April 1942 we were briefed for a 'fire blitz' on Rostock; we were told that the town was to be burned to the ground and that we should keep on going back until the job was finished. In fact it took 4 nights and we were on the first and third. Rostock was a city built like a pair of spectacles: the old town to the East and the new town to the West. Because the lighter coloured buildings were in the new town and more easily seen, they were pasted on the first and second nights with relatively little damage to the old town.

In our bomb dump at Dishforth (Yorkshire) we had a number of 250lb incendiaries which we were not then permitted to use because they were said to give-off noxious phosphorous fumes and the powers that be were afraid that we would be accused of using poisonous gas and face retaliation. But by then the G.A.F. was, more or less, beyond giving trouble and my C.O. Wg Cdr Percy Pickard (one of the few outstanding bomber leaders of the war) asked for permission to arm a couple of aircraft with 250 pounders to mark the target. Up until then we had used flares, but these were often shot-down by the enemy light flak. Permission was received and my aircraft and P/O Lambert's were sent off first with two incendiaries to mark the old town. It is now history that the third and fourth nights finished the job (there was no need to mark on the fourth night).

---

matter of days. But this was largely unimportant, the psychological bonus for Bomber Command at the time was immense.

Sandwiched between the Lubeck and Rostock raids was one of the more spectacular raids that Bomber Command staged from time to time – the low level raid on the submarine diesel engine factory at Augsburg in distant Bavaria on the 17th April. It was intended partly as a dramatic 'entree' for the new Lancaster bomber and partly as yet another attempt to resuscitate daylight precision bombing. Twelve aircraft of Nos 44 and 97 Squadrons led by Squadron Leader J D Nettleton took off at 1500 hours to fly to Augsburg and back, over 1200 miles, at very low level without fighter escort. Four aircraft of 44 Squadron had already been downed shortly after crossing the coast and three more succumbed over the heavily defended target. Just 17 bombs landed on the factory of which 5 failed to explode; damage to the target, which in any case was by no means critical, was not excessive. Nettleton, who survived, received the Victoria Cross and members of every crew which returned were decorated. But nearly 50 very experienced airmen were killed and seven of Bomber Command's newest aircraft destroyed with the rest damaged. Although the raid earned valuable publicity as a daring feat of skill and courage, it was in truth an unnecessary act of bravado which did little to further the war.

For Harris, the first two months was an auspicious start to his reign at Bomber Command: innovatory tactics were being

Lancasters of No 44 Squadron participated in the low level raid on Augsburg which was partly intended as a dramatic introduction of the aircraft to operational service. **IWM**

Sqn Ldr J. D. Nettleton was awarded the Victoria Cross for leading 12 Lancasters on a daring, but largely unproductive and costly daylight raid on Augsburg on the 17th April 1942. **IWM**

constantly refined and the techniques of target illumination and marking were soon to lead to a dedicated pathfinder force. But most of all, Harris' vigorous leadership was restoring the confidence of the crews. By the beginning of May he needed just one more coup to set the seal on Bomber Command's burgeoning reputation – he was to find it in the 1,000 bomber raid.

'Millenium' – The 1,000 Bomber Raids

It appears that Harris first broached the idea of the 1,000 bomber raid in early May in conversation with Air Vice Marshal Robert Saundby, his Senior Air Staff Officer at Bomber Command. He mentioned it to Portal on the 18th May who in turn passed it on to Mr Churchill – both approved, it no doubt appealing to the latter's penchant for the melodramatic gesture. But it wasn't only just a propaganda ploy. It had taken four separate raids on Rostock on successive nights to destroy the major part of the town, how much greater the impact would have been if the same number of aircraft could be concentrated into a single short time span, thus saturating the defences and inhibiting recovery. But where would the aircraft come from? On a good night Harris might assemble about 400 front line

Air Marshal Sir Robert Saundby, the Senior Air Staff Officer at Headquarters Bomber Command, was an invaluable foil to Sir Arthur Harris and carried out much of the detailed planning. IWM

aircraft, with sufficient warning a few more might be squeezed out of the squadrons. The Operational Training Units were now very large, with the added bonus of most of their instructional crews having already completed an operational tour. But even including these, he could muster only some 700 aircraft. He attempted to borrow the rest from Coastal Command to which a large number of bomber aircraft had been transferred since the escalation in the Battle of the Atlantic. Although the Commander-in-Chief, Sir Philip Joubert, was enthusiastic, the Admiralty soon vetoed the idea; their aim was to sequester more of Bomber Command's assets, not risk losing those they had. Flying Training Command was approached and thought they could produce 30: in the event they managed four. If the 1,000 total was to be reached, they had to come from within Bomber Command. In the end, virtually every aircraft in the Command which could be made serviceable and provided with a crew was added to the list. No 91 OTU Group provided no less than 259 aircraft, 51 with student crews, and No 92 OTU found 108. The final roll call was 1,043 aircraft: 598 Wellingtons, 131 Halifaxes, 88 Stirlings, 79 Hampdens, 73 Lancasters, 46 Manchesters and 28 Whitleys. Marshalling and preparation required some time, but eventually all assembled on 52 different airfields.

The first choice objective was Hamburg with Cologne as an alternative and the mission had to be mounted during the last week of May which was a full moon period. The most striking feature of the meticulous plan was that the whole force was to be concentrated over the target in 90 minutes. Given that only two months previously 120 an hour over the target was considered very creditable, this concentration in time and space was quite remarkable. Three separate aiming points about one mile apart were selected and crews directed to maintain a strict circuit pattern. No flares were to be used and although Groups could select their own height from which to bomb, the minimum was 8,000 feet. No 2 Group and Fighter Command were tasked with diversionary raids.

The deciding factor was one which Harris could not control – the weather. On three successive days the operation was postponed and initially Saturday the 30th May did not look much more promising: thundery clouds over the North Sea, but breaking towards the south and dispersing in the middle Rhine. Hamburg, the more northerly target, was more likely to be shrouded in cloud. Following the weather briefing, Harris continued to contemplate the charts, slowly his finger moved across the map and stopped – Cologne it was to be. There were more alarms from the weather forecasts during the day, but at 12.25 pm the executive order was given: the raid was on.

Briefing at most stations started soon after tea. With so many aircraft concentrated over the target – nearly 700 per hour – there was obvious concern over the risk of collision. At Swinderby the Station Commander announced at briefing that the statisticians had calculated that no more than two aircraft would collide over the target – which two asked a wag at the back. As darkness settled, the busy drone of over 1,000 bomber aircraft shattered the silence of the still and sombre countryside of Lincolnshire, Yorkshire and East Anglia.

The bomber stream almost immediately ran into unpleasant weather with icing over the North Sea, but after crossing the Dutch coast the cloud slowly thinned as forecast and Cologne was clearly visible under only small amounts of high cloud. Most crews, with the benefit of Gee, had little difficulty finding the target and many remarked on the prominence of the medieval cathedral, its twin facetted spires glinting in the moonlight. Zero hour was 0055 and all bar a handful bombed within the scheduled 90 minutes, but a few disobeyed the instruction to depart by 0230 whether they had bombed or not and isolated attacks continued until 0315. 898 crews claimed to have found the target, dropping in all nearly 1,500 tons of bombs: it was later calculated at 31 tons per square mile. Later crews arriving over the target commented upon the large number of individual fires; the ratio of incendiaries to high explosive was about two to one. To rub salt into the wound, four Mosquitos visited Hamburg at 0500 on their first bombing mission of the war. As the statisticians predicted, there was one collision over the target (and another, not expected, over Lincolnshire on their return). Casualties were within tolerable limits; it was estimated that 22 aircraft had been lost over the target, most having succumbed to flak rather than night fighters, and another 28

This Halifax is being loaded with 500lb bombs for the 1000 bomber raid on Cologne on 30th May 1942.

IWM

Flt Lt R. Waite

My conversion training from Whitleys to Halifaxes in May 1942 was interrupted in order to do 'second dickey' trips on the first 1000 bomber raids. I was expecting to complete my conversion when I was surprised to find my name on the Operational Crew List as captain of BB195 for operations that night. I was nearly equally surprised to find at briefing that the target was Hamburg. I didn't know my crew, we introduced ourselves at briefing. Up until this time I had no experience of 3 engine flying and had never carried out a night cross country flight. My night flying on Halifaxes as pilot was 1 hour 45 minutes (6 circuits and landings). The grand total of all my solo night flying was 10 hours 20 minutes! That night my port inner engine failed about 80 miles from Hamburg, so this was my first cross country and first three engine flying and landing. My crew, fortunately, were I believe unaware of my lack of experience.

were lost elsewhere on the sortie including crashes and ditchings. The overall loss rate was 4.78 per cent, similar to the average for the previous year over Germany as a whole. Only 30 of the returning crews reported that they had been attacked by fighters, suggesting that the tactic of saturating the defences had succeeded.

Despite the optimistic reports of the crews on their return, the success of the mission could not be finally evaluated until reconnaissance photographs were available. At dawn one of the Mosquitos reported a great pall of smoke over the city with many fires still burning and later photographic evidence confirmed that damage was heavy and widespread, 600 acres, much of it in the city centre, had apparently been devastated. That considerable damage was caused is indisputable, but it was subsequently estimated that only one months war production had been lost and that within two weeks the life of the city was functioning almost normally. It is difficult to concede the validity of this latter point with 60,000 people homeless.

However, this was of no consequence at the time. The raid had been marvellously stage managed and Harris had achieved his 'coup dramatique'. He made the most of it and fully deserved the accolades which were showered upon him. It had required enormous courage as well as skill to execute 'Millenium', for if his gamble with the OTU crews had failed, he could have destroyed the training capacity of the Command for months to come. The magnitude of his decision has to be seen in the context of the widespread denigration of the Command within senior military and political circles just two months earlier. If, indeed, the raid had been a disaster, Harris would no doubt

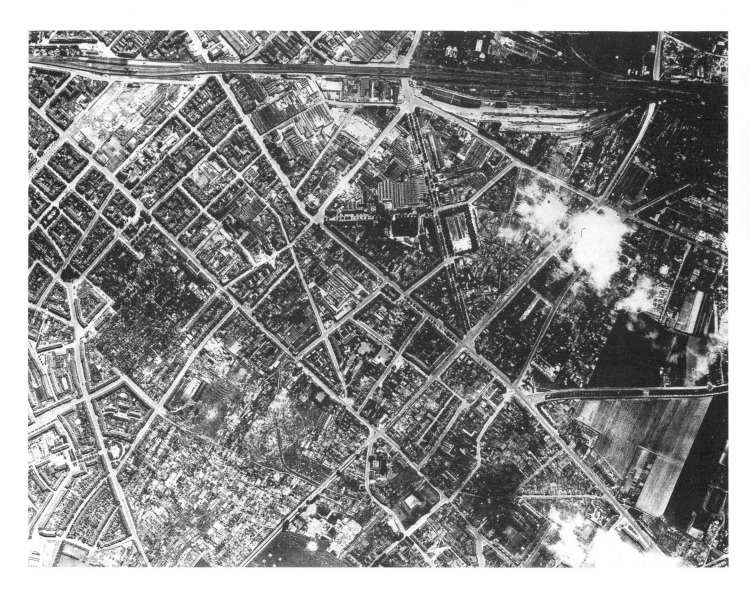

have been dismissed as a reckless gambler – but every great leader in history has at some time been prepared to take a calculated risk, and Harris' 1,000 bomber raid was very carefully calculated.

Harris made two more attempts to repeat the formula. Almost incredibly, only two nights later he managed to launch 956 bombers against Essen, but the weather and this notoriously difficult target defeated them. Photographs showed that very few crews actually bombed the town and the main aiming point, the Krupp factory, was again missed altogether. On the second occasion, with the help this time of Coastal Command, he squeezed 1,003 aircraft into the air against Bremen on the 25th June. Again hampered by the weather, damage was less than had been expected, but none of this detracted from the great practical and political success of the first of the 1,000 bomber raids. The confidence of Bomber Command itself and the prestige it enjoyed in the country at large was well under way to being restored. Furthermore, they were about to be joined by a formidable comrade in arms – the United States Army Air Force.

Wide areas of Cologne were devastated by the first of the spectacular 1000 bomber raids in May 1942.   IWM

Probation – The 8th Air Force Goes to War

Although a USAAF planning team arrived in England promptly after the Americans joined the war, it was not until July 1942 that their first combat aircraft, a B-17E of the 97th Bombardment Group landed at Prestwick: they had much to prove. The American concept of strategic operations had from the outset been based on daylight precision bombing by tightly grouped formations reliant on a bristling array of guns for self defence, a method of operation which their British colleagues had all but completely abandoned by this time. The Air Staff in London were, to say the least, sceptical of the ability of 8th Air Force to survive in daylight over Germany and laboured long and hard to persuade the Americans to join-in the night offensive. But there was no real alternative. Trained to operate in packs in which some of the difficulties of the newest crews

The crews of the Fairey Battle had an unenviable task in trying to stem the German thrust into France in 1940. These aircraft are from No 12 Squadron, the 'Dirty Dozen'.

The Blenheim Mk IV, unsuitable for strategic bombing, found a role in anti-shipping strikes in 1940-41.

The slow and ungainly Whitley was the RAF's main night strategic bomber at the outbreak of war. This is a Mk V of No 102 Squadron.

The Wellington became the mainstay of Bomber Command's night strategic force until 1943. This is a Mk 1A taking-off in the twilight for a strike against Germany.

The Hampden was increasingly used for aerial minelaying in the early war years. This aircraft belonged to No 44 Squadron at Waddington in 1940-41.

The Manchester was one of the less successful bomber designs of the war. On the ground is the second prototype and above it an aircraft of No 207 Squadron.

The two outstanding heavy bombers of the war were undoubtedly the Avro Lancaster and the Boeing B-17. This shows a Mk 1 Lancaster of No 207 Squadron and a B-17G of the 381st Bombardment Group.

The Stirling was the first of the new heavy bombers to enter operational service. These aircraft are from No 1651 Heavy Conversion Unit based at Waterbeach.

The Halifax gave admirable support to the Lancaster in the strategic role during the last three years of the war. This is a No 35 Squadron aircraft.

The Flying Fortress became a legend in the history of aerial bombardment. This B-17G belongs to the 709th Bombardment Squadron based at Rattlesdon in Suffolk.

After a sticky start, the B-24 Liberator consolidated its reputation in the raid on the oil refinery at Ploesti in August 1943.

The Lockheed Ventura was the slowest of the new medium bombers which replaced the Blenheim and was often employed on 'Circus' operations. This No 21 Squadron aircraft is escorted by a Spitfire Mk IX of No 402 (Canadian) Squadron.

The Douglas Boston was more often seen in RAF colours in the European theatre, but also briefly served with the 8th Air Force.

The Martin B-26 Marauder had a short-lived and disastrous experience in low level operations before converting to a medium level role.

The B-25 Mitchell provided good service to No 2 Group, Bomber Command, before playing a major role in ground attack operations in the re-invasion of Europe in 1944.

The most versatile aircraft of the Second World War, the Mosquito was an outstanding low level bomber. This aircraft belongs to No 105 Squadron at Horsham St Faith in 1942.

could be shouldered by their more experienced colleagues leading the formation, they had more than enough problems in daylight coping with the often murky weather over Europe without the added problems of navigating and bombing individually at night. Furthermore, it was to a certain extent alien to the American temperament to accept the constraints of area bombing which had been forced upon Bomber Command – their weapon was to be the scalpel rather than the bludgeon.

The newly arrived crews of the 97th Bombardment Group at Polebrook and Grafton Underwood in rural Northamptonshire soon buckled down to serious training. In many ways their ethos and approach were so different to the more sober, battle scarred mien of Bomber Command. Confident, brimming with vitality, far more disposed to the cult of the individual and

as far as their limited range allowed; a development congenial to Fighter Command who looked upon it as an enhanced 'Circus' operation for a force which was in danger of becoming under-employed. After several false alerts due to weather, they launched their first raid on the 17th August with General Eaker, the VIII Bomber Command leader, along for the ride. Two squadrons mounted an elaborate feint along the Channel to distract the enemy fighters whilst the main force of just 12 aircraft escorted by no less than four squadrons of the latest Spitfire Mk IXs made straight for the extensive railway marshalling yards at Rouen. The weather was good, some of the bombs fell on the target, the Luftwaffe gave the heavy fighter escort a fairly wide berth and only two aircraft were slightly damaged by light flak. It was adjudged a great success and was

sensitive to the arrows of fate, most American airmen placed enormous faith in good luck tokens and omens of success or disaster. Their aircraft sported flamboyant motifs, often based on the scantily clad female form, and descriptive titles which soon became household names. 'Memphis Belle', the first aircraft to complete 25 missions, is perhaps the best known as a result of William Wyler's eulogistic film of 1943 and David Puttnam's dramatically photographed sequel in 1990. As they settled into their strange new home, redolent with the greyness and deprivation of three years of war, they created pockets of 'Little America' across the length and breadth of the flat lands of East Anglia which, warmly welcomed though they were, often bewildered and occasionally antagonised their English hosts.

Formation training and instrument flying in cloud were the highest priorities for the pilots whilst air gunnery practice was badly needed by the rear crew members. The work-up went well under their experienced commander, Colonel Frank Armstrong, and the 97th was soon champing to have a crack at the real thing. Despite their reliance on self defence, it had already been agreed that RAF Spitfires would escort the B-17s

From August 1942 when they made their first raid on Rouen, the B-17s of VIII Bomber Command brought another dimension to the air war over Europe.   IWM

duly celebrated by the assembled crowd of senior officers and press correspondents when all aircraft returned safely. But most of those present, not least a jubilant General Eaker, recognised that there were far sterner tests ahead.

The following day the first squadron of the 92nd Bombardment Group (BG) arrived through Prestwick to join the 97th and 301st. The two latest groups were equipped with the superior B-17F and the first B-24 Liberators of the 44th BG joined in September: hopes were high that the 8th would soon be able to put together a formation of a more realistic size and penetrate unescorted deeper into enemy held territory. Such expectations were soon dashed, for the 8th Air Force was now tasked with supporting the American landings in North Africa, draining much of its experience as well as diverting aircraft and equipment. Furthermore, groups originally destined for England were now diverted to the Pacific theatre. East Anglia

became a training ground for Operation 'Torch' and the expected build-up of strength to pursue the bombing offensive over Europe was seriously diminished – an ever recurring problem for General Eaker until 1944. It highlighted, of course, the different view the Americans held of the task of the USAAF in Britain; to them 8th Air Force was seen primarily as a supporting element for the re-invasion of Europe, to Sir Arthur Harris it was a strategic force in its own right.

Over the last two weeks of August, the 97th BG made seven more visits to France or the Low Countries. Most raids were uneventful with no contact with the Luftwaffe. Only once, on the 21st, when the B-17s failed to adhere to the agreed assembly time with the escorting Spitfires did they encounter problems. After the fighters had turned back, FW 190s pounced out of the cloud and severely mauled a straggling B-17 although it still managed to regain its base. This was of course typical of 'Circus' operations in which the Luftwaffe would only take-on the opposition on its own terms. The first losses were suffered on the 6th September on the second of two visits to Rouen on consecutive days. On this occasion VIII Bomber Command had raised its effort to 36 aircraft, the largest number so far, but lost two to the most determined attack they had yet encountered. One feature which was consistently to distort the true picture of operations was already apparent: on an operation to Rotterdam on the 7th September the air gunners claimed 34 enemy aircraft destroyed or damaged against no loss to themselves. It only gradually became apparent that the gunner's claims were wildly exaggerated.

The Autumn weather was now increasingly impacting on operations, for any significant cloud or poor visibility would prevent the bombers from identifying the target and thus cause the mission to be abandoned or aborted. Although the RAF crews were inclined to believe that any bomb dropped on German soil was a bonus whether or not the target could be located, it was certainly not desirable to scatter bombs indiscriminately over the towns and villages of our erstwhile allies in France. By October 21st it was possible to launch 66 B-17s and Liberators against the Biscay submarine base of Lorient, but only the experienced 97th was able to locate the target in marginal weather suffering three aircraft lost and six damaged – the worst day so far. The submarine pens remained as impervious to bombing as ever. The two most experienced

Left: The 'Memphis Belle' was the first 8th Air Force aircraft to complete 25 missions after which it carried out a triumphant tour of the United States. RAFM

Below: The Liberator took a long time to settle down in England, suffering from reliability and maintenance problems. WWE

Groups, the 97th and 301st, now departed for North Africa leaving the learning process to start all over again. It was a process that had to be conducted by trial and error. On one sortie against St Nazaire in November the main force bombed from less than half the normal height at 7,500 feet; it lost three aircraft to flak and did not repeat the experiment.

The FW 190 pilots were beginning to have a healthy respect for the exuberant American air gunners and it was towards the end of November that Oberstleutnant Mayer of JG2 developed a new tactic of head-on attacks. With the high closing speed of up to 600 miles an hour, this was a difficult and potentially dangerous approach, but it exposed the weakness of the B-17's nose armament and several successes were achieved – with the occasional collision as well. It was also a tactic which tended to break-up the bomber formation, an additional bonus.

A raid of 101 aircraft against Rouen on the 20th December illustrated again the exaggerated claims of the air gunners. Fifty six German fighters were claimed, but post war study disclosed that in fact the Luftwaffe lost only five aircraft. As six B-17s were destroyed and 29 damaged, this was hardly a sustainable rate of exchange, particularly as the bombing results were proving variable and certainly less accurate than pre-war experiments in ideal conditions had led the USAAF to expect. In contrast to the earlier missions, losses were now being experienced on almost every raid from both flak and fighters. But the 8th was also developing its tactics and improving both bombing accuracy and the concentration of their defensive fire power. The one critical factor was formation discipline, stragglers were almost invariably snapped-up by the rapacious FW 190s.

At the turn of the year the daylight campaign was still very much on probation albeit strongly defended by General Arnold at the Casablanca conference. Although casualties were mounting, the loss rate was still comparable with that suffered by the RAF at night who themselves were increasingly suffering from the attentions of General Kammhuber's night fighters in the latter half of 1942. The very high claims of enemy aircraft destroyed also tended to reveal the campaign in a rather more favourable light than was subsequently proved justifiable. Most important of all, confidence was still buoyant; both the crews and their commanders, who at all levels frequently flew on combat sorties, believed in the success of their mission. But in truth, VIII Bomber Command was still operating on a

The advent of the Fw 190, which had a generally better performance than the Bf 109, brought added complications to VIII Bomber Command until long range fighter escorts became more readily available. This is the A-4 version. IWM

shoestring, only four bombardment groups were normally available which could raise at best about 100 aircraft, many of whose crews were 'rookies' still learning their trade. Furthermore, the Command had as yet only attacked targets in the occupied territories whereas Bomber Command raided Germany itself almost nightly throughout most of 1942. The fact that the RAF regarded targets in France as almost training runs for inexperienced crews began to rankle amongst the American crews – they too wanted to tackle Germany and they believed they were ready.

The Creation of the Pathfinder Force

On the night of the 14th November 1940, 449 German bombers had attacked the Midlands city of Coventry with unprecedented precision and devastating effect: nearly 400 people were killed and many more injured. The bombers were directed to their target by the He 111s of the specialist Kampfgruppe 100 which marked the target with incendiaries released automatically using a beam guidance system called 'X-Gerat'. Although this very precise navigation system was soon countered by radio jamming, the pathfinder technique pioneered in Germany had been developed to a very high degree of effectiveness before its use was even contemplated by the RAF.

The undoubted achievements of the Spring of 1942 had stemmed the controversy over the future of Bomber Command, but neither the Air Staff or Harris himself were complacent. The more successful raids were achieved in ideal conditions of weather and moonlight and against straight forward targets – those which could be easily identified and were lightly defended. The problem of the Ruhr had not been cracked as the largely abortive attacks on Essen showed only too clearly, and

whilst bombing concentration had been improved, it achieved little if the concentration was not on the designated aiming point. It was evident that decoy fires were frequently successful in attracting a large weight of attack and if the leading aircraft failed to designate the target accurately, the effort of the follow-up force was invariably misdirected.

Much has been made of the controversy surrounding the creation of the Pathfinder Force and of Harris' alleged opposition to it. That there were differences of view regarding the implementation of a target marking concept is undeniable, but there was little real argument regarding the concept itself. Indeed the introduction of Gee which was fitted only to a limited number of aircraft had ensured that these crews had fulfilled a target marking role in the raids on Essen in March. Nor did Harris dispute the need for the more experienced crews to be responsible for target marking, his objection rested on the creation of an independent force, a *corps d'elite*, to undertake the task.

The idea of a special force had been simmering in the Air Ministry for some time and first found formal expression in a letter by Group Captain Sidney Bufton to Sir Arthur Harris in March 1942. He was promptly rebuffed by Harris who claimed he was reasonably satisfied with the methods in use; an understandable reaction perhaps to a letter from a comparatively junior officer questioning the tactics in use within his Command. That Harris was not satisfied is readily apparent from letters to his own Group Commanders around the same period. There was, however, one conceptual difference which was now beginning to emerge. The concept of area bombing had never been universally accepted within the Air Ministry and there were those, Bufton included, who hankered for a return to precision bombing. Harris, on the other hand, had now veered in the opposite direction and whilst content to nominate specific targets, gave greater weight to the dislocation and morale effect of those bombs which were generally spread across an urban area.

Harris' objections to an independent force stemmed partly from a natural aversion to a *corps d'elite*, but also because of the dilution it would impose upon the operational squadrons who were already overloaded with inexperienced crews. It is not surprising therefore that the Group Commanders were adamantly opposed to the creation of a special force outside of their own control and feared that the removal of the most experienced crews would have a debilitating effect on skill and morale in the depleted squadrons. However, Bufton had done his homework within the Air Ministry and on the 14th June Sir Charles Portal himself wrote a carefully reasoned letter to Harris recommending the establishment of a Pathfinder Force. Sensing that this was a battle he was going to lose, Harris did not wait for the formal directive which followed on the 11th August, but almost immediately charged Group Captain D C T Bennett with forming what undoubtedly became an elite force, contributing greatly to the successes Bomber Command was to enjoy from 1943 onwards.

An Australian by birth and only thirty one years old, Don Bennett was outspoken and egotistical, but he had wide and varied experience in both civil and military aviation and was an acknowledged expert in long distance flying and navigation. He was also single minded with an almost demonic drive in support of causes in which he believed – and he passionately supported the concept of an independent target marking force. Bennett had rejoined the RAF only in September 1941 after helping to set-up the Atlantic ferry service, but by the Autumn of 1942 he had already commanded two bomber squadrons, Nos 77 and 10, and gained a lot of experience in a very short time.

Despite his antagonism towards an elite force, Harris immediately contributed to the image by authorising the highly esteemed pathfinder badge – a small but distinctive gold wing worn beneath the medal ribbons. Furthermore, he decreed that crews should complete 60 operations rather than the normal 30 to gain the maximum benefit from their experience. Bennett established his headquarters, not yet formally recognised as a group, at Wyton with another airfield at nearby Oakington and two satellites at Graveley and Warboys. His allotted squadrons came one each from the established groups bringing with them a variety of aircraft – No 7 Squadron (Stirlings) from 3 Group, No 35 Squadron (Halifaxes) from 4 Group, No 83 Squadron (Lancasters) from 1 Group. He also had one more unusual squadron, No 109, which was not affiliated to any group. Vickers had produced a pressurised Wellington for high altitude bombing using Oboe (a line of sight device) and No 109 under Wg Cdr MacMullen had been given the task of developing this concept. They quickly decided, however, that the Mosquito of

Air Commodore D.C.T. Bennett (then a group captain) was selected by Sir Arthur Harris to lead the Pathfinder Force when it was created in July 1942. IWM

which there were a few spare within the Command at this time was a much more suitable vehicle for this specialised role. The Mosquito went on to play a vital role in the subsequent development of the Pathfinder Force as well as making a useful contribution as the Light Night Striking Force of which more later.

Bennett immediately tackled the two main problems of the pathfinding concept – target identification and target marking. Gee had proved a useful navigation aid but was not sufficiently accurate for blind bombing and already susceptible to jamming over Germany. Two other devices, Oboe and H2S, were just appearing on the scene and these became the main tools of the new force, Oboe in the Mosquito and H2S in the heavy bombers. Visual target acquisition was also used when weather conditions were favourable, generally with the assistance of flares to illuminate the area. The latter were soon equipped with barometric devices to control the ignition height and umbrella shaped hoods to prevent the bomb aimer being blinded by their glare.

To mark the aiming point, high powered candles called

Target Indicators were produced in a wide range of colours. A combination of colours which was selected and briefed just before the raid made it much more difficult for the Germans to provide credible decoys, and different coloured indicators could be used to indicate a new aiming point if the bombing was beginning to drift. The Target Indicators were set barometrically to ignite at about 200-500 feet above the ground resulting in a cascade which again made the German task of replicating or extinguishing them more difficult.

Target Indicators were of course only effective when cloud did not obscure the ground and the Indicators. For such conditions Bennett developed a sky marking technique – parachute flares emitting star shells which were visible for up to five minutes. The sky markers drifted in the wind and so had to be carefully placed upwind of the target using Oboe or H2S. Timing of the arrival of the main force, which now had to fly through the target on a steady predetermined heading, was therefore the essence of accurate bombing using this method. The three methods of marking were given code names which became very familiar to all bomber crews in subsequent years. 'Newhaven' was the code for ground marking by visual methods, 'Parramatta' for ground marking by H2S, and 'Wanganui' for sky marking. These terms remained in general use for the rest of the war and formed the basis of the many more sophisticated techniques developed later.

The first independent pathfinder operation was flown against Hamburg on the 18th August 1942 and operations continued regularly thereafter. The Pathfinder Force, not yet equipped with the more sophisticated aids and techniques which were soon to appear, was not at first conspicuously successful, re-opening with the Groups some of the dissensions which had marked its creation. Nevertheless, in January 1943, the Pathfinder Force became a separate group – No 8 – and Bennett, promoted to Air Commodore, its AOC.

The story of the Pathfinder Force from now on is the story of Bomber Command. Although harmony within the Command was rarely possible for long given Bennetts's forthright and often irascible temperament, the target marking techniques perfected by the Group's elite crews became a byword for efficiency, skill and courage, and perhaps more than any other single initiative contributed to Bomber Command's enhanced success during the last two years of the war.*

Consolidation

Following the highly acclaimed 1000 bomber raids in May and June, the remainder of 1942 might almost be regarded as an anti-climax, but is perhaps better described as a period of consolidation. After the raid against Bremen on the 25th June by 1006 aircraft, Bomber Command never again mounted an attack of comparable size until well into 1943. The largest force assembled was 630 aircraft against Dusseldorf on the 31st July, but nevertheless the Command ranged widely across Germany and to Italy on every night that bombing was feasible.

Sir Arthur Harris' main concern was that his resources were not increasing sufficiently fast to counter the increasing losses, not only in action, but also by the transfer of squadrons to other theatres and to Coastal Command. On the other hand, the four engine heavy bombers were steadily replacing the less effective twins which had carried the brunt of the effort so far: The Manchesters departed unlamented after the last 1,000 bomber raid in June and the Hampden flew its last operational mission over Germany on the 14th September. The remaining Whitleys had already been transferred to Coastal Command earlier in the

This impressive demonstration of target marking showing ground markers, flash and flak was taken over Pforzheim in 1945.　　　　IWM

*For a German view of the Pathfinder Forces, see Appendix.

The Pathfinder Force soon acquired Oboe equipped Mosquitos to supplement their heavies and eventually employed them in an independent bomber role as well as for target marking. This is a B Mk IV. IWM

year. Not only were they replaced by the Halifax and the Lancaster, but larger and more effective weapons were arriving on the scene; the 8000 high explosive in April and 4000lb incendiary bomb (Pink Pansy) in September. By the end of the year the Canadian squadrons equipped with the Halifax were ready to be formed into a Group of their own, No 6, and the Oboe blind bombing aid was ready for operational service, shortly to be followed by H2S. If by the end of the year the force available to Harris had not increased dramatically in size, it had made immeasurable strides in quality.

The Command had still not totally abandoned its penchant for daylight operations despite the losses on the Augsburg raid and on the 17th October mounted a similar but much larger scale attack on the Schneider armament factory at Le Creusot on the Franco-Swiss border. Led by Wing Commander L C Slee of No 49 Squadron, 94 Lancasters made a wide detour over the Bay of Biscay and crossed France at 100 feet to reach Le Creusot at dusk, climbing to about 5000 feet for the bombing run itself. The force achieved total tactical surprise and the low level navigation was immaculate, but the bombing results disclosed

by the ubiquitous photographs soon dispelled the optimistic assessments of the crews. The fading light, smoke which soon covered the target and inadequate training for a new aiming technique led to the bombs being widely scattered. Although only one aircraft was lost, probably not as a result of enemy action, the potential risk was clearly very high and it was apparent that crews accustomed to high level bombing at night could not adapt to low level bombing by day without unacceptable training penalties. Daylight bombing for the heavies was at last put on ice until the final months of the war. There were, however, increasing signs that Bomber Command was not having it all its own way at night as well, and this is a timely moment to review the progress the Luftwaffe's night fighter defences had made since 1940.

Night Fighter

Lancasters at low level over Chattilon sur Loire en-route to Le Creusot on the 17th October 1942. IWM

Although Bomber Command had been largely driven from the skies of Germany in daylight, from 1939 to 41 they operated almost with impunity at night. The elements rather than the enemy were the greater hazard, and the deficiencies of the German air defences were alleviated only by the inability of the bomber crews to hit, or even find, their targets with any degree of regularity or precision. The Luftwaffe did not possess a specialised night fighter force at the outbreak of war. A few Bf 109 units were detailed for night flying training, but this was very much a subsidiary activity to their daylight operations. The Bf 109 was by no means well suited to night operations; it had no navigation or blind landing aids and, like the Spitfire and the Hurricane, it was not an easy aircraft to land at night. Take-off and landing accidents were numerous and the pilots were not encouraged in an unfamiliar environment by the rarity of even seeing an intruding bomber. Even if they managed to catch a glimpse of one in a searchlight cone, they were usually blinded by the glare and lost it before they could close to within the firing zone. Furthermore, they had the distraction of 'friendly' flak which fortunately was more unnerving than lethal. Nevertheless, in February 1940, one 'gruppe' of JG 2 equipped with the Bf 109D was formally designated as a night fighter unit.

The failure of the Bf 110 to match the RAF's more agile fighters in daylight over the Channel allowed them to be concentrated in a role for which they were rather better suited. The original night flying 'gruppe' of JG 2 converted to

Bf 110s in June 1940 and were joined at Dusseldorf by two more 'staffel' for concentrated night flying training. On the 20th July 1940 the first dedicated night fighter wing was formed, Nachtjagdgeschwader (NJG)1 under the overall command of Colonel Josef Kammhuber, one of the brightest of the young officers absorbed into the Reichscheer in 1919 and eventually destined to become the Commander of the West German Air Force within NATO after the war. By this time a few Dornier Do 17s and Junkers Ju 88s had also been converted to night fighter duties to reinforce the Bf 110s. Contact with bombers was still sporadic and it was very clear to Kammhuber that a dedicated ground control organisation was essential if the success rate was to be improved.

In the interim period there was, however, another more profitable outlet for the night fighter crews. One sure way of locating the elusive bomber was to catch it over its own airfield, a tactic we have already noted being used by No 2 Group's Blenheims. The Luftwaffe's intelligence service was sufficiently advanced at this period to have a good idea of when Bomber Command raids were planned and the night intruders attempted to intercept the bomber as it was taking-off or landing, at which time not only were the airfield lights ablaze to indicate its position, but the aircraft was at its most vulnerable in terms of height, speed and manoeuvrability. Although this was inevitably a rather hit or miss affair, NJG 2, with rarely more than 20 aircraft available for this task, had claimed 143 victims

Most of the routine maintenance was undertaken in the open at the bomber dispersal and it could be arduous work in the Winter months. This Halifax ground crew shelter from the elements. IWM

by October 1941 when it was transferred to the Mediterranean theatre.

The first specialised aid to night interception which was fitted on the Do 17 was an infra red spotlight known as 'Spanner Anlage' which was connected to the gunsight. It was not particularly effective as it penetrated only about 600 feet; the difficulty was always finding the bomber in the first place to enable the pilot to close to that range at which point it could often be seen silhouetted against the sky or by its exhaust flames which could only be partially concealed. What was needed was an airborne radar, and that was still a little way ahead.

The availability of ground based radar was, however, improving. The introduction of the Wurzburg radar allowed the creation in October 1940 of three night fighter zones, each with two radars, one linking the fighter to a ground control

organisation and the other feeding information to a master searchlight which could then link with others to produce the familiar cone. A plotting control room completed the defensive zone and the Luftwaffe had its first embryo ground control organisation. At the end of 1940 the 'Giant Wurzburg' which doubled the radar range to 40 miles was another step forward.

This development led directly to the 'Himmelbett' system in which a line of boxes (raum) about 30 miles deep were established from the north of Denmark, south west across northern Germany and Holland and then later down through Belgium and France as far as the Italian border. Each 'Himmelbett' box contained a 'Freya' long range search radar, two 'Wurzburg' narrow beam radars and a 'Seeburg' plotting table. The initial contact on the bomber was made on the 'Freya' and subsequently plotted when it came within range on the 'red Wurzburg'. The 'blue Wurzburg' meanwhile locked-on to the fighter. The plots from the two radars were telephoned to the control room in which two assistants sitting beneath the grid lined plotting table projected upwards two coloured lights. The fighter controller sitting above the plotting table now directed

The Douglas Boston, these are Mk IIIs, was an impressive replacement for the Blenheim in No 2 Group in 1942. IWM

the fighter (blue spot) by radio to intercept the bomber (red spot). If the pilot failed to see the bomber before it left the box, as frequently happened, he returned to a radio beacon to await the next interception. The major limitation of the 'Himmelbett' system was that only one fighter could be controlled at any one time. As the RAF became aware of this arrangement, which they called the 'Kammhuber Line', they could easily swamp a box by directing 40 or more aircraft through the same sector in close succession, of which only one unlucky crew was likely to be intercepted before the whole stream had cleared the box. Nevertheless, the Luftwaffe achieved some success until Bomber Command could develop the appropriate counter tactics. If the night fighter, of which there were five 'gruppen' by the end of 1940, gained visual contact with the bomber, its fate was almost invariably sealed. Creeping-up astern with its superior speed, the first indication to the bomber crew was often the hail of shells splintering the fragile fuselage of their lumbering Whitley or Wellington. Even if the fighter was spotted, the 0.3 in machine guns in the rear turret were no match for the lethal fire of the two 20mm cannon of the fighter.

Despite the limitations of the 'Himmelbett' system, the night

fighter 'staffel' began to collect their 'aces' as did all the other branches of the Luftwaffe. One of the first was Hauptmann Werner Streib who shot down his first Whitley, caught in a searchlight cone in the Ruhr on the 19th July 1940. Streib was to claim another 30 victories within the next two years. Heinrich Wittgenstein joined NJG 2 in August 1940 and eventually achieved 83 victories and Hauptmann Helmut Lent flew night fighters for most of the war and became one of its legendary experts. Some of the fighter controllers also became renowned for their prowess and along with experience came technical and tactical improvements: the honeymoon period for Bomber Command was fast drawing to a close. At the end of 1942 the Americans were already convinced that the Luftwaffe fighter defences had to be neutralised, but Bomber Command still relatively secure within the cloak of darkness was more sceptical. Within the next year, the need to defeat the night fighter became very real to Bomber Command as well.

Operation Oyster – 6th December 1942

1942 proved to be the watershed for which No 2 Group had been waiting. Although the Blenheim soldiered on throughout the first eight months, the year was mainly notable for the re-equipment of the Group with a new range of better armed and more effective aircraft. The first to arrive was the Douglas Boston which eventually equipped three squadrons and was mainly used in 1942 on 'Circus' operations. After a flirtation with the Albermarle, a slow, ponderous British built bomber which the Group quickly discarded with relief, two squadrons slowly re-equipped with the Mosquito and in June three squadrons began to form with another American newcomer, the Lockheed Ventura. Finally, towards the end of 1942, the Mitchell II, which eventually equipped four No 2 Group squadrons began to approach operational status. Operations were rather restricted during this period as squadrons learnt how best to use their new aircraft, not without some heart searching in the case of the Mosquito which belied its superb operational record later in the war. Nevertheless, by November the Group was ready to carry-out one of its most daring and spectacular feats of the war, a raid against the Phillips factory at Eindhoven in Holland.

Attacking targets in the occupied countries was always a controversial subject because of the likelihood of killing civilians who had but recently been allies. Airfields, railway installations and naval facilities were generally considered legitimate military targets in which the risk, if not exactly negligible, was acceptable. The Phillips factory, however, lay well within the town perimeter and was surrounded by the worker's houses. It was, nevertheless, an enticing objective producing over one third of the radio valves used by the German armed forces as well as specialised radar equipment. Its location within a heavily built-up area already gave it some indirect protection, but it was also only 50 miles from the heavily defended Ruhr and within a German fighter zone as well as being protected by its own anti-aircraft guns. Furthermore, it was outside of the range of escort fighters.

Planning for the projected raid against this formidable target was initiated by Bomber Command on the 9th November 1942. It clearly had to be a low level attack both to achieve bombing accuracy and reduce the risk of interception, and was not considered a suitable objective for the Lancaster. It was a target best suited to No 2 Group, but after a difficult period of reconstruction it was now equipped with four different types of varied performance ranging from the slow, cumbersome Ventura to the fast, agile Mosquito. Numbers were inadequate to employ a single aircraft type and it was originally intended to use all four which made timing and co-ordination critical from the outset. But as training progressed, it became evident that the newly formed Mitchell squadrons were not quite ready for a precision operation of this complexity and they were withdrawn.

The crews were well aware that something special was at hand as they pounded incessantly round the flat East Anglian

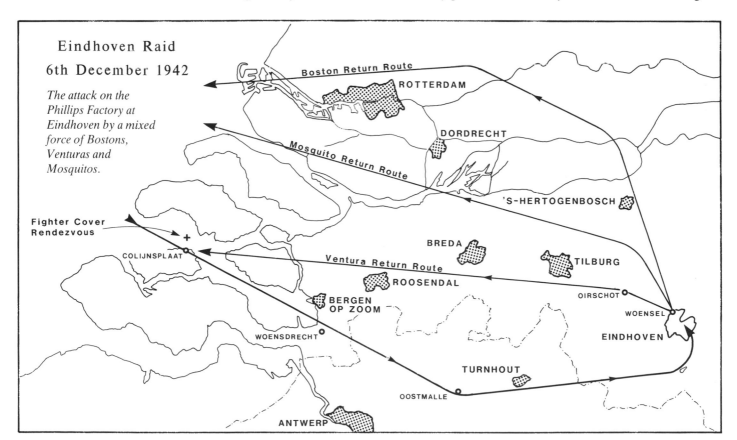

Eindhoven Raid
6th December 1942

The attack on the Phillips Factory at Eindhoven by a mixed force of Bostons, Venturas and Mosquitos.

The pillars of smoke against the wall are incendiaries in this impressive photograph taken on the raid on the Phillips factory at Eindhoven on the 6th December 1942. IWM

countryside at tree top height honing their low level navigation skills after a protracted period of medium level 'Circus' operations. A route simulating the raid plan including a sea crossing from Flamborough Head to Cromer and ending at the town of St Neots was flown by the tasked aircraft on the 17th November and on each of the following two days. Valuable lessons were learned which caused the plan to be totally recast, moving the Venturas from first to last in the bombing cycle. The final plan came out on the 23rd November with the code name 'Oyster' – the target was still a heavily guarded secret to all but a select few.

There were two distinct objectives within the town, the main factory and a subsidiary building making valves and lamps. The final raid plan required the attack to be complete within ten minutes with 12 Bostons, 12 Mosquitos and 30 Venturas attacking the main factory and 24 Bostons and 12 Venturas targeting the subsidiary building; a snake of 90 aircraft crossing the town at the comparatively low speed of 220 knots. Elaborate decoy raids were planned, principally by 8th Air Force B-17s against Lille, and four squadrons of Spitfires were tasked to cover the return flight from just inside the coast. On the way out, the raiders were dependent only on speed, ultra low level flying and surprise to evade the defenders. The day set for the operation was the 3rd December, but as so often the weather intervened and it was not until the 6th that cloud conditions, although marginal, were considered suitable.

Leading the raid was entrusted to Wg Cdr J E Pelly-Fry, CO of No 88 Boston Squadron, and there were many other very experienced crews in the formation including Wg Cdr Hughie Edwards VC leading the Mosquito element and Wg Cdr R H Young the Venturas. On the day there was a small deficiency of Mosquitos but the numbers were more than made-up by five extra Venturas. The basic tactical formation was six aircraft in a shallow echelon to port and starboard of the leader, with the sections themselves displaced laterally to cover the width of the two targets.

The join-up went according to plan and the landfall on the Dutch coast to the north west of Antwerp was accurate. But two Bostons had already aborted with technical problems and a Ventura crashed into the sea, possibly after a bird strike – an expected problem which caused damage to several aircraft. Flak on the coast accounted for two more Venturas although the Bostons and Mosquitos escaped serious damage. The formation was now nicely lined-up in a snake about 30 miles long with the Venturas striving to stay in touch and the Mosquitos flying uncomfortably slowly to stay behind the Bostons. Picking-up a convenient railway line and wheeling left towards the target, the Bostons pulled-up to bomb from about 2,000 feet with their 11 second delay 250lb bombs. The main factory, a five storey building, was clearly visible just as predicted in the photographs at briefing, but so was the flak and the alert gunners soon claimed a hit on Pelly-Fry's leading Boston. The weight and speed of the attack, however, soon disconcerted the gunners and most aircraft passed over the target with comparatively minor damage. Bomb after bomb hammered into both buildings, the only real difficulty, as at Le Creusot two months earlier, being to identify the blazing factories in the smoke. The Venturas carrying incendiaries and 30 minute delay bombs attacked at low level and most found the target although some bombs overshot hitting houses near the factory. Two Venturas were shot down close to the target and one damaged Mosquito eventually crashed into the sea.

The return route was not quite flown with the precision of the outbound leg with the Bostons in particular taking a more dangerous northerly route around Rotterdam after the damage to the lead aircraft had disrupted the formation. They missed their fighter escort and three were shot down by FW 190s over the sea. The Venturas returned in accordance with the plan, met their fighter escort and suffered no more casualties. Many aircraft suffered flak damage, one ditched off the Norfolk Coast and four crash landed.

A few minutes after the last attacking aircraft had left, a lone Mosquito of No 139 Squadron roared across the target, its mission to take photographs of the damage. Although harassed by two Bf 109s, the pilot confirmed that the factory buildings were consumed by flames and smoke. Virtually every building in the complex had been hit and although some of the machinery survived, output was seriously restricted for many months. It was later reported that only 25 civilians had been killed although several houses had been inadvertently destroyed. The cost for such a difficult operation was not excessively high – four Bostons, nine Venturas and one Mosquito. It was a fitting end to a difficult year for No 2 Group and augured well for 1943.

'Gardening'

As we progress through our account of Bomber Command's operations during the war, 1942 is a convenient moment to consider aerial mine laying. Development was continuous from 1940 through to 1945 in both scope and sophistication, and for continuity the whole period will be discussed in this section. The mine had played an important role in the 1914-18 conflict, claiming more U boats than any other offensive system, but as a new war approached there was no tradition or experience of laying mines from the air. That it was feasible was self evident, but the development of an air laid magnetic mine was so leisurely between the wars that none became available for use until the Spring of 1940 even though economic blockade was once again the primary strategy for the defeat of Germany. Nevertheless, there were many discussions between the Admiralty and the Air Ministry in 1939 when the former was developing a magnetic mine for free fall sowing from a torpedo bomber with Coastal Command's Beauforts as the intended carrier. The Beaufort, however, did not have the range to reach Germany's Baltic ports and thus Bomber Command had to be brought into the loop in which they were to remain for the rest of the war.

Aerial mining has had little exposure in most accounts of bomber operations between 1939-45, often being regarded as little more than a diversion for aircraft and crews who could not be used more profitably in bombing Germany. Indeed, there were long periods when the Air Ministry and Bomber Command regarded it in just this light, as for example in the Nuremberg raid of 30th March 1944 when a large scale mining operation was laid-on as a decoy to distract attention from the main force. Nevertheless, Bomber Command made a major contribution to the war at sea, and until the beginning of 1943 it was to prove one of the most rewarding uses of the strategic bomber force.

Aerial mining throughout the war was known as 'Gardening' and individual areas were designated by the names of trees, flowers and fishes. The Admiralty was responsible for target selection and Bomber Command was initially allocated to the Western Baltic, the Kattegat and the approaches to the Elbe, with Coastal Command aircraft responsible for the areas closer to home. It will be recalled that by the Spring of 1940, the Hampden and the Wellington had largely been driven from the daylight sky over hostile territory and it was the former that was chosen to undertake aerial mine laying. One snag surfaced immediately, for the minimum practical speed and height from which a mine could be dropped by a Hampden was too high for free fall and it was first necessary to develop a drogue parachute to retard the entry into the water. This was soon achieved and on the 13th April 1940, 15 Hampdens mounted the first mine laying operation in the Greater and Little Belts. Each aircraft could carry only a single mine and thus laying a field was a somewhat protracted affair, but even so 128 mines had been sown in 12 different 'gardens' by the end of the month, 109 of them by Bomber Command for an overall loss of eight aircraft. There was still a shortage of mines in May, a total of only 71 being sown, but the area of operation had been extended to Oslo Harbour, now in the hands of Germany after the invasion of Norway, and to the Keil Canal, the vitally important artery between the Baltic and the North Sea. After the fall of France two months later the Biscay ports became increasingly important as U boat bases and 'Gardening' was extended to

The number of mines which could be sown increased significantly when the Stirling, which could carry 6, was introduced to this role in March 1942. These mines are being loaded into a Stirling of No 7 Squadron. RAFM

Lorient, Brest, St Nazaire and La Pallice in September. By the end of the year, despite a continued shortage of mines and a refusal by Bomber Command to commit more than one squadron to the task, over 1,100 mines had been laid for the loss of 30 aircraft: post war analysis showed that these had claimed no less than 82 German and neutral ships.

The Air Ministry was still somewhat reluctant to be diverted from its primary role of bombing Germany, pointing out in January 1941 that air mining was not included in the recently issued War Cabinet directive on bombing objectives. In consequence they directed that Bomber Command aircraft could only be used for mining as a function of crew training and only reluctantly later accepted that no more than 15 experienced crews could be so employed when the weather was not suitable for bombing. This was all rather unfortunate, for although not so apparent at the time, aerial mining, given the meagre effort provided, was arguably achieving as much damage as that obtained from bombing Germany at night: in fact one ship was sunk or damaged for about every 15 mines laid. A particularly satisfying coup in February 1942 was the damage caused to the *Scharnhorst* and the *Gneisenau* by mines hurriedly laid at Terschelling after their embarrassing dash through the

Channel from Brest despite the undivided attention of Bomber Command.

A significant milestone in mining capability was passed when the heavy bombers were engaged, of which the first was the Manchester on the 12th February 1942. The great advantage brought by the larger aircraft was the ability to carry more mines on each sortie; the Manchester and Halifax could each carry four and the Stirling and Lancaster six. The Air Ministry was now being rather more co-operative and the first Stirling operation was carried-out on the 23rd March. The Admiralty planned to produce 4,000 mines a month by June although that figure was soon shown to be excessive. In the Summer months, however, mining was largely restricted to the Bay of Biscay because of the shorter nights in the north which would have precluded completing the sortie in darkness.

The Germans were initially caught unprepared by the aerial minelaying offensive in 1940, but rapidly instituted buoyed

Although quickly out-classed as a day bomber, the Hampden found an invaluable niche for itself in aerial mine laying.

IWM

channels and more effective mine destruct vessels – 'Sperrbrechers'. Thereafter aerial mine warfare developed along similar lines to that of electronic warfare: as ever more sophisticated circuitry was developed by the British, the Germans in turn introduced counter measures which more or less maintained a reasonable balance. One disadvantage of mine warfare is that the enemy can fairly easily recover and examine an intact weapon, thus facilitating the introduction of an appropriate antidote. Even so, acoustic mines which were introduced in September 1943 caused particular problems even though the Germans had been developing a similar weapon over the previous two years. Destruction was made more difficult by the British practice of indiscriminately using different types of mines in the same field.

By 1943 all the major Bomber Command Groups were involved in minelaying, dropping on average about 1,200 mines per month in areas ranging from Danzig in the north to Bayonne in the south. From March onwards, however, the introduction of H2S enabled blind bombing over Germany and thus the nights when the weather was unsuitable for strategic bombing decreased with an inevitable reduction in minelaying. Inevitably, the wrangling resurfaced between the Admiralty, who wanted the RAF to lay 1,000 mines a week, and the Air Ministry who were only prepared to countenance 1,000 a month. Nevertheless, nearly 14,000 mines were sown over the year although the success ratio diminished and aircraft losses increased.

The main developments in 1944 were the capability of dropping mines from a higher level which reduced the danger from flak, the use of H2S for minelaying, and the introduction of pathfinding techniques prompted by the accidental deposit of 54 mines on Swedish territory. In May 1,000 mines were laid between the Scheldt and Le Havre in support of Operation 'Overlord' and the same month saw another innovatory development with the Mosquito adding minelaying to its ever widening repertoire. A new mine for laying at high speed in shallow water had been developed and the first operation was mounted against the Kiel Canal, with another more spectacular mission to the Dortmund-Ems Canal on the 9th August. Towards the end of the year the emphasis turned towards Norwegian waters as the Biscay ports became untenable for the U boats. The same pattern continued in 1945 until the last operation was tasked, albeit subsequently recalled, just a few days before the war drew to a close.

The results of the mining campaign in North West Europe

are impressive. 18,532 sorties for the loss of 484 aircraft (4.2%) leading to 627 vessels sunk and 521 damaged, or put another way there was a positive return for every 16 sorties. This compares very favourably with direct attacks on ships, not as we have seen an easy target, in which three times as many sorties resulted in little more than a third of the number of enemy vessels sunk or damaged. Aerial minelaying, however, had a number of other advantages. It was the sole means of harassing shipping in areas immune to other forms of attack and tied-up considerable enemy resources in combatting the threat, not only in mine destroying, but in anti-aircraft defences to protect coastal areas. Port closures, pressure on dockyard repair facilities and the restriction of training were other positive factors. Indeed, in the Baltic it proved a major constraint on U boat trials and training from 1940 onwards which by 1944 had become very serious. The one disappointment was that aerial mining had very little direct impact on U boat operations, only 16 sunk and 20 damaged. In every other respect, 'Gardening' was a much underrated activity within Bomber Command's wide repertoire, and up to the beginning of 1943 was perhaps the most successful of all its varied operations.

Towards the end of the war, H2S was used in the Lancaster for more accurate minelaying in coastal waters. This Mk III aircraft is from No 619 Squadron.   IWM

CHAPTER SIX

Gathering Momentum–False Dawn–1943

The 'Pointblank' Offensive

Although in retrospect it is easy to recognise that the tide of war was turning in favour of the Allies, it did not appear quite so self evident as 1942 drew to its close. German troops still controlled most of Western Europe from the North Cape to the Mediterranean, increasing numbers of U boats were exacting a terrible toll in the sea lanes of the world and the Japanese hovered menacingly on the borders of India. Although the United States had been in the war for over a year, the enormous fighting potential of this vast country was only now emerging from the chrysalis of isolationism. Bomber Command began the new year apparently little stronger than it had started the last, mustering only a daily average of little more than 500 aircraft available for operations. But one third of these were now Lancasters, H2S was about to enter service as was the Oboe equipped Mosquito, and the Pathfinder Force was beginning to find its feet. The 8th Air Force, after a gentle apprenticeship over France, was also now ready to commence operations against mainland Germany.

The new year began with the meeting at Casablanca between President Roosevelt and Mr Churchill with their Combined Chiefs of Staff. The leaders had already agreed a 'Germany first' policy at the Washington Conference in December 1941 and now made another far reaching decision that the war could only be ended by her unconditional surrender. The most important decision of the Casablanca Conference for our story was the decision to embark upon a Combined Bombing Offensive with the objective of 'the progressive destruction and dislocation of the German military, industrial and economic system, and the undermining of the German people to a point where their capacity for armed resistance is fatally weakened'. These fine words, with which few could object as a general statement of intent, were to be the catalyst of considerable controversy between the Air Ministry, Bomber Command and 8th Air Force as the months unfolded. The same directive also went on to lay down target priorities – submarine construction, the aircraft industry, transportation, oil plants and other war industry targets. It also made reference to such diverse objectives as attacks on Italy, the German fleet and the containment of the enemy fighter force. In other words, there was something in there for everybody and Sir Arthur Harris had no doubts as to

his interpretation of this highly ambiguous document. Sir Charles Portal, who was given strategical direction of all bomber operations from Britain, increasingly took a divergent line.

The argument revolved yet again around the question of selective as opposed to area bombing. Harris was now firmly attached to the area concept and indeed went much further than the clear intention of the Casablanca Conference that strategic bombing was but a prelude to a land invasion of Europe. He was convinced that if sufficient resources were devoted to the strategic offensive, this alone would bring Germany to defeat. The Americans on the other hand were committed to daylight precision raids and in general they were supported by the Air Staff who further refined the target priorities to submarine construction, the aircraft industry, the ball bearings industry, oil production, synthetic rubber plants and military transport. There were, however, two snags. The 8th Air Force was still too small to carry out this task effectively alone and it was essential that Bomber Command's heavier weight reinforced at night the attacks on the targets chosen for the Americans by day. Secondly, the Americans had not yet proven that their unescorted bomber formations could withstand the inevitable onslaught of the still formidable German fighter force. Admittedly the B-17 was much better equipped to achieve this than the Wellington had proved in 1940 and the American crews were well drilled in formation flying. Nevertheless, the Combined Offensive could succeed only if the Americans gained air superiority over the greater part of the German mainland and defeated the enemy's fighter defences. On the other hand, Bomber Command, who depended upon deception and evasion tactics at night, did not have the same overriding priority, or at least this was not so perceived in the first half of 1943. General Eaker proposed therefore that the 'intermediate' objective of the Combined Offensive, with priority over all others, was the defeat of the German fighter force, a strategy which became known as the 'Pointblank' offensive.

General Eaker's plan was approved by Portal and not objected to by Harris, and in a rather watered down version endorsed by Roosevelt and Churchill at their Washington Conference in May. On the 3rd June the Air Ministry circulated

The Allied leaders and their Chiefs of Staff at the Casablanca Conference in January 1943. IWM

a new bombing directive in draft which faithfully reproduced the 'Pointblank' concept, giving priority to the 'intermediate' objective of destroying the Luftwaffe's fighter force and the industrial infrastructure which supported it. In part justification, it conceded for the first time that the fighter was a threat to the night bombing campaign as well as that of 8th Air Force during the day. Unfortunately, this new concept was totally alien to Harris' tactics of deceiving and avoiding the fighters rather than confronting them head-on, for with some justification he believed that once a fighter had a bomber in its sights, its destruction was all but inevitable. Between the draft directive and its issue in final form seven days later, Harris had managed to drive a steamroller through its intentions. It was both obscure and in parts contradictory, but its effect was to consign the 'intermediate' objective to the 8th Air Force whilst Bomber Command would adhere to the more general Casablanca objective of the destruction of the 'German military, industrial and economic system'. The key draft reference to the need for selecting targets based on 'the immediacy of their contribution to the weakening of German fighter strength' was omitted. The 8th Air Force for all practical purposes was to be left to defeat the Luftwaffe on its own whilst

Harris pursued his own objective of total victory. It was an extraordinary about face by Portal given the universal agreement at all levels to the 'Pointblank' plan, which it must also be remembered was an essential plank in the primary strategic aim of a second front in France. Whilst Harris was correct in recognising that Bomber Command was still limited even in 1943 in its ability to attack selective targets, whether or not associated with the aircraft industry, the directive of June 1943 was a wilful disregard of the strategy agreed at the higher level for the conduct of the war.

Although we shall examine the performance through 1943 of both the 8th Air Force and Bomber Command in more detail later, we must record here that the 'Pointblank' offensive was in danger of foundering by the Autumn. The 8th Air Force had not achieved its projected size by the end of September when only 850 of a forecast 1,192 bombers had been delivered. Even more crucially, the German fighter strength on the Western Front had doubled in size since January. In the circumstances, it is not surprising that the Americans were now facing crippling losses and increasingly having to constrain their penetration into the more heavily defended areas of Germany. Furthermore, as indicated by a raid against Munster in October, the 8th Air Force was itself beginning to turn towards area rather than selective bombing.

As the American effort declined, Harris continued his inexorable progress across Germany from the Ruhr through Hamburg to Berlin, but as the Deputy CAS pointed out in September, in the process Harris had not once attacked the six towns which had been indicated to him as the main centres of aircraft production. Furthermore, the failure to achieve air superiority was seriously jeopardising the prospects of 'Overlord', now projected for early in 1944. It was difficult to avoid the analogy of the German's Operation 'Sea Lion' when the crucial switch of the Luftwaffe from attacking the fighter airfields to an attack on London led inevitably to the abandonment of the invasion plan.

The contradictions contained within the June directive which allowed Harris to press on regardless with his own strategic policy could no longer be ignored. The dispute began to centre upon Schweinfurt. To one faction, the ball bearing industry concentrated in this town was the crucial key to the defeat of the German aircraft industry, to Harris it was just another 'panacea' target, a symbol of a concept which he now totally abhorred. On the 14th October the 8th Air Force mounted a major raid upon Schweinfurt with 291 aircraft: it was a disaster, 60 aircraft were shot down and another 138 damaged. In one week this brought the American losses to no less than 148 aircraft, a rate which could not be sustained. Intelligence estimates at this time also clearly suggested that the Allied strategy was facing a serious crisis. Whilst it was calculated that in July there had been 1,210 German fighters on the Western Front, it was estimated that by the end of the year this figure would rise to 1,560 – by mid 1944, the projected date for 'Overlord', the total German fighter strength would have risen to 2,865. This was certainly not a recipe for air superiority over the invasion front.

It was the opportune moment for Sir Arthur Harris to stop paying lip service to 'Pointblank' and openly espouse the strategy he had actually pursued throughout the year. Typically he went straight to Mr Churchill to seek his support for a new combined offensive, his letter concluding, 'We can wreck Berlin from end to end if the U.S.A.F. will come in on it. It will cost between 400-500 aircraft. It will cost Germany the war'. But it was difficult to see how the Americans could assist; it was out of the question for the 8th Air Force to be re-trained to operate at night in any reasonable timescale and there was no reason to believe that an attack on Berlin by day could be any less catastrophic than the Schweinfurt raid a few weeks earlier. Furthermore, there could be no recourse to 'Overlord' without air superiority if the Berlin strategy failed. It was a gamble that Churchill and Portal, and certainly Roosevelt and Arnold, were not prepared to take – the German fighter strength must be neutralised if 'Overlord' was to go ahead. 'Pointblank' must be continued.

The Battle of The Ruhr

This then was the policy for the Combined Bomber Offensive throughout 1943, the reality as we have seen was rather different; in fact the action which ensued was rarely combined either strategically of tactically. In many respects this was inevitable, the two concepts of daylight precision and night area bombing were so diverse that correlation was often difficult if not impossible. What is incontrovertible is that Sir Arthur Harris made little effort to reconcile them; for him 1943 was to be an unremitting onslaught on the major industrial, political and commercial centres of Germany, with little concern for the finer nuances of shifting policy.

The battle against the U boat reached a critical stage at the beginning of 1943 and much of Bomber Command's effort was directed, unproductively, against the submarine repair and replenishment bases in the Bay of Biscay. Even so, there was sufficient spare capacity to develop pathfinding techniques in medium scale raids against targets in the Ruhr, Hamburg and Berlin, and thus when the Command was finally released from its commitment to the U boat war on the 6th April, Harris was well prepared to start along the road to the east which was to culminate in the Battle of Berlin at the end of the year. Although the campaign from March to July 1943 is generally described as the Battle of the Ruhr, it was by no means the only area attacked during these four months. It was essential to keep the defences stretched across the width of Germany to prevent their concentration in any one area and raids ranged from the Ruhr to Berlin in the east, to Turin in the south, with even an occasional return to the Biscay ports.

Harris precisely defined the beginning of the Battle of the Ruhr as the night of the 5th March with a raid against that old adversary, the Krupp factory at Essen. The first two raids in the campaign set the tactical pattern for the whole battle and may thus usefully be described in some detail. The key to success in the Essen raid was the Mosquito target marking force of No 109 Squadron. Only eight Oboe equipped Mosquitos were designated to mark the target, the first of which was to drop blind a salvo of red target indicators at precisely 2100 hours. The first Mosquito was to be followed two minutes later by a pathfinder who would reinforce the red markers with green. A second Mosquito, again using Oboe, was to re-mark the target one minute later with a third seven minutes after that. In between the Mosquitos, the pathfinders would reinforce the reds with greens at one or two minute intervals. The pattern was to continue throughout the 40 minutes in which the main force of 412 Halifaxes, Wellingtons, Stirlings and Lancasters was concentrated. To help the less well equipped bombers, yellow target indicators would be dropped 15 miles short of the target to act as a lead-in point. The main force was ordered to bomb the reds if visible, otherwise to concentrate on the greens. The whole attack, therefore, was dependent upon blind bombing, not one crew needed to see the target. The bomb load was to consist of two thirds incendiaries with the remainder high explosive, some with delayed action fuses.

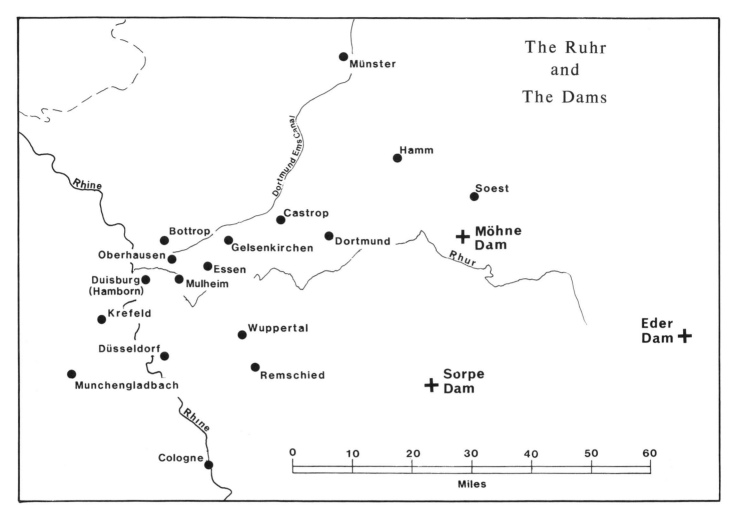

Such was the plan. Out of the 442 crews detailed, 56 sorties were for various reasons aborted including three of the Mosquitos. The first Mosquito indicators, dropped two minutes early, were apparently well placed and immediately fastened onto by the leading aircraft of the main force. The first green indicators were also correctly placed and despite the gaps in the Mosquito marking, the target was accurately marked right-up to the last greens 38 minutes after zero hour. In all, 345 crews of the main force claimed to have bombed the target. As always, however, the photographic reconnaissance sorties were vital to the true assessment of the raid and the first of these was not available until the 7th. The results were not disappointing, an area of 160 acres in the middle of the town had been 'laid waste' with significant damage over another 450 acres. The aiming point, the Krupp factory, had been severely damaged – a stark contrast with the results achieved on the first Gee equipped raid on Essen a year previously. The losses were also acceptable; 14 aircraft failed to return, including two Wellingtons which collided on the way out to the target, and 38 were damaged. It was a most encouraging beginning to Harris' Spring campaign.

The second raid on the 8th March was not against the Ruhr, but a target which lay outside the range of Oboe-Nuremberg. The tactics were therefore entirely different and this time H2S was the primary bombing aid. Zero hour was 2315 at which time

five aircraft were to drop illuminating flares blind by which the crews would, hopefully, visually identify the target. If this could be achieved, the target was to be visually marked with green target indicators. A further nine H2S equipped aircraft were to repeat the process two minutes later after which 22 backers-up would mark the target at one minute intervals. If the target could not be identified visually, red target indicators were to be dropped blind on H2S. It will be recognised immediately that the plan was rather less precise than the Oboe designated raid on Essen, depending as it did on the cloud and visibility found over the target. Predictably the results were less accurate, but even though bombs were scattered over a much wider area, a daylight reconnaissance disclosed that many industrial complexes had suffered heavily including the M.A.N. factories producing submarine engines. Nevertheless, the concentration achieved over Essen was much more effective where incendiaries formed the bulk of the bombload.

Targets beyond the Ruhr were regularly attacked during the first two months of the campaign, but as the nights shortened the Ruhr increasingly attracted attention. Essen, Duisburg, Cologne, Dusseldorf, Dortmund and Bochum were frequently attacked with forces which generally ranged in size from 400 to over 700 aircraft. Furthermore, because of the shorter distances, a far higher proportion of the available payload could be

Duisburg was attacked 5 times, more than any other city except Essen, during the 'Battle of the Ruhr' in the Spring of 1943. IWM

devoted to bombs rather than fuel. Most of the targets in the Ruhr were marked by Oboe which was quickly recognised to be a far more precise aid than H2S. Even the use of Oboe was not totally unconstrained. If the cloud was too thick for the ground target indicators to be seen, the pathfinders had to use sky markers which were much less effective in that they soon drifted away from the area in which they had been placed. Two sizeable raids on Essen using this technique in April and May were far less successful than two earlier attacks when clear skies allowed ground markers to be employed. The campaign in the Ruhr disclosed beyond doubt that Oboe initiated raids using ground marking target indicators were invariably most successful, a reminder that despite the new aids, the weather still played a significant role in success or failure.

Whereas the Ruhr consistently sustained heavy damage with comparatively few failures, raids on Berlin at the end of March failed to achieve worthwhile concentrations and attacks against Munich and Stuttgart were almost total failures. In one attack against the Skoda works at Pilsen, only six crews out of 249 placed bombs within three miles of the target. A more successful raid was mounted against Stettin, another distant target, on the 20th April when 256 out of 304 crews appeared to have hit the centre of the town. The key was always the accuracy of the pathfinders, if these could ground mark the target accurately

and, equally importantly, sustain the marking throughout the raid, the results were usually successful. Even so, Bomber Command in 1943 was still an area bombing force. With the exception of such remarkable feats as the raid on the Ruhr dams on the 16th May and the much larger Peenemünde raid of August, individual targets such as the Krupp works were destroyed or damaged only as a side effect of the vast concentration of bombs brought to bear over a much wider area – it was the success of the bludgeon rather than of the rapier. Nevertheless, Bomber Command had at last 'cracked' the Ruhr; after three years of disappointing results, large areas of this industrial heartland of Germany had apparently been laid waste. It is perhaps unsurprising that the impact upon her economic potential was widely exaggerated at the time. In fact, the actual results as disclosed after the end of the war were far less dramatic. Although vast areas of industrial buildings were damaged, the machinery they housed was often left intact and quickly put back to work; and the morale of the workers, far from being destroyed, was frequently fortified by the deprivation they endured. The inhabitants of the Ruhr, like those of Coventry, Liverpool and London, were showing remarkable durability in the face of this onslaught from the sky.

The devastation of the Ruhr, or 'Happy Valley' as it was known to the bomber crews, was not achieved without serious losses. The Mosquito operating up to 30,000 feet was almost immune to attack, indeed No 109 Squadron lost only one crew throughout the year. The heavy bombers were not so fortunate. Of 18,506 sorties mounted during the four months of the Battle of the Ruhr, 872 failed to return and no less than 2,126 aircraft were damaged, often severely. Whilst the overall loss rate was a just containable 4.7 per cent, some raids were particularly hard hit, none more so than one of the last against Oberhausen on the 14th June when 8.4 per cent were missing and a further 21.4 per cent damaged. The truth was that the German night defences, although under great stress, were also proving remarkably resilient, and whilst most damage to aircraft was caused by flak, about 70 per cent of the losses actually fell to the night fighters: flak was dangerous, but night fighters when they achieved a visual contact were lethal. The trend was significant, perhaps Harris could not ignore 'Pointblank' as blithely as he had until now.

The Dams Raid – 16th May 1943

Whilst Sir Arthur Harris was intent on bludgeoning the Ruhr into submission in the Spring of 1943, one individual small scale raid was entirely different in conception and technique. The attack on the Ruhr dams was undoubtedly the most celebrated single raid in the course of the war, but although the details are already well known, they must be recounted again here if only because the tactics used had a significant influence on wider Bomber Command policy and tactics in the subsequent two years.

The impact of the uncontrolled release of the water contained in the Mohne, Sorpe and Eder reservoirs had been recognised, perhaps over optimistically so, in the relevant ministries in London from before the war. The Mohne in particular supplied a high proportion of the water needs of the Ruhr both for domestic and industrial use and, furthermore, the resulting inundation would have a widespread affect on the morale of the people over a vast area. The Eder was of lesser economic value as its main function was to equalise the water-level between two canal systems. But even if the rewards were high, the difficulties of achieving sufficient damage to the huge concrete structures of the dams were considerable and the Sorpe, of earth construction, was well nigh indestructible. The problems were approached in two directions. Dr Barnes Wallis of Vickers Armstrong designed a weapon, technically a mine rather than a bomb, of sufficient power to fracture the structure of the concrete. He was also responsible for the technique by which it could be placed accurately against the wall without either destroying itself on impact or the aircraft which released it. The second problem, the actual delivery of the weapons, was entrusted to Wg Cdr Guy Gibson who selected and trained the crews to the very high level of precision flying needed to accomplish the task.

The mine designed by Barnes Wallis was in the shape of a barrel about five feet deep and four feet in diameter containing five tons of high explosive. It had a hydrostatic detonation pistol designed to explode the device at about 30 feet below the water surface. It was so large and cumbersome that the Lancaster had to be modified to hold the mine which protruded below the bomb bay. The genius of Barnes Wallis was strikingly evident in the technique he devised for delivering the weapon: it was to be dropped from a very low level (60 feet) well short of the dam retaining wall from where its momentum would enable it to skip over the surface of the water and, very importantly, over the protective torpedo nets, to nestle against the lip of the dam. By the time it had sunk and exploded, the aircraft which released it would be well clear. After several disappointments, the mine was eventually successfully tested off the south coast of England.

The flight profile for the delivery of the weapon was no less difficult and complex, for of course at this time Bomber Command's heavy force was employed almost solely on high level area bombing. Wg Cdr Gibson, although only 25 years of age, already had a distinguished operational record in both fighters and bombers which had earned him the DSO and DFC and he had just completed a tour as OC No 106 Squadron. A new squadron, initially Squadron X, but eventually designated No 617 was formed to carry out this single operation. Gibson had a free hand in selecting the air and groundcrew – some 700 personnel in all – and they quickly came together at RAF Scampton near Lincoln. Of the many difficulties, one of the more intractable was that the crews could not be told the target for security reasons with the consequential problem of organising realistic training. But it was known to be a very low level mission in formation at night – that was quite sufficient in itself to exercise their minds for the time being.

The problem of flying precisely at 60 feet was eventually

Dr Barnes Wallis designed the mine which was used against the Ruhr dams on the 16th May 1943.

IWM

solved by fitting spot lights fore and aft which joined together in a figure of 8 on the surface of the water when the aircraft was at the required height. A simple bomb sight was locally manufactured in which the release point was indicated when two vertical projections on the sight were seen to be exactly aligned with the towers at either end of the dam. Two conditions constrained the timing of the raid; it had to be within a near full moon period and the water in the dam had to be at the maximum level so that the mine would explode as close as possible to the narrowest section through the retaining wall.

All of the necessary conditions for the raid came together on the night of the 16th May 1943. The weather was excellent, new

looking like stirred porridge in the moonlight' was cascading into the valley below. 'Nigger', the codeword for a successful attack, was triumphantly flashed back to Scampton.

The attack on the Eder dam was more of an academic exercise in that it was unprotected by flak. It was though well hidden in a valley and difficult to approach, and there were only three mines left. Sqn Ldr Maudslay released his mine too late which exploded on the parapet taking the aircraft with it, but after several abortive runs, both Flt Lt Shannon and Plt Off Knight laid their mines accurately. The resulting collapse was even more spectacular than that of the Mohne. The Sorpe attack was unsuccessful, not unexpected in the light of the earth

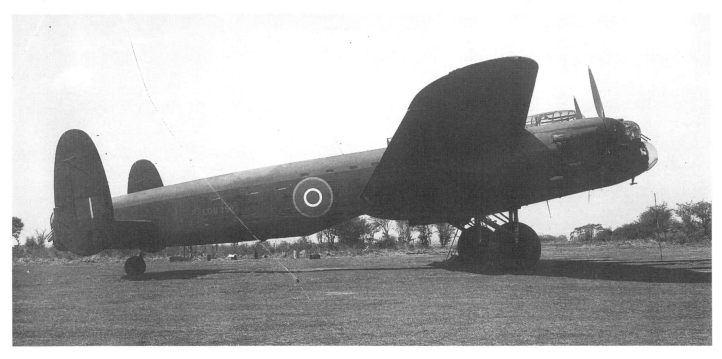

The Lancaster had to be specially modified to carry the dam's mine: note the cut-out in the bomb bay. This aircraft was used on the raid by Flt Lt Joe McCarthy.   IWM

aircraft had arrived and been tested and training was at a high pitch. The tasked force consisted of 18 aircraft – nine led by Gibson himself to the two main targets and five by Flt Lt Joe McCarthy, a large bluff American, which were to proceed independently to the Sorpe: there were four reserves. McCarthy's formation was decimated well before the target; two were shot down by flak crossing the coast and two had to return, one after hitting the sea and the other with flak damage. Their places were filled from the reserve flight. Gibson's flight was luckier with only one failing to reach the target area, probably because the pilot flew into the ground after being blinded by searchlights.

After a careful reconnaissance around the Mohne, Gibson made his run-in along the lake and successfully released his mine in the right place despite the intensive, albeit inaccurate light flak and small arms fire. The second aircraft (Flt Lt Hopgood) was hit by flak and crashed, but the third and fourth (Flt Lt Martin and Sqn Ldr Young) made successful runs. The dam still held. The fifth, however, flown by Flt Lt Maltby was spot on. As the Lancaster climbed away, Gibson circling the lake saw that the top of the dam had simply 'rolled over and the water,

construction of the dam. In all eight aircraft were lost from the 18 which had set-out; a very high ratio, but justified by the nature of the operation. Gibson was awarded the Victoria Cross and 32 other crew members received decorations. Of the 56 crew shot down, 54 died – there was little chance of survival from 50 feet.

The impact on the Ruhr industry was less severe than expected even though more than 1,000 civilians died and thousands were made homeless. One indirect benefit was that 7,000 men had to be transferred from preparing the Atlantic wall defences to rebuild the Mohne dam which was accomplished within four months. Although the economic results were in retrospect somewhat disappointing, the boost to Allied morale was enormous, not least in Bomber Command itself. Full advantage was made of the publicity fall-out even if secrecy was maintained as to the methods employed. Of greater significance, however, were the pointers for the direction which

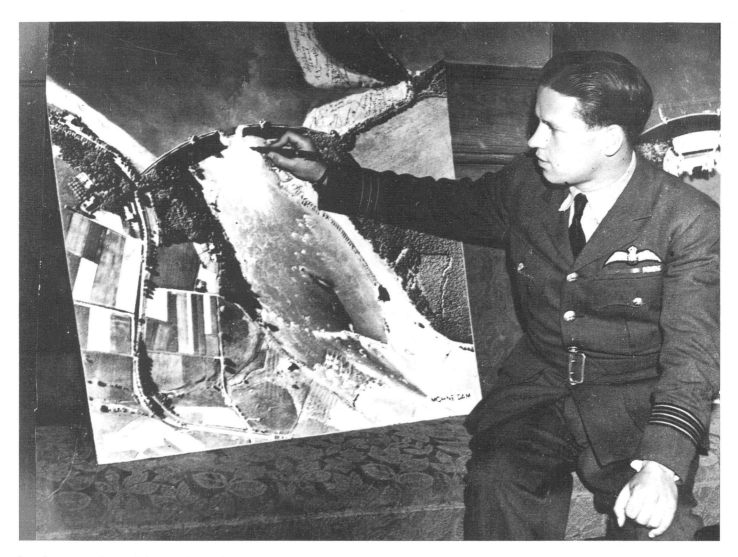

Wing Commander Guy Gibson pointing out the breach in the Mohne Dam after the raid of 16th May 1943. RAFM

bomber operations might take in the future.

The dams raid was a unique operation; indeed, it had been intended to disband No 617 Squadron after its completion although in the event this direction was countermanded. It had achieved with the heavy bomber what had previously been possible only with the light or medium bomber when conditions were favourable – a very high degree of accuracy in bomb aiming against a small target. The key to precision was the low level attack, for although Bomber Command had moved into the Oboe/H2S era which was undoubtedly improving accuracy, it still fell only within the parameters of area attack – a bomber force could now be expected to hit a town with some consistency rather than the countryside surrounding it. But the degree of expertise needed for precise low level flying, the culmination of experience and intensive training, could not be expected to exist across the whole command. The obvious answer was to combine the two, to mark the target visually with great precision from low level and to ensure that it remained highlighted throughout the main force raid which would continue to be conducted from high level; the role in practice of a 'master bomber'. There was one serious snag, low level operations and visual marking could only successfully be employed in moonlight periods, the

very time when the main force was most vulnerable to the night fighter. It was, therefore, a system which required air superiority, a state which Bomber Command was not to enjoy until well into 1944. Nevertheless, the lesson was well recognised in No 5 Group with No 9 Squadron now joining 617 in developing precision techniques so that when the opportunity arrived in the approach to Operation 'Overlord', Bomber Command could be rapidly adapted from an area into a precision force. Even more significantly, the door was at last beginning to open to those elusive 'panacea' targets, the synthetic oil production plants.

To Germany at Last

Whilst Bomber Command at the outset of 1943 was beginning to get its act together, culminating in the impressive onslaught against the Ruhr in the Spring, the 8th Air Force, after an almost equally tentative apprenticeship, had still not ventured across the borders of Germany. General Eaker was eager to cross this rubicon as soon as possible as the war entered its fourth year.

With the battle of the Atlantic as yet unresolved, submarine construction yards were still the highest priority target in the early months of 1943 and Vegesack on the River Weser just 30 miles from the North Friesian coast thus seemed to provide a suitably gentle introduction to 8th Air Force's German campaign. Led by Colonel Frank Armstrong, who had flown on the first mission to Rouen just six months previously, 64 B-17s launched at dawn on the 27th January to follow a wide detour over the North Sea to achieve maximum surprise. The promised clear weather over the target did not, however, materialise and the secondary target, Wilhelmshaven, was bombed instead to little effect. Flak was light and the formation was not intercepted by German fighters until it was returning home, and even then their attacks were not pressed home. One B-17 was lost and seven fighters actually destroyed out of a claim of 22. Not surprisingly, the first raid over German territory was hailed as a creditable achievement.

Rather more ambitiously, the Command now set its sights on the Ruhr and a number of sorties were flown in February, mostly against Hamm. All were aborted because of bad weather over the target, but the formations did not escape unscathed, and including one very costly trip to St Nazaire, over a quarter of the force available at the beginning of the month was lost. The 91st BG redressed the balance to a certain extent on the 4th March when just 15 B-17s scored a clean hit on the marshalling yards at Hamm, but four aircraft were destroyed and all the rest carried the marks of flak back to their base at Bassingbourne. A far more decisive strike occurred a few days later when the force went back to their first German target, Vegesack, which was damaged sufficiently seriously to curtail production for at least two months. Despite ending on a highlight, the first two months operations against Germany could only be considered moderately successful; the American concept of visual precision bombing demanded clear skies and such conditions are rarely found in Europe in Winter. On the other hand, the Luftwaffe was far less inhibited by the weather and its relatively inexperienced day fighter squadrons in central Germany were gaining markedly in confidence and capability as the daylight raids increased.

VIII Bomber Command was also working hard at developing tactics to combat the fighter menace. Often in the lead in such

Flooding of the Ruhr Valley at Froendenberg-Boesperde 13 miles below the Mohne Dam. IWM

developments in the early months was the commander of the 305th Group, Colonel Curtis Le May, a blunt, single minded but perceptive airman who was later to achieve fame as a commander of the post war Strategic Air Command (SAC). The basic grouping within a fairly widespread bomber formation was the vic of three aircraft, but whilst manoeuvrable in combat and certainly the most effective arrangement during the bombing run, it did not pack the collective defensive punch to repel a determined fighter attack with aircraft on the extremities of the formation particularly vulnerable. To provide the necessary concentration of fire power, a much tighter box of 18 aircraft with vics staggered vertically as well as horizontally became the standard formation. However, this brought difficulties for the bomb aimer because his pilot's freedom of action was constrained by the proximity of other aircraft. The obvious solution was for the whole group to bomb in unison on seeing the bombs released from the lead aircraft, but whilst this tactic guaranteed concentration of effort, it could equally lead to the whole group missing the target if the lead bombardier's aim was amiss. Nevertheless, variations on the 18 aircraft group and synchronised bombing on cue from the lead aircraft became the basic tactic for the rest of the war. Although the air gunners were commendably enthusiastic, bolstered by claims which we now know were greatly exaggerated, the more perceptive commanders began to recognise that much of the shooting was wild, out of range, and occasionally self destructive: it was by no means unknown for a waist gunner to hit his own aircraft's tailframe. Other aircraft in the formation or even the target towing aircraft in training were too often the victims of exuberant airgunners. Inexperience was still a major handicap, the first crew member to complete a tour of 25 operations did not achieve this goal until April 1943. In such a formative period, it is hardly surprising that results were erratic, depending as much on luck or individual instances of inspiration and courage as on a sustained application of skill and experience. Fortunately, the poor weather which curtailed operational flying allowed ample opportunity for further training.

A raid on the Focke-Wulf factory at Bremen was an early indication of the increasing ascendancy of the German fighter. It was the largest concentration, 115 aircraft, that VIII Bomber Command had yet managed to assemble for a single raid and the formation was unlucky in that it was spotted over the North Sea by a stray German reconnaissance aircraft. The fighter defences were thus ready and waiting and after early skirmishing on the approach to the target, two gruppen of JG 1 unleashed a furious head-on onslaught on the leading group as it opened-up for its bombing run. Sixteen B-17s were destroyed, all but one falling to the fighters; 48 more were damaged. Although 63 fighters were claimed by the gunners, the actual loss could be no more than 10. This was the worst set-back suffered by the Command so far, made more ironic by the fact that aircraft production had ceased in that particular factory six months earlier.

Although most of the attention was devoted to the B-17 Wings during this period, there were also two B-24 Liberator

B-24Ds taxying-out from an unnamed airfield in East Anglia in 1943.
IWM

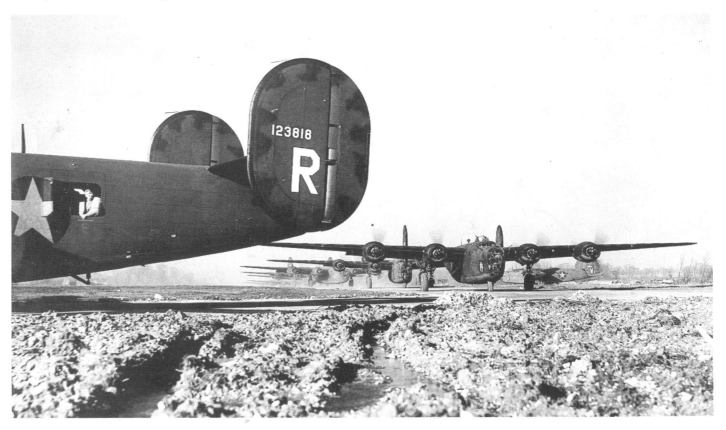

This B-24 came to grief after landing at Ashill, a satellite airfield in Norfolk.   WWE

Groups in England – the 44th and the 93rd. Dogged by shortage of aircraft and crews and by diversions to North Africa and maritime patrol in support of Coastal Command, B-24s frequently supported the B-17 operations or mounted their own smaller scale sorties. But although in some respects superior to the B-17 in performance, the B-24 was mechanically unreliable and more vulnerable to damage, its losses were thus generally higher than its more glamorous counterpart. Morale inevitably suffered and relations between the Liberator and Fortress groups were often less than cordial. By May 1943, the 2nd Bomber Wing had been severely mauled in combat with few real achievements to show for its efforts.

April 1943 signalled the end of the USAAFs first phase of operations from England. The intention of building-up 8th Air Force into a formidable striking force had not materialised and diversions to the Pacific and North African theatres had not only deprived Spaatz and Eaker of aircraft and crews, but had dissipated experience. The campaign so far had largely been mounted by just four groups, the 91st, 303rd, 305th and 306th, and between them these had already lost nearly 100 aircraft and two thirds of their original complement of crews. Results had been very patchy. Despite the weight of effort directed against them, the submarine pens in the Biscay ports had remained intact even if the towns around them had been devastated. Isolated successes had been scored, particularly against railway targets, Vegesack on the second attempt, and the Renault factory in Paris. Morale was still surprisingly high, sustained largely by the damage which the groups believed they were inflicting upon the enemy fighters. Post war analysis was,

however, to show that the exorbitant claims, which had already been scaled down by subsequent evaluation, were still nearly as large as the total number of fighters in France and north west Germany at that time. In fact only 50 fighters had been destroyed and the Luftwaffe was numerically stronger in May 1943 than it had been when the 8th's operations commenced. The daylight campaign had of course introduced an increased claim on German resources and much was made of the beneficial impact that this brought upon the Eastern front, but there is little evidence that this was in any sense decisive.

Most importantly, the central question which had divided the Americans and the British in 1942 had still not been conclusively answered – could a precision bombing campaign be sustained over central Germany in daylight? In retrospect, we may perhaps conclude that in May 1943 there was sufficient evidence to suggest that a daylight campaign could be sustained only when the bomber force was supported by a strong fighter escort. For those most closely involved at the time, further experience was still required – and obtained – before they were convinced that this was in fact so.

Firestorm – The Battle of Hamburg

The Ruhr, shrouded in smoke or haze and heavily defended, had proved a too difficult nut to crack in 1942, but the advent of Oboe and target marking techniques had enabled Bomber Command to unleash a trail of destruction in the Spring of 1943 which at last began to justify some of the expectations of the early proponents of strategic bombing. But other targets in the heart of Germany were outside the range of Oboe and the deeper penetration gave the night fighter defences greater opportunity to marshal their forces and capitalise on their increasing expertise and experience. Raids beyond the Ruhr in the first six months of 1943 had consequently proved relatively less successful, but Harris was determined to extend the war of attrition right across the heart of Germany to Berlin. The next stage in the process was to be Hamburg.

Bomber Command had depended until now on evasion and deception techniques, but above all upon the cloak of darkness. The Luftwaffe was, however, beginning to pierce that cloak by the introduction of better night fighting and interception techniques and by the more flexible and responsive organisation of their fighter forces. The cannon equipped fighters could seal the fate of a bomber well before it entered the lethal range of the latter's small calibre machine guns even if the air gunner managed to spot his adversary at all.

The long range day escort fighter had so far always been out of favour with the Air Staff, but the superior performance and acknowledged immunity of the Mosquito suggested that, with a suitable Airborne Interception (AI) radar, it could be used at night to counter the Bf 110s which were increasingly successful for the Luftwaffe. Harris had proposed this course of action to Fighter Command as early as October 1942, but the latter was usually reluctant at this stage of the war to venture their Mosquito force far beyond the boundaries of the North Sea. It was not therefore until June 1943 that an experiment was mounted with Beaufighter Mk VIs of No 141 Squadron equipped with a device known as 'Serrate' which enabled them to home on to the AI transmissions of German fighters. 'Serrate' was effective out to 100 miles, but whilst providing a bearing of a transmitting source, it gave no indication of range. The technique employed therefore was to home towards the enemy fighter until it could be identified on the AI radar from where a normal interception could be completed. Of the 233 'Serrate' sorties mounted in the three months from June, 1,180 contacts were made, but this led to only 20 occasions when the Beaufighter was able to bring its guns to bear on its opponent. It was not so much the failure of the technique or the equipment itself, but the totally inadequate performance of the Beaufighter which caused the experiment to fail. There can be little doubt that by 1943 when Fighter Command was relatively under employed in the air defence of the homeland, a more aggressive and co-operative attitude in the use of its Mosquitos could have paid a handsome dividend.

There was, however, one other unused expedient which had been available for some time. This was the radar jamming device known as 'Window', one of the simplest yet most

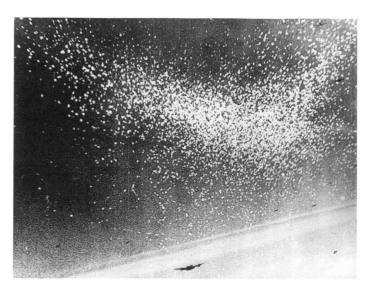

A Lancaster dispersing 'Window' which was first used in the 4 raids against Hamburg in July 1943. This photograph was taken later in the war in a raid against Essen in March 1945.   IWM

effective techniques ever employed in war. Its use over Germany had so far been vetoed on the rather negative grounds that if the technique became known to the Germans, it could equally easily be used by their bombers to jam the radar defences of the UK. In fact, not surprisingly, the Germans were also well aware of 'Window' which they called 'Duppel' and were not using it for the same reason. Nevertheless, it is surprising that Sir Arthur Harris did not press even more strongly than he did for the earlier introduction of 'Window' by Bomber Command and it was not until towards the close of the Battle of the Ruhr when bomber losses were beginning to approach an unacceptable level, and following a personal intervention by the Prime Minister, that its use was finally authorised. There were, however, still problems: the metallic strips already produced were of the wrong size (the reflecting qualities of the strip varied with the wavelength of the radar) and no automatic launcher was available. The only method of distributing 'Window' was for a crew member to throw bundles out of the flare hatch at prescribed intervals.

This rather long preamble to the Battle of Hamburg illustrates the extent to which the 'Pointblank' concept of neutralising Germany's fighter defences was by the middle of the year becoming as important to Bomber Command as it was to 8th Air Force although there is still no evidence that Harris was as yet prepared to be deflected in any way from his strategy for defeating Germany by the might of Bomber Command alone. Nevertheless, the stage was now set for the assault upon Hamburg, codenamed Operation 'Gomorrah', and 'Window' was to be used for the first time in the raid planned for the 24th July. Although Bomber Command still ranged widely across Germany at this time with occasional sorties to easier targets in France and Italy, Harris viewed Hamburg as a vital objective on his road to Berlin. One of the important Hanseatic free ports, it was now Germany's second largest city and an important industrial centre. Its shipbuilding yards were responsible for almost half of the U boats constructed in Germany during the war and it also had important factories connected with aircraft production.

As already indicated, Hamburg was beyond the effective range of Oboe and thus H2S was to be used as the primary bombing aid. The city showed up particularly well on the H2S display being close to a distinctive coast line and centred astride the River Elbe. The composition of the bomber force was also indicative of the growth in destructive capability during 1943. Whereas in May 1942 over half of the first 1,000 bomber raid consisted of Wellingtons, by July 1943 Harris could launch a force of 791 bombers of which 347 were Lancasters and 246 Halifaxes, with only 125 Stirlings and 73 Wellingtons making-up the numbers. The Pathfinder Force now played a major role in the tactical plan, laying lead-in yellow route markers and disseminating an up-to-date wind velocity calculation for the main force. The main attack was to open at 0100 with 20 aircraft dropping yellow target indicators blind on H2S followed by eight attempting to place red markers visually. Throughout the raid, which was planned to last only 50 minutes, backers-up were to place green markers at roughly one minute intervals with some of them making a positive attempt to re-identify the target rather than just reinforcing the existing markers. Measures were also to be taken to eliminate creep-back which had become a feature of large scale raids.

Weather conditions for the first raid were near perfect, there was no cloud and only a little haze as the first pathfinders made their run-in to the target. Most of the yellow markers were concentrated in the target area, but the visual marking was less satisfactory, leading to four areas of concentration up to three miles from the target. The backers-up managed to keep the main force reasonably well centred on the target for about the first third of the mainstream bombing, but thereafter an

Flt Sgt (later Sqn Ldr) Wally Lashbrook MBE, DFC, AFC, DFM – 35 Squadron

We lost our hydraulics over Hamburg (in a Halifax) and the under-carriage fell down of its own accord, so we were late back to base and very short of fuel. Thankful to be home, I was not best pleased therefore when they switched-off the runway lights just as we made our approach thinking that we were an enemy intruder. We overshot the approach but ran out of fuel before we could line-up with the runway again. I was therefore committed to landing straight ahead. It was very dark, but when it got really black I just pulled back on the stick and hoped for the best. We were doing all right until we hit a tree which brought us to a very abrupt stop. I scrambled out of the top hatch, but immediately fell 10 feet to the ground as I hadn't realised that the fuselage had broken off right behind the cockpit. In fact the aircraft had broken into 5 pieces, most of it wrapped around this large tree. The rest of the crew were alive, but two were not in very good shape so I set off to look for help. It was still pitch black and almost straight away I walked into a large drainage ditch – up to my neck. I eventually reached a cottage, but had considerable difficulty persuading the owner that I was not a German (probably my Scots accent). I managed to convince him however to ring the station for help. It later transpired that the ambulance had turned over on the way to the scene of the crash! Still soaking wet, all I could borrow from Sick Quarters when I eventually got there was a plain airman's blue uniform with no wings or rank badges, but it was at least dry and warm. But my warm feeling was soon shattered when I got home where my wife, seeing the plain uniform, simply wouldn't believe that I hadn't been stripped of rank and wings for some dreadful and degrading misdemeanour. It was not my best day in the war.

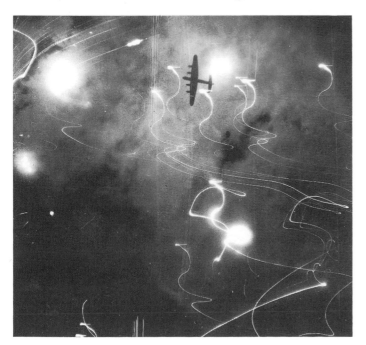

increasingly marked creep-back occurred towards the north west, the direction of the run-in. The on-board cameras disclosed that rather less than half bombed within three miles of the target, which in terms of previous performance was not unreasonable for a H2S marked target. 'Window' proved a great success. Intercepted radio transmission between the controllers on the ground and their fighters disclosed just how confused they were by this new situation, and the radar controlled searchlights were seen to be aimlessly scanning the night sky for aircraft which were now hidden in a mass of clutter. The radar laid guns were equally frustrated and chance played the major role in the few unlucky bombers which were either intercepted or claimed by the gunners. Only 12 aircraft failed to return, a significantly better loss rate than that which was being sustained at the end of the Battle of the Ruhr. All in all, it was a very satisfactory nights work for Bomber Command.

A startling photograph of aircraft enveloped by flak which was taken on one of the Hamburg raids.   IWM

The RAFs onslaught on Hamburg had for once been co-ordinated with the 8th Air Force who followed-up on the two succeeding days. General Eaker could not match the numbers which Bomber Command could now raise and managed only 235 sorties, but it kept the pressure-on, frustrating rubble clearance and casualty evacuation as well as preventing the restoration of services to those homes still left reasonably intact. The pressure was continued overnight by small scale raids by Mosquitos, now increasingly operating independently.

Bomber Command returned with another major raid on the 27th by 787 aircraft. The tactics were similar except that on this occasion the attempt to mark the target visually, which had not been very successful on the previous raid, was abandoned. The number of crews who managed to bomb within three miles of the target was roughly the same as before with the creep-back less apparent. 'Window' was still largely successful, but the Germans were already beginning to counter this new development by introducing a broadcast type of control which gave the location of the bomber stream rather than trying to identify individual targets. Seventeen bombers failed to return,

not quite as satisfactory as the first raid, but still well within a containable figure.

Two nights later Bomber Command returned again with 777 aircraft, but for reasons which are difficult to determine, the blind marking was much more dispersed and thus the main force bombing, which could only rely on the markers, was also spread widely. It was evident that the initial impact of 'Window' was now declining as 30 aircraft were lost on this raid and it was estimated that night fighters had made as many as 100 interceptions. The final raid of the series occurred on the 2nd August with 740 bombers. Unlike the previous three nights, the weather this time was appalling with cloud rising to 15,000 feet and sometimes higher in storm clouds. The yellow markers were barely visible and half the force failed to find the target at all. The weather did not, however, keep the night fighters grounded and 30 aircraft were again lost.

In little over a week, Harris had despatched 3,095 sorties to

Hamburg after the bombing, the prominent building in the foreground is a Flak Tower.   IWM

Hamburg dropping 9,000 tons of bombs, roughly half of which were incendiaries. The overall loss was 89, slightly under 3 per cent, which compared favourably with, for example, the 4.5 per cent sustained in the five raids on Essen earlier in the year. There is no doubt that 'Window' had played an important role in the smaller loss rate although it was disconcerting that within the space of four raids to Hamburg and one to Essen on the 30th July, the Luftwaffe was already showing signs of coming to grips with this new defensive technique. But as a sustained and concentrated attack, it reinforced even more strongly the recognition that Bomber Command was coming to possess the awesome power that had been promised but not delivered in the early years of the war.

Despite the limitations in bombing accuracy, particulary in the disappointing final raid, the impact on Hamburg was spectacular. The greatest damage was caused in the second raid when a firestorm swept through the densely packed older quarters of the city. For several hours an uncontrollable furnace raged over nearly five square miles of residential areas north of the river from which there was little chance of escape. Most of those who survived the bombing were burned or suffocated in their basement shelters. The great majority of the 45,000 civilians who died in Hamburg succumbed on this dreadful night, a toll exceeded in a single raid only by the Dresden raid of February 1945 (although the figures for that raid are uncertain), the incendiary attack on Tokyo by the USAAF in March 1945 and the two atomic bomb attacks which brought the war in Japan to a close. In material terms, the raids were even more devastating; over 50 per cent of the housing stock of Hamburg was destroyed along with nearly 500 public buildings. The damage sustained by the industrial enterprises was less spectacular and it was estimated after the war that output returned to 80 per cent of normal within five months: once again factories, and the machinery they contained, proved remarkably resilient to high explosive attack.

Finally, if further proof was needed, the unprecedented devastation of Hamburg proved beyond doubt that, totally contrary to pre-war expectations, civilian morale cannot be destroyed by bombing in a well structured and controlled society. Shocked and scarred though they undoubtedly were, the mass of the people drew ever more closely together to rebuild their lives and their homes. Area bombing had reached the apex of its concentrated fury in one week in Hamburg: it had made but a minor contribution towards the ending of the war.

The Peenemünde Raid – 17th August 1943

Bomber Command followed-up its successful onslaught on Hamburg by another of its special operations which, quite apart from its own intrinsic value, like the dams raid earlier in the year was a valuable pointer towards the direction in which tactics would develop in the future. This time the target was Peenemünde, a seemingly obscure village on the Baltic coast.

By September 1944 Hitler was in need of a miracle to turn the course of a war which after the Allies had secured their

Air Vice Marshal Sir Ralph Cochrane, AOC No 5 Group, was one of the most innovative of the Allied bomber leaders who complemented, and sometimes rivalled, Bennett in the development of precision bombing techniques.   IWM

beachhead in Normandy was moving inexorably towards its inevitable finale. But if no miracle, there was one weapon which might just conceivably have turned the tide of battle if it had been ready a few months earlier. This was the Vergeltungswaffen (weapon of revenge) better known to us simply as the V-2. It was a weapon against which there was no defence, a liquid oxygen powered rocket carrying three quarters of a ton of high explosive over a range of 200 miles. Its development had started in 1937 under Wernher von Braun near the little village of Peenemünde, midway between Stettin and Rostock. Peenemünde sat on the tip of a peninsular reaching out into the Baltic, its experimental facilities hidden in a forest of pine. That the V-2 was not ready in time to influence the course of the war was at least partly due to a visit by Bomber Command on the night of 17th August 1943.

British Intelligence was somewhat slow to recognise what was actually happening at Peenemünde bearing in mind that activity at the site began two years before the war started and that the 'Oslo' report, an anonymous document forwarded to the British Embassy in Norway in 1939, drew specific attention to rocket activity at that named location. It was not until 1943 that further intelligence material was taken seriously and

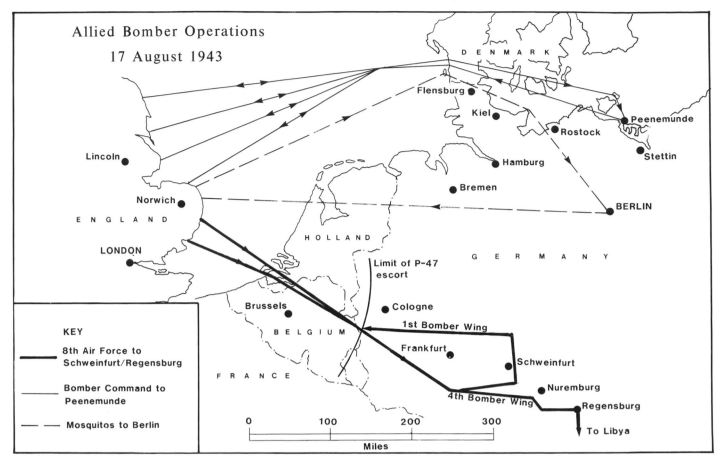

Allied Bomber Operations
17 August 1943

KEY

—— 8th Air Force to
Schweinfurt/Regensburg

—— Bomber Command to
Peenemunde

– – – Mosquitos to Berlin

0   100   200   300
Miles

Mosquito reconnaissance photographs actually disclosed the presence of a rocket on the test stand. The Special Committee set-up under Mr Duncan Sandys to report on this matter reacted promptly and a proposal to mount a bombing raid against Peenemünde was approved by the War Cabinet Defence Committee under Mr Churchill's chairmanship on the 29th June. It is perhaps rather surprising that the 8th Air Force was not asked to carry-out the attack, for it was a small precision target ideally suited to a daylight operation whereas the RAF at this stage was in the midst of its area bombing campaign and had little experience of precision attacks at night. Politics rather than pragmatism seems to have guided the Combined Bombing Offensive on this occasion.

Sir Arthur Harris soon decided that this raid had to be a major effort and discounted a small specialist operation by No 617 Squadron, or even the whole of No 5 Group which had a growing reputation for innovatory tactics. The Peenemünde site was not thought to be heavily defended by flak; but once alerted, it would be very dangerous to have to return for a second bite at the cherry. Furthermore, because it was a precision attack, it had to be carried-out in moonlight conditions in which Bomber Command did not normally operate and in which the risk from night fighters was very high.

The key to a successful operation was the target marking, the province of Bennett's pathfinder squadrons. For the first time No 8 Group was to employ a master bomber whose duty it was to remain over the target and to control the subsequent marking

and the mainforce bombers. It was not, of course, a totally new technique, it had been used by Gibson in the dams raid and by No 5 Group subsequently. On this occasion No 5 Group was to employ an entirely different technique, time and distance bombing, which was dependent on clearly identifiable lead-in points to the target, a condition which was well satisfied at Peenemünde because of its coastal location. Following a carefully timed leg between two recognisable pin points on the approach to the target, the actual wind conditions could be determined accurately from which the required aircraft heading and elapsed time from another prominent point to the target could be precisely calculated. On crossing over this latter point, the final run-in to the target was carefully flown and the bombs dropped after a specific elapsed time: as long as the Initial Points (IPs) could be identified, it mattered not at all if the target was covered in smoke, and smoke flares were known to be sited at Peenemünde. Furthermore, since every crew was acting independently, inaccurate marking would not detract from the main force effort. There were thus two relatively new tactics to be explored in this raid; the Cochrane time and distance method and Bennett's established marking technique enhanced by the introduction of a master of ceremonies. A comparison of the results was eagerly awaited, for an element of rivalry had developed between two equally determined and dogmatic leaders.

As always the raid was dependent upon the weather, but after several days of disappointment, the right conditions were forecast for the night of 17th August – full moon, clear skies over north Germany and good landing conditions back in England. Fortuitously, the Americans had planned a major raid against Schweinfurt/Regensberg on the same day and this could hopefully be expected to attract both day and nightfighter defences from the North German airfields. The final raid plan envisaged an approach from the north across Denmark and the three individual targets at the site were allocated, unusually, to the participating groups. The first target, the workers accommodation area, was allocated to Nos 3 and 4 Groups, the factory building the missiles to No 1 Group and the experimental workshops to Nos 5 and 6 Groups. The normal mixed load of incendiaries and high explosives was strongly weighted in favour of the latter. A diversionary Mosquito raid on Berlin would break away from the main force north of Kiel. Again, unusually for this stage of the bomber offensive, no other diversionary raids were mounted. It was not quite a maximum effort, but the first of 596 heavy bombers – 324 Lancasters, 218 Halifaxes and 54 Stirlings – lifted off soon after 8.00 pm, still in broad daylight, joined later by the eight Mosquitos for Berlin.

The assembly over the North Sea was accomplished satisfactorily and only two aircraft which had wandered off track were shot down by flak over Flensburg and Sylt. Almost no threat emerged from the fighter defences. The bombing was to be conducted from medium or even low level and the stream started to descend from their cruising altitude on a beautifully clear night in which navigation over the Baltic was particularly

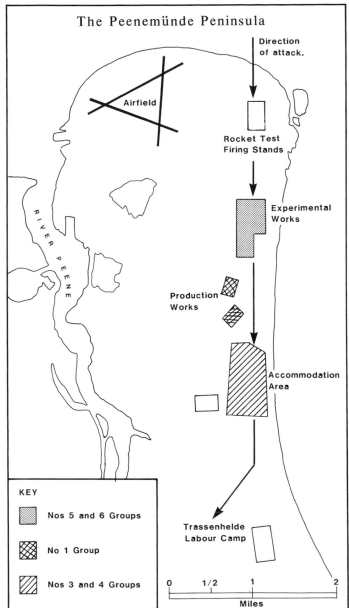

The Peenemünde Peninsula

Direction of attack.

Airfield

Rocket Test Firing Stands

Experimental Works

Production Works

Accommodation Area

Trassenhelde Labour Camp

RIVER PEENE

KEY

Nos 5 and 6 Groups

No 1 Group

Nos 3 and 4 Groups

0 1/2 1 2
Miles

straight forward. Meanwhile the Berlin diversion had been very successful, attracting as had been intended a large number of fighters which claimed only one Mosquito.

The pathfinders had mixed fortunes. The plan was to mark the first target, the accommodation area, by blind marking using H2S from around 15,000 feet. Unfortunately, the radar picture was not quite as well defined as expected and not only were the lead-in markers incorrectly positioned, but most of their red target indicators were placed to the south of the target. The visual markers did rather better and their yellows were generally accurately placed, but despite the efforts of the master bomber, Group Captain John Searby, several of the mainforce aircraft bombed on the inaccurately placed reds. The main force

Gp Capt John Searby who acted as the 'Master Bomber' on the Peenemünde raid seen here leaving Bently Priory, the Headquarters of Fighter Command, with Air Commodore Bennett.   IWM

The Experimental Site at Peenemünde before and after attack on the 17th August 1943. ('A' are light flak positions, 'B' is a cradle for moving rockets and at 'C' are two V-2s.) IWM

bombing was conducted for accuracy from between 4,000 and 10,000 feet, a height which would usually have been very susceptible to light flak. But surprise had been achieved and the first wave crossed the target unimpeded by either flak or fighters over a period of 15 minutes after zero hour, 0015.

They were followed immediately by No 1 Group's Lancasters whose objective was the production factory. Again the marking was variable and although the master bomber recognised clearly which of the red indicators had actually found the correct spot, communicating this to the main force crews was more difficult and many of the bombs from this wave also went astray, with the original incorrect marking still attracting a lot of attention. The odd night fighter had now entered the fray, but the flak was still generally light.

The marking was by now becoming generally chaotic and the ground was largely obscured by smoke and flames, but this should not have affected the third wave, for this incorporated No 5 Group's time and distance technique. Unfortunately, in a last minute outbreak of indecision, the bomb aimers had been ordered to bomb the markers if they were visible rather than depend entirely on the timed bomb run. Furthermore, the night fighters had now arrived in force which made many timed runs nugatory as the bombers were forced to weave and dodge. The end result was that very few bombs from the third wave actually fell on their assigned target, although several overshot and hit the production facility. However, the main feature of the final

wave of the attack was the intense air battle that developed as the fighters belatedly arrived on the scene. The fighter control organisation had almost entirely collapsed, but many fighters orbiting over Berlin were attracted to Peenemünde by the markers and fires. Some 40 Bf 109s, Fw 190s and Bf 110s made visual acquisitions in the clear moonlight and the reflected fires from the ground and 28 bombers were destroyed within a matter of minutes. Many of the returning crews later said that it was the most intensive air battle they had witnessed in the course of the war. The return flight was largely uneventful for the first two waves, but the final wave suffered again when half a dozen stragglers were picked-off by night fighters over Denmark.

In all 40 bombers were shot down, a casualty rate of nearly seven per cent, well above the average. Furthermore, a higher than normal proportion of men were killed and the loss of experienced crews from Nos 5 and 6 Groups was also much larger than usual. Nevertheless, in many respects the Peenemünde raid had proved a success. Nearly all the crews who bombed had done so in the immediate vicinity of a small precise target, a feat rarely achieved at night other than by No 617 Squadron. Although the pathfinder's efforts were at best mixed, the innovation of the master bomber had done a lot to alleviate the failings. Only in the final wave when the intervention of the fighters created considerable confusion did the close control of the bombing begin to run completely astray. For the same reason, the results of time and distance bombing were encouraging if by no means conclusive. All three targets were hit with the accommodation area suffering particularly severely. The production factory and experimental area were also damaged but not crippled. One unfortunate aspect of the overshooting markers was the near destruction of a forced workers camp at Trassenheide in which about 500 Poles and Russians were killed. It is difficult to assess the effect of the raid on the V-2 programme, estimates of the ensuing delay varying from two to six months. In fact, the experimental work at Peenemünde was considerably run down and the effort transferred to other centres in Germany. The raid did not, as has been claimed occasionally, decide the course of the war, but it certainly reduced the number of casualties which would have accrued in London and Paris from the full scale deployment of this crude but effective terror weapon.

The Raid on Ploesti – 1st August 1943

The 8th Air Force's B-24 Liberators had not had an auspicious beginning to their operational life, indeed the 44th BG, 'the Flying Eightballs', had developed something of a reputation as a *jinx* unit after losing 27 aircraft, exactly the number with which the Group had first arrived at Shipdam in Norfolk in October 1942. The inability of the Liberator groups to establish themselves was hardly their own fault: they were small in number and suffering the inevitable teething problems of a new aircraft, exacerbated in the case of the 93rd by a detachment to North Africa. They had a variety of tasks thrust upon them ranging from maritime support to 'Moling' – single aircraft sorties using Gee for blind bombing which were soon abandoned. Thus, they never had the opportunity to develop their skills and experience in a sustained role in the way afforded to the other groups. Furthermore, regarded rather disdainfully by the Command staffs, they resented the attention and adulation reserved for their apparently more glamorous colleagues in the B-17 units. Nevertheless, in June 1943, the 8th's B-24s were selected to participate in one of the most daring and difficult raids of the war – an attack on the oil refining plants at Ploesti in Romania.

It will be recalled that oil was the first of the 'panacea' targets adopted in 1940, but only fitfully pursued because of the difficulty of hitting the synthetic processing plants in Germany. In any case, Germany obtained a substantial amount of oil at that time from Romania and Russia which were out of reach of the RAF even if it had been politically possible to regard them as belligerents. But although little progress had been made in disrupting the flow of oil to Germany, other than as an indirect result of 'Barbarossa', it still remained in 1943 one of the most critical resource areas within the German military machine.

In June 1943 the two B-24 Groups were surprised to be relieved of all offensive operations and directed to begin an intensive period of low level training. At this stage only the most senior commanders were aware of their intended role in Operation 'Statesman' which was the planning responsibility of 9th Air Force in North Africa. The acquisition of airfields in Libya and the advent of a long range bomber had at last opened-up the possibility of reaching the complex of oil refineries at Ploesti which had become even more important to the Germans after the cessation of supplies from Russia. An attempt had been made to mount a night attack on Ploesti in 1942, but none of the bombers had found the target which lay a thousand miles from the nearest bomber base, nearly all of it over enemy occupied territory. The new plan involved a low level attack with a force of 200 Liberators, more than half of which were to be provided by 8th Air Force. The two existing Liberator groups had been joined in England in June by the newly formed 389th BG which immediately buckled down to intensive low level training to catch-up with their more experienced colleagues. By the end of the month, 124 Liberators set-out for Benina and Benghazi where they came under the control of IX Bomber Command.

The raid on Ploesti was not mounted immediately as the aircraft were first used to support the invasion of Sicily and for other raids on Italy and Crete. Towards the end of July, however, training recommenced for their main objective. The preparation was thorough – a mock up of the Ploesti plant had been constructed in the desert – and by the 1st August all was ready. 9th Air Force provided two groups, the 98th and 376th, with the latter leading the whole force of 179 aircraft.

The raid did not get away to a good start as the two leading groups became separated from the remainder, but surprise had been achieved and there was little opposition during their long transit to the target. Further confusion arose as the two leading groups mistook the Initial Point (IP) and turned away from the target, but the 93rd soon recognised their mistake and were able to make a bombing run on one of the targets allocated to another group. They encountered heavy anti-aircraft fire and were intercepted by BF 109s, but managed to drop their bombs despite losing nine aircraft over the target area. The 44th's complement of 37 aircraft was divided into two groups. That led by the Group Commander, Colonel Johnson, had the misfortune to attack the target already alerted by the 93rd and had their bombing run disrupted by heavy flak. The second group of 21 aircraft led by Lieutenant Colonel Posey was more successful, bombing so accurately that this plant never re-entered production throughout the duration of the war. The 389th had been given the most distant but most lightly defended target at Campina. Although their run-in was disrupted by a navigation mistake which led them down the wrong valley, they soon rectified this error and totally destroyed their target.

Although the approach to Ploesti had been relatively quiet, the defences were now thoroughly alerted and the whole formation was subjected to both fighter and anti-aircraft attack throughout its long passage home down the Ionian Sea. The 93rd and the 44th were harassed with great determination by both German and Romanian fighters as they left the target area

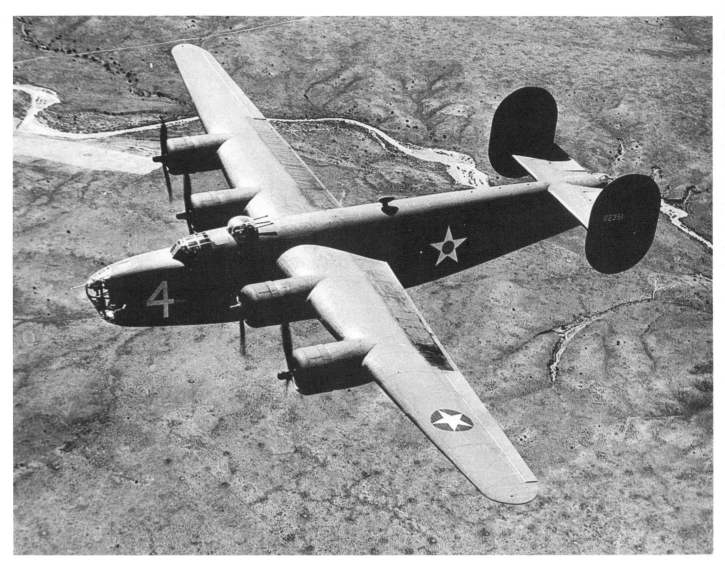

Three groups of B-24 Liberators were detached from 8th Air Force to assist the 9th in the epic raid against the oil installations at Ploesti in Romania on the 1st August 1943. IWM

and the steady stream of casualties grew as they fought their way home through several running battles. Some damaged aircraft landed in Turkey where their crews were promptly interned. In all 52 bombers were missing – a high total, but still less than the 50 per cent forecast before the raid by General Brereton commanding 9th Air Force. There were many conspicuous examples of individual bravery and an unprecedented five Congressional Medals of Honour were awarded for this one raid. It was indeed a considerable feat, and although it had not progressed exactly according to plan, considerable damage had been achieved albeit at a loss rate of some 30 per cent. Although this casualty rate was completely unsustainable, oil was the Achilles' heel of Germany's war effort and in the end it was a deficiency of aviation spirit rather than any other material shortage which eventually grounded the Luftwaffe and severely curtailed the mobility of the Panzer groups during the invasion of France the following year.

The Ploesti raid was not the end of the 8th Air Force's contribution from North Africa. Another long range raid was ordered on the 13th August against the Messerschmitt factory at Wiener Neustadt in Austria, a centre of BF 109 production.

Again it started as a combined effort of 101 aircraft, but the two 9th Air Force groups turned back over the Adriatic. Opposition was light as the defences again appeared to have been taken completely by surprise. Although the target was obscured by thin cloud, the factories were successfully bombed and production reduced by about a third. Three further raids were flown against targets in Italy, on one of which the 44th enhanced its reputation as a *jinx* unit by losing eight more aircraft although the other two groups escaped virtually unscathed. The unlucky 'Eightballs', for the second time since its arrival in England, had been virtually destroyed as an operational unit. At the end of August the three groups returned to England; their exploits had given a considerable uplift to the standing of the Liberator and their crews within the 8th Air Force. A further valuable if less spectacular detachment to North Africa followed in September when once again a successful raid was mounted against the aircraft factory at Wiener Neustadt.

The Schweinfurt/Regensburg Raid – 17th August 1943

The 8th Air Force laboured under an acute shortage of aircraft and crews for almost the whole of its first year in England. It usually had less than a hundred aircraft available on any one day for operations and could rarely mount a sufficiently concentrated mission to provide a real chance of achieving significant damage without suffering undue losses. In May 1943, however, this situation improved dramatically with the arrival of five more B-17 groups with more to follow. Another innovation was the introduction of 12 YB-40s, a heavily armed B-17 gunship intended to act as a bomber escort; but this was not conspicuously successful as this heavier aircraft tended to slow down the whole formation. The newcomers arrived with all the enthusiasm and confidence of youth, fortified by a more intensive and effective training programme in the USA, although this infectious brio was inadequate compensation for their lack of battle experience. Nor were the new groups given much time to settle-in with nominally 'easy' targets, if such existed in mid 1943, before being thrust into the heart of Germany. Even before the end of May the 8th was able to launch more than 200 aircraft against Kiel, an unprecedented weight of attack compared with their earlier efforts.

New tactics were evolved for the greater number of aircraft available, staggered raids and deceptive routeing were now regularly used to confuse the enemy defences and individual hot spots had been identified. Nevertheless, losses now occurred on almost every mission and from time to time there were some very black days. One such was June 13th when 26 B-17s were lost on a raid on the submarine yards at Kiel, nine of them within sight of the English coast on their return journey. 8th Air Force had no alternative but to turn their attention increasingly towards the 'intermediate' objective in the Combined Bomber Offensive – the destruction of the Luftwaffe fighter defences. It was becoming a battle of attrition which, although not recognised as clearly at the time, the USAAF was losing. It was also, as we have already seen, an objective for which little direct help was coming from Bomber Command where Harris was relentlessly pursuing his trail of destruction towards Berlin. A new fighter group, JG 11, had been established in North Germany and by August 1943 the Luftwaffe had 630 day fighters in the Western European theatre compared with only 270 in April. This contrasted markedly with the public perception in Britain and even more in the USA that the Luftwaffe was on the verge of defeat.

The last week of July ended a period of unusually cloudy summer weather over Europe leading to a renewed effort. A successful raid was mounted against factories in Norway followed by two major attacks on Hamburg to reinforce Bomber Command Operation 'Gomorrah'. By the end of the week the sustained operations had taken their toll, an effective strength of 330 aircraft had been reduced to below 200 with 90 crews killed or missing. Nevertheless, reinforcements were still flooding into England and by the beginning of August there

Like their British counterparts, the American ground crew had to undertake most of their routine servicing in the open air.

were no less than 19 B-17 groups settling into East Anglia, although not all were yet ready for operations. The stage was being set for one of the most ambitious and undoubtedly the most disastrous raid of the American campaign so far – the attack on Schweinfurt/Regensburg on the 17th August, the same day that Bomber Command visited Peenemünde.

Schweinfurt was a typical 'panacea' target and had already figured prominently in the argument between the Air Ministry and Sir Arthur Harris on the efficacy of attacking such objectives. The city produced just under half of the total ball bearing production in Germany, but although its criticality to the German war effort had long been a matter of dispute, there can be little doubt that the complete destruction of the Schweinfurt factories would in the medium term have been a serious blow to several diverse areas of military aircraft and vehicle production. Regensburg was a more obvious target in the context of the 'Pointblank' 'intermediate' objective. Together with Weiner Neustadt, its factories were responsible for nearly half the German fighter aircraft production, predominantly Bf 109s which, despite the advent of the newer Fw 190, were still the main threat to the USAAF's bombing campaign. Over 500 miles from England, these targets were regarded hitherto by the Germans as being reasonably safe from

A mass formation of B-17s setting out for a raid over Germany.

IWM

daylight attack because of the long transit over hostile territory which would have exposed the attacking force to an unacceptable risk. It was intended originally that a combined raid would be made against Weiner Neustadt and Regensburg with the former, much further to the south, being attacked by the 9th Air Force from Libya. But the weather delayed the mounting of the raid from England and as we have already seen, Weiner Neustadt was successfully attacked by B-24s on the 13th August.

A new and unusual feature of the Regensburg mission was that after completing their bombing run, the aircraft would fly-on to land in North Africa, thus depriving the Luftwaffe of a second bite at the cherry on their long home run to East Anglia. The 4th Bomber Wing with seven groups of 21 B-17s each was tasked with this part of the operation, and it was regarded as a sufficiently important raid for back-up aircraft to fly as far as the Dutch coast to replace any bombers which turned back for technical malfunctions. The Schweinfurt operation was entrusted to the 1st Bomber Wing with a total of 230 B-17s

which would return to their bases in England. The timing of the Regensburg raid was critical if the bombers were to reach North Africa in daylight and the 4th Wing was to launch first with the maximum possible P-47 escort. This was expected to generate a major Luftwaffe response, and whilst the fighters were on the ground refuelling and rearming, 1st Wing would slip through the window of opportunity and hopefully escape major attention. This at least was the plan.

The uncertain weather delayed the mission for some days and even when favourable conditions appeared likely on the 17th August, early morning mist over the airfields for a time put the operation in jeopardy. Eventually, however, the visibility improved sufficiently for the first Wing to take-off although cloud hampered their join-up and they were still too dispersed even after crossing into enemy territory at 17,000 feet. Far more serious was the failure of one of the two P-47 escort groups to rendezvous with the rear groups in the formation and this was quickly seized upon by the first wave of Fw 190s which ignored the escorted leading aircraft and scythed head-on through the two rearward groups. All too soon the escorts had to turn back towards England leaving the whole force vulnerable to fighter attack in the cloudless blue sky into which they now emerged. For the next 150 miles, a constant stream of both Fw 190s and Bf 109s harried the bombers unmercifully and one after another peeled away from the formation and descended streaming smoke and parachutes. Bf 110s and Ju 88s replaced the single engine fighters, but the main damage had already been done, 17 aircraft had been downed with another 250 miles still to run to the target. Exhausted of fuel and ammunition, the relentless harassment gradually died away and the final run-in was uneventful. The bombing conditions were excellent and the accuracy in the wake of such a gruelling mission so far was surprisingly good. The Wing pressed on as planned to North Africa and a surprised Luftwaffe only managed the occasional desultory attack on the final leg. Even so, five aircraft had to

ditch in the Mediterranean, either because of fuel shortage or combat damage. Twenty four were lost in all. Whilst the first phase of the operation had suffered greatly, No 1 Wing was to be even more grievously afflicted.

The second wave to Schweinfurt, as already indicated, was intended to slip through the enemy defences in the wake of the Regensburg force. However, the fog persisted through to the late morning at the 1st Wing bases, which were further inland than those of the 4th Wing, and it was soon decided that their take-off would be delayed until the P-47 escorts could refuel and rearm. This respite of course applied equally to the Luftwaffe and thus they too were ready and waiting when the second wave appeared. The Schweinfurt force followed a similar track initially to that of 4th Wing, but this time the fighter defences were even better prepared with reinforcements brought down from North Germany bringing their numbers up to about 200.

A solitary B-17 flying over Regensburg on the 17th August 1943. Loose formation keeping almost invariably led to heavy losses; this aircraft was lucky to survive. IWM

The attacks commenced around Antwerp and persisted, with some lulls, all the way to the target and throughout the return trip to the coast. A steady stream of crippled aircraft fell out of the sky, this time many from the leading formations which had escaped attention on the first wave. Nevertheless, the ever diminishing number doggedly pressed-on and eventually bombed Schweinfurt, albeit with only limited success. The Wing lost no less than 36 aircraft during this horrendous four hour assault, bringing the total from the combined raid to 60 – over twice as many as had been lost on any previous raid. Despite ridiculously inflated claims of nearly 300 enemy fighters shot down, the Luftwaffe in fact lost just 27 aircraft. Not only was the American loss rate in itself unsustainable, but the war of attrition against the German air defence system was being lost not only in aircraft destroyed, but even more importantly in crews. Many of the downed German pilots, parachuting into their own backyard, were fit to fly again almost immediately, but the 10 man Fortress crews were almost invariably lost into captivity even if they survived the destruction of their aircraft. The intensity and duration of the air battle in the Schweinfurt/ Regensburg raid was never again equalled in subsequent operations, and indeed for the next six weeks VIII Bomber Command rarely ventured beyond the Channel coast except for one very costly mission to Stuttgart in which losses arose from poor planning as much as enemy action.

The lesson was unavoidable, the daylight formation simply could not depend upon its own internal fire power for adequate protection. Either the fighters had to be defeated or the bombers provided with escorts throughout their mission, not just over the opening and closing stages.

Salvation – The Escort Fighter

The 8th Air Force had been on probation in 1943, as much in the eyes of its own leaders as in those of a sceptical Air Ministry in Britain. After Schweinfurt/Regensburg it began to look as though the dire predictions of the many British opponents of daylight bombing had been vindicated. In the sense that the unescorted bomber was untenable they were generally right, but it was those same philosophers of air power, led by Sir Charles Portal, who had derided the viability of the long range escort fighter, and it was in this that the 8th Air Force was to find its salvation.

It was not that the Americans were unaware of the benefits of close escort, they simply did not have the means to provide it for the most vulnerable parts of the mission. It was generally accepted by mid 1943 that bomber formations escorted by fighters suffered only about half the casualties sustained in the unsupported missions. To a certain extent this comparison was invalid, for the Luftwaffe generally concentrated its attack beyond the point at which the fighter escort had to turn back, but no one could deny that an escorted formation was less vulnerable than one without the benefit of such protection.

The problem with the concept of fighter escort which had always constrained its development was the trade-off between range and agility: the larger and heavier the fighter became in order to carry the fuel to achieve the range, the less it was able to match the manoeuvrability of the much lighter Bf-109 and FW 190s. The occupied buffer zone of Holland, Belgium and France was of enormous benefit to Germany, for it allowed the Luftwaffe to choose the point of engagement at which the escort was most constrained by lack of fuel or after it had to break-off altogether. The assault could then be sustained all the way to the target and back to the point at which the escort could once again gather-in its flock.

The early VIII Bomber Command operations were escorted by RAF Spitfires with an increasing number of American pilots and squadrons swelling their ranks, but the radius of action of this agile fighter did not extend very far beyond the coast of northern France and thus its operational viability was very limited. The USAAF fighter groups assigned to 8th Air Force were intended primarily from the outset to provide bomber escort and the aircraft selected were the Lockhead P-38 Lightning and the Bell P-39 Airacobra. The latter, however, proved a great disappointment and does not figure in this story. The Lightning was a twin engine, twin boom aircraft of unconventional design but with a good performance, superior to any other American fighter of this period. Even so, although fast and manoeuvrable at the lower levels, it could not match the climb rate of the FW 190s and its performance deteriorated markedly at high level. Furthermore, of complicated construction, it proved technically unreliable and took a long time to settle into operational service. Although the P-38s escorted a few of the early tentative B-17 sorties over the occupied countries, they were soon withdrawn for transfer to 12th Air Force in preparation for Operation 'Torch', leaving only the 4th Fighter Group comprising the celebrated 'Eagle Squadron' still flying their Spitfire Vs. But they numbered only 36 aircraft and were integrated into Fighter Command operations.

The next American fighter to arrive in Britain at the end of 1942 was the P-47 Thunderbolt: it was viewed with extreme scepticism by the 4th Group pilots. It did not even look like a fighter with its ugly shape and massive radial engine, and inevitably attracted unfavourable comment when compared with the sleek feline lines of their beloved Spitfires. It was soon nicknamed the 'Juggernaut' for obvious reasons, but later when it had proved itself in combat it became more affectionately known simply as the 'Jug'. It was quickly evaluated against a captured FW 190 and began to show itself in a rather better light. Provided air combat could be contained above 15,000 feet, the powerful P-47 could acquit itself quite well against its adversary. It was first committed to escort duties in a raid against Antwerp on the 4th May 1943, but at this stage the Thunderbolt's radius of action was under 200 miles; of little comfort to the bomber crews when even the Ruhr just across the German frontier was over 300 miles distant. Their tactics were derived from RAF practice with two squadrons of the group flying about 4,000 feet above the bombers and another squadron 2,000 feet higher still to provide top cover.

The means of extending the range of the Thunderbolt

Above
The P-38 Lightning was the first escort fighter to support the 8th Air Force in England.   IWM

Below
The rather more robust P-47 Thunderbolt soon replaced the Lightnings in England, but suffered initially from an inadequate radius of action.
IWM

without unduly inhibiting its performance became the most pressing need during the summer of 1943, for although the 'green' pilots were gaining experience, the Luftwaffe was generally avoiding intercepting the formation until the fighters were forced to break away. Although by no means a new idea, one solution was the jettisonable fuel container known appropriately enough as the 'drop tank'. There were two problems areas, the tank had to be pressurised to provide fuel above about 20,000 feet and had to be jettisoned before the aircraft entered combat because the drag incurred radically reduced the performance. The American ferry tank was initially unavailable and 8th Air Force therefore designed and built its own metal 100 gallon tank which was suspended beneath the belly of the aircraft, but these were not ready until September because of a shortage of steel. American unpressurised 200 gallon ferry tanks began to arrive in July and these were used for fuel on the climb although they had to be jettisoned above 23,000 feet when the fuel feed dried-up. Nevertheless, this extended the radius of action of the Thunderbolt another valuable 75 miles. A custom built pressurised metal tank arrived from America in August which, although of much less capacity, was far more versatile and could be retained at any height. By the late Autumn the radius of action of the P-47 had been almost doubled to around 350 miles from their homebase and more

The contrails of fighters are seen weaving above a formation of bombers on route to Germany. IWM

than once caught the Luftwaffe fighter pilots by surprise when they were expecting to confront only the bombers. On the 27th September a force of P-47s escorted B-17s to Emden, well into the heartland of Germany, opening another phase in the ever increasing capability of VIII Fighter Command. The Luftwaffe was quick to respond and devised new tactics themselves. If a small force of fighters engaged the P-47s as they crossed the coast, they could force them to jettison their tanks thus once again restricting their range. It was an ingenious and enthralling game of cat and mouse with a prize of the highest order – the very survival of the daylight bomber offensive.

The Autumn of 1943 also saw the return of the P-38 to the European theatre providing a further increase in the radius of action of the escort fighter to about 450 miles. There were, however, operational problems still to resolve; the close co-ordination of the fighter and bomber groups was of course vital and in the early days this was not always achieved satisfactorily. The bombers themselves had to form-up over England and then rendezvous with the fighter escort over the sea; timing and accurate navigation were essential and both were often constrained by poor weather conditions. Relays of fighters were provided, some with long range tanks to stay close to the

The B-26 Marauder had a somewhat chequered career with the 8th Air Force. This aircraft of the 386BG is taking off from Boxted in Essex.
IWM

bombers, others without tanks to fend off any early Luftwaffe counter attack. Although their task was to protect the bombers, the fighters increasingly began to actively search-out combat. The 'Pointblank' directive requiring the neutralisation of the Luftwaffe's air defences was ever more pressing and destroying a fighter in combat was a far more satisfying and immediate way of achieving this than bombing an aircraft factory. By November 1943 the P-47 crews had claimed nearly 400 aircraft destroyed or damaged, and unlike the grossly inflated claims of the bomber air gunners, most of these could be confirmed by camera film.

As this traumatic year for 8th Air Force drew to a close, the survival of the daylight bomber offensive was still not assured. The escort fighter had proved its value, but its radius of action still generally only encompassed the Ruhr and Rhineland. What was needed was an agile fighter which could reach Berlin and other similarly distant targets. The solution was in sight when the first of the P-51 Mustangs arrived to equip the 9th Air Force in November. From early 1944 until the end of the war, this magnificent aircraft will increasingly come to dominate the continuing story of the escort fighter.

Low Level Interlude – Marauder Operations in England

The twin engine medium bomber is not normally associated with the 8th Air Force and indeed the main contribution to the concept of intruder operations in north west Europe is traditionally assigned to No 2 Group of the RAF and in the USAAF to the 9th Air Force. As we have already seen, the RAF did not quite know how best to use it's light and medium day bombers after the fall of France and they were not really to come into their own until the lead-in to Operation 'Overlord'. The Americans had, however, developed four medium bombers before Pearl Harbour, the Mitchell, the Boston/ Havoc, the Ventura and the Marauder. All of these were used quite extensively by the RAF, but it was the B-26 Marauder which was assigned to 8th Air Force in 1942.

The Marauder had already acquired an unenviable reputation before it even arrived in England following a number of crashes. It was a difficult aircraft to fly, particularly on one engine, and its two Pratt and Whitney Wasp power plants were not noted for their reliability. On the other hand it had acquitted itself quite well in the Pacific theatre although without the range to be really effective. It was thus perceived that operations in Europe might lie more within its capabilities and three groups were authorised to join VIII Bomber Command in the Autumn of 1942. However, Operation 'Torch', the American landing in North Africa, was now in progress and after a period of low level training in England, all three groups were re-assigned to 12th Air Force. Before the end of 1942 four more Marauder groups were allocated to England and assigned to the 3rd Bombardment Wing with its Headquarters at Elveden Hall in Suffolk. Despite some scepticism in official quarters, it was intended from the outset to use the Marauders at low level to complement the RAF's Boston and Mosquito squadrons which were just beginning to show their potential in this role.

It was not until March 1943 that the first aircraft began to arrive in England. They immediately settled into a period of rigorous low level training, although this did nothing to improve the reputation of this controversial bomber. A major accident in April and other hair raising incidents only seemed to confirm the hazards of low level flying in a somewhat temperamental aircraft. Nevertheless, by the 14th May two squadrons were considered ready for operations and a power station at Ijmuiden on the Dutch coast was the selected target. It was not an easy objective, being close to a German E boat base which was particularly well protected by anti-aircraft guns.

Twelve aircraft, each carrying four 500lb bombs, set-out from their base at Bury St Edmunds at mid morning and flew at very low level across the North Sea to escape radar detection. Speed and surprise are the essence of low level operations, but on this occasion the German batteries were wide awake and accounted for one aircraft as the formation coasted-in: it was fortunate to regain England on one engine and minus a sizeable portion of its rudder. The remaining aircraft pressed on following a canal and a railway line, favoured navigation features for low level flying, and the target soon appeared under the nose of the leading Marauder. The defences had already been alerted and all bar one aircraft received some flak damage even though only one was lost, crashing near its home base whilst trying to make an emergency landing. The crews were nevertheless tolerably well satisfied with their days work, confident that the objective of the mission had been achieved. They were both mystified and disappointed therefore to find two days later that their aim had not been as accurate as they thought and even more disenchanted when they were ordered to repeat the raid on the following day.

Only 11 aircraft could be mustered for this occasion and the outcome was a major disaster, indeed the story of the raid could only be pieced together two days later when two survivors were plucked out of the North Sea. Again the raid was launched in mid morning in bright Spring sunshine, but the formation was fairly soon reduced to ten aircraft as one returned with electrical problems. The rest pressed-on, but a navigation error led to a landfall near the Maas estuary which was one of the most heavily defended areas in Holland. Three aircraft were shot down and two more collided and crashed whilst the formation was regrouping. The remaining five, still unsure of their navigation, now blundered into the heavy defences surrounding Amsterdam. Cutting their losses, they hurriedly bombed a gas

This dramatic photograph shows a B-26 shortly after being hit by flak on a medium level operation.   IWM

holder and headed for home, but four aircraft were so badly damaged that they soon crashed into the sea. The sole remaining Marauder then had the misfortune to encounter three Bf 109s and it too fell into the sea, but with the two aforementioned survivors. Only 20 other airmen survived to enter prisoner of war camps. The 17th May was a black day for 8th Air Force and particularly for the 322nd Bombardment Group.

Low level operations over hostile territory were temporarily suspended although training continued for the other Marauder groups which were by now arriving in England. Another fatal low flying accident before the month was out hastened the inevitable review of American low level operations in Europe, but in fact 8th Air Force agonised for some time over what they should do with the 250 or so Marauders now based in England. The crews were only trained for low level operations and the aircraft were not fitted with a bombsight suitable for use at higher levels. Moreover, if the far more heavily armed B-17 was having difficulty defending itself at high level, what price the chances of the Marauder succeeding at medium level where the light flak was so much more intense. On the other hand, the RAF was operating its Mitchells reasonably successfully at medium levels and the Marauder in North Africa was also performing quite well, low level operations in that theatre already having been discontinued. A decision was eventually made to use the Marauders at medium level with a fighter escort and the aircraft were re-equipped with a Norden bombsight and their crews retrained. As with the Liberator, VIII Bomber Command was never very fond of its Marauders and soon transferred them to VIII Support Command, an embryo organisation dedicated to the support of ground forces which had barely found its feet at this stage.

This change of command did not in practice materially affect their targeting and the first medium level raid against the marshalling yards at Abbeville, heavily escorted by RAF Spitfires, was mounted on the 16th July. No more disasters ensued, but the Marauders radius of action and bombload were limited and no more than 36 could normally be launched in any one mission because of the limited number of escorts available. Bombing results were, to put it kindly, rather mixed, but aircraft casualties also declined quite markedly compared with the disastrous results at low level. Before the Marauders were eventually withdrawn, over 4,000 sorties had been flown for the loss of just 13 aircraft in action, an achievement which can largely be attributed to the Spitfire escorts as was generously acknowledged by the Marauder crews who were now beginning to gain some confidence in their heavily maligned machine.

Nevertheless, the bombing results, albeit improving, were hardly commensurate with the effort involved and in October 1943 it was decided that the four Marauder groups should be transferred to the 9th Air Force which had just arrived in England to prepare for the invasion of Europe to be mounted the following year. 8th Air Force now concentrated upon what it had long believed was its real business; the operation of its beloved Flying Fortress in long range high level missions deep into the heart of Germany.

Searching for a Role – No 2 Group in 1943

1942 had proved a watershed for No 2 Group with the replacement of its Blenheims by Bostons, Venturas, Mitchells and Mosquitos, aircraft which were potentially far more effective than their predecessor. Nevertheless, there were many technical and training difficulties to be overcome which inhibited their operational capability for much of the year despite the resounding success of the Eindhoven raid in December. 1943, for rather different reasons, was to prove an equally trying year. In fact, Bomber Command did not quite know how best to employ No 2 Group. Although regarded essentially as an army co-operation group, it did not at this stage of the war have ground forces to support, and yet on the other hand it did not fit easily into the pattern of strategic operations by heavy bombers which was the mainstay of the rest of the Command.

And so 1943 began with the usual round of 'Circuses' and 'Ramrods' for which the Ventura squadrons were usually tasked and which were still no more popular with the crews than in previous years. The Boston and Mosquito crews were happier,

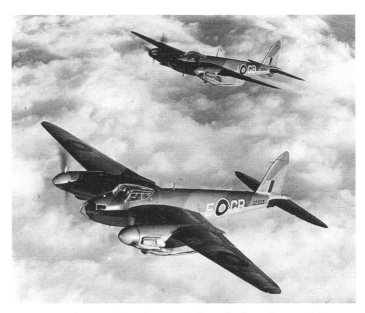

Mosquitos of No 105 Squadron carried out the first of many visits to Berlin in January 1943.   RAFM

for they had the more stimulating role of low level intruder operations against the familiar range of targets including airfields, power stations and railway marshalling yards. In addition, the Mosquitos were often tasked for photo reconnaissance, a role for which their speed made them ideally suitable.

There was, however, the understandable urge to really exploit the unique qualities of their new wooden bomber which the RAF had been so reluctant to order and which at this time was still regarded with suspicion in some quarters. A spectacular opportunity appeared at the end of January with the first Mosquito raids on Berlin, not once, but twice on the same day. Furthermore, the two raids were timed to coincide with mass rallies in the city to be addressed by Goering at 11 o'clock and Goebbels at 4 o'clock. It was hoped that the irony of hearing Goering's speech on a radio broadcast overlayed by air raid sirens would not be lost on the population of the Reich.

The major part of the outbound leg was to be flown at low level to avoid radar detection followed by a rapid climb to 25,000 feet for the bombing run. The return flight was either to use the shelter of cloud or descend again to low level. The first three aircraft of No 105 Squadron launched just before 0900 and despite rain and low cloud deposited their bombs on the 'Big City' dead on the dot of 11 o'clock – unfortunately the speech was delayed until 12! Their return was equally uneventful apart from some wayward flak and distant fighters; it was the perfect example of the type of profile for which the Mosquito was so ideally suited.

If the plan to disrupt a senior German leader's rallying cry by the RAF's first Mosquito raid on Berlin was inspired, to have attempted it for a second time on the same day may perhaps be thought foolhardy. But three more Mosquitos from No 139 Squadron were already on their way when the first formation

Air Vice Marshal Basil Embry, who had served as a squadron commander in No 2 Group in 1940, returned to take over the Group in May 1943. He is seen here later in the war with Air Commodore D F W Atcherly at 2 Group Headquarters.   IWM

landed. Following a similar route, the aircraft reached Berlin unscathed; but the Luftwaffe was not to be caught napping twice and had a reception committee waiting. Sqn Ldr Darling's aircraft was shot down although the other two escaped. It was a great propaganda coup and a tremendous boost for the growing reputation of the Mosquito.

Nevertheless, all was not sweetness and light within No 2 Group. The Mitchells were still having technical problems and not yet ready for full operational use and a further blow came in February when the Boston squadrons were ordered to give-up their aircraft for service in North Africa. Although they were to be replaced in due course by Boston IIIAs, this necessitated a further period of proving and training. Building on the success of the Berlin raid, the Mosquitos undertook ever more difficult specialist attacks, noteworthy among which was another No 139 Squadron success with a raid on the molybdenum mine at Knaben in Norway, one of the most important economic resources of that country now in German hands. The Venturas continued with their medium level 'Circus' operations, sometimes with good results, but also quite often with heavy casualties. None, however, matched the disastrous raid against Amsterdam on the 2nd May. No 487 Squadron was intended only to provide a diversionary 'Circus' raid against a power station just to the north of Amsterdam to cover a more

important Boston low level attack upon the Royal Dutch Steel Works at Ijmuiden. The 12 Venturas, led by Sqn Ldr Leonard Trent, met up with their three squadrons of escorting Spitfires at 1700 for a low level transit across the sea. One aircraft turned back, but the rest began the slow climb to their bombing height of 12,000 feet as they approached the coast. Unfortunately, and unknown to them, another diversionary Spitfire raid on Flushing had arrived 30 minutes early, attracting about 70 Fw 190s and Bf 109s into the air which, by chance, were now ready and waiting for the Venturas. The Spitfire escort was immediately cut-off from its charges and almost 30 Bf 109s had a free run at the bombers. One Ventura was badly damaged immediately and turned for home; it was to be the only one to return. The fighters continued to pick-off the bombers one by one until Trent's aircraft was the only one remaining as the target was reached. Still he pressed on and bombed, unfortunately causing only blast damage to the target, before turning for home. It was a forlorn hope, his aircraft controls were soon shot away and Trent and his navigator were fortunate to escape the disintegrating aircraft into captivity. When the story was finally patched together at the end of the war, Leonard Trent was awarded the Victoria Cross.

At the end of May, No 2 Group was transferred out of Bomber Command to the 2nd Tactical Air Force. It was a separation which was not greatly regretted by either side; to many at Bomber Command the Group was a misfit and they in turn were not always entirely enamoured by the support they received from above. What was regretted, however, was that Bomber Command retained the two Mosquito squadrons at the parting of the ways although in return No 2 Group gained Air Vice Marshal Basil Embry as its Commander. A former squadron commander within the Group, Embry was one of the most charismatic, forceful and courageous senior officers to emerge from the RAF during the war, one of a number who served with the Command's 'Cinderella' formation. Embry recognised the qualities of the Mosquito only too clearly and from the moment he assumed command continually badgered higher authority to replace his more vulnerable medium bombers with this real thoroughbred.

In fact the change of ownership did little to alter the tasks of the Group and they continued as before to mount a mix of 'Circuses' and intruder raids until towards the end of the year when there was a change of emphasis which also impinged upon Bomber Command. The Air Ministry had been carefully monitoring throughout 1943 the developing threat of attack by pilotless aircraft and rockets. In the Autumn there were unmistakeable signs of the construction of launch sites in northern France and by October no less than 88 had been identified. Shaped like a ski jump and pointing towards London, concrete platforms about 30 feet long were mushrooming in the Pas de Calais with similar sites elsewhere orientated towards Portsmouth and Bristol. The Mitchells and Bostons of No 2 Group were immediately directed towards these 'Crossbow' targets, as were elements of Bomber Command and 8th and 9th Air Forces. These raids attracted surprisingly little attention

Gp Capt Charles Pickard who led the precision attack on Amiens prison in February 1944. This photograph was taken immediately before take off on this raid in which he lost his life. IWM

The raid on Amiens prison was marred only by one stray bomb which hit the main cell block killing a number of prisoners. IWM

from the enemy fighters, but a powerful array of anti-aircraft weapons surrounding the sites ensured that they were no picnic. Furthermore, hitting such a small target under heavy flak attack from medium level was not easy and several sites had to be revisited on a number of occasions. In the two months either side of Christmas, 1,362 sorties were made against the 'V' sites with varying degrees of success.

Meanwhile, Embry had succeeded in his battle to reintroduce Mosquitos to No 2 Group and by January 1944 they were ready for one of the most spectacular and well publicised raids of the war. Along with the dams raid, the attack on Amiens prison is perhaps the most celebrated special operation of the bomber offensive: certainly in terms of the precision required, it must rank alongside that earlier epic feat. Amiens prison, some 70 miles north of Paris, held 700 inmates of which 180 were resistance workers and 200 political prisoners – the rest were ordinary criminals. The Germans habitually showed little mercy to those caught aiding the Allied cause, but of particular

relevance to this raid, it was learned that a number of their leaders were due to face a firing squad on the 19th February.

A daring plan was conceived to breach the outer wall of the prison and the cell block itself to allow the prisoners to escape in the ensueing confusion. The raid was planned to take place in mid February, but in the event did not occur until the 18th because of bad weather – just in time. No 140 Mosquito Wing at RAF Hunsdon was allotted the task: it was truly a Commonwealth affair – No 487 was a New Zealand squadron, No 464 Australian and No 21 was nominally British. The station was commanded by Group Captain Charles Pickard, DSO, DFC, a former Whitley and special operations squadron commander who had led the Bruneval raid and was regarded by many as one of the outstanding bomber leaders of the war. Typically, he decided to lead this difficult raid even though he had only recently converted to the Mosquito, and it was only with great difficulty that Embry was dissuaded from going along himself.

An elaborate plaster model of the prison was constructed to aid in the briefing and the intended plan was that No 487 Squadron would go in first from the north west to breach the outer wall followed immediately by No 464 Squadron from the north east who would bomb the guards accommodation and try to break down the wall of the main block. No 21 would be held in reserve. The formation took-off at 1100 accompanied by an escort of 12 Typhoons and immediately ran into severe snow storms at low level which caused four Mosquitos and four Typhoons to lose contact with the formation and return. The approach to the target was made at 50 feet, guided by a conveniently sited poplar avenue pointing like an arrow towards the prison. Two of the first wave aircraft scored direct hits on the outer wall with their 500lb 11 second delay bombs: the wall was breached. The second wave neatly took-out the guards accommodation and opened a gap in the inner wall, but unfortunately also scored a direct hit on the main cell block. By now the flak defences had recovered from their surprise and a squadron of Fw 190s appeared on the scene, shooting down two Mosquitos and two Typhoons and badly damaging others which had to make emergency landings. Charles Pickard was one of the casualties, both he and his navigator were killed when a Fw 190 shot-off the tail of their Mosquito.

The raid was only a qualified success: 258 prisoners escaped, but among these were 179 criminals and only 50 resistance workers. Over 150 were killed by the bomb which hit the main block and more civilians died in the town. It could so nearly have been the perfect operation.

Berlin after attack on the 3rd September 1943. The 'Battle of Berlin' did not start in earnest until November. IWM

The Battle of Berlin

Returning to the mainstream of strategic bombing, the third and last of the great 'battles' of 1943 was that of Berlin. It was the culmination of Harris' relentless drive to lay waste the face of Germany, the climax of his attempt, despite the official policy, to defeat Germany by strategic bombing alone. After the successful assault on Hamburg at the beginning of August, Bomber Command continued to employ the tactics pioneered in the Spring and Summer. Oboe was used with increasing success for attacks against targets which lay within its restricted range and H2S for those more distant. A new aid, G-H, was used with some success in November. We have seen how Hamburg was clearly identifiable on the H2S display, but many of the targets attacked in the three months following were often far more difficult to detect with certainty. Indeed, the results were frequently very disappointing if the weather was not sufficiently clear to allow visual marking on top of an initial H2S blind marking. There were nevertheless notable attacks using this technique during these three months against Mannheim, Frankfurt, Hannover and Kassel. In each case heavy damage was caused to large parts of the town, and in the raid on Kassel on the 22nd October, no less than 380 of the 444 crews who attacked the target laid their bombs within three miles, a far better average than was achieved at Hamburg. Against this, however, a number of raids were much less successful and few more so than the three on Berlin before the 'battle' was commenced in earnest.

The three preliminary strikes against Berlin were made on the 23rd and 31st of August and the 3rd September. In stark contrast to Kassel, the evidence of the cameras suggested that of 1,719 sorties dispatched on these three nights, only 27 had dropped their bombs within three miles of the aiming point. Despite its rivers and lakes, Berlin simply did not show-up as a good target on H2S at this stage; there were so many returns on the screen that it became a confusing mass of light even to crews who were becoming more experienced in its use. Furthermore, losses to German night fighters were higher with the Halifaxes and Stirlings suffering far more heavily than the Lancasters. Stirling casualties in particular at over 10 per cent were simply not sustainable and the last raid of this opening period was left to Lancasters alone. These three raids did not augur well for the main onslaught upon Berlin which was to start in November.

In advocating the assault on Berlin to Winston Churchill, Harris had called for a joint British/American action: in the event it was almost solely a Bomber Command effort with the 8th Air Force only joining-in during the final month in March 1944. This was in fact inevitable as Harris must have known, for there was no way that the Americans could be trained to operate at night in this timescale even if they had been of a mind to do so, and their inability to penetrate safely that far into Germany in daylight had already been conclusively demonstrated, not least by the very costly raid on Schweinfurt/Regensburg on the 17th August and the equally expensive return to Schweinfurt on the 14th October. It was not until the P-51 Mustang was available to cover operations as far as Berlin that such a course of action could even be seriously contemplated.

As before, the heavy raids during this period were by no means confined to Berlin; in fact 16 major sorties were sent to Berlin before March 1944 compared with 19 to a dozen other major targets. It was ever more necessary to disperse raids widely so that the increasing potentcy of the Luftwaffe night fighter force should not be allowed to concentrate in one area. The Lancaster was now the major asset in Bomber Command and over 80 per cent of the sorties flown against Berlin were entrusted to this aircraft with the Halifax making-up all but a handful of the remainder. The Lancaster was, however, being asked to carry an ever increasing bombload over the 600 miles to Berlin resulting in the removal of some of its armour plating and reducing its performance. In fact, this dimunition in performance was no longer of significance, for the night fighter, superior in both speed and fire power, was very likely to achieve a kill if the crew managed to acquire a visual sighting. Safety now depended upon deception and electronic counter measures, it was not practicable to try to out-run the predatory fighter.

The Battles of the Ruhr and Hamburg both had the benefit of new devices – Oboe and 'Window' respectively – but no such innovation was available for Berlin. The German defences had quickly found a partial answer to the latter by using a broadcast control technique which in fact increased the efficiency of the night fighters by allowing more of them to be concentrated in the bomber stream. Bomber Command was increasingly forced to fall back on its old tactics of deception to evade the fighters and on some notable occasions this was very effective, as in the raid against Peenemünde on the 17th August. Given the unexpected failure of H2S to clearly delineate the target, the main problem for the Pathfinder Force in the raids on Berlin was identification of the aiming point. Another serious obstacle, not surprisingly over central Europe in mid winter, was the weather. Berlin was often blanketed in cloud which posed great problems for the main force crews when the marking was confused or scattered, and throughout the whole period bombs were spread over a wide area with extensive creep-back.

The first raid occurred on the night of the 18th November and operations continued until the final attack on the 24th March. In all, 9,111 sorties were dispatched to Berlin in 16 major raids which were supplemented by another 208 Mosquito and Lancaster harassing attacks on other nights. Berlin was an important target in two senses. The psychological impact of a sustained assault on the nation's capital needs little further explanation. Although after three years of intermittent bombing it could hardly be expected to generate the alarm caused by the Gotha raids on London in 1917 which gained impact by their very novelty, the apparent freedom with which Britain could bring widespread devastation to the very heart of Hitler's Reich could not but bring home to the population of the capital the feeling that the war was moving towards an

---

Flt Lt M.C. Wright – IX Squadron

We were stationed at Bardney in Lincolnshire and had completed 11 operations together. Our trips had ranged all over Germany including Hamburg, Munich, Mannheim, Hannover and the Rhur, and so it could be said that we were settling down into an experienced team. Nevertheless we still had to come face to face with the enemy and were not to know at briefing on the 3rd October 1943 that this was to be the night.

Our Squadron was putting on 12 aircraft in the first wave and the crew sat around our table in the Briefing Room looking anxiously at the black screen which covered the wall map that held the answer to all our thoughts – the target. The Squadron Commander pulled the screen to one side to reveal the answer – KASSEL. The route would take us in north of the Ruhr and out to the south. There was nothing unusual about the target and as usual we were warned to expect a strong concentration of searchlights and anti-aircraft guns.

Within a few minutes of time on target the pilot reported no sign of pathfinder activity, nor anything else for that matter. Suddenly we were lit up like the fairy on a Christmas tree and almost at once both gunners sighted a Focke Wulf 190 at about 700 yards passing from starboard to the port quarter. The rear gunner told the pilot to start the standard corkscrew manoeuvre, but the fighter hung-on and at 600 yards both our gunners opened fire. The Fw 190 replied with cannon and his initial burst cleanly shot away the cupola of our mid-upper turret, also severing the electrical and oxygen supplies to both turrets: the mid-upper gunner was killed by a shell through the head. At 300 yards the fighter and Wally Mullet, the rear gunner, exchanged fire again and the latter could see his shots hit the fighter's engine. It turned sharply to port, rolled over on its back, and when alongside the Lancaster at about 100 yards it exploded. Pieces of fighter thudded against the side of the Lancaster; Wally lost consciousness through lack of oxygen.

Ron Walkup, the pilot, decided to lose height until oxygen was no longer needed and in the end Wally suffered nothing more than mild frostbite as a result of the loss of electricity to his heated flying suit. After a lonely return flight at low level we eventually landed at Ford at 0400. A quick examination by the Squadron engineer soon confirmed that the aircraft was a write-off, riddled from the middle to the tail with bullet holes, and the upper turret disappeared altogether. But of greatest interest were pieces of Fw 190 embedded in the fuselage. This was one claim that couldn't be denied.

Wally was awarded the DFM and we all went to Boston to celebrate.

German civilians going to work in Berlin in December 1943 at the height of the onslaught against their city. The strategic offensive was to prove that the impact on the morale of the population had been grossly exaggerated before the war. IWM

inexorable conclusion. Berlin was, however, an important industrial target in its own right. The third largest city in the world, it housed important aircraft engine, machine tool and instrument factories as well as one third of Germany's electrical engineering industry and a quarter of its tank production capacity. It was also an important communications centre between the eastern and western fronts. There was no doubt that if the scale of destruction perpetrated upon Hamburg could be wrought in Berlin, it might just have brought the war to a premature end as Harris had promised. That serious damage was sustained is undeniable, but it was not as concentrated as in many other smaller cities and longer recovery periods were allowed between successive raids. In fact, post war records show that armament production actually increased during this period and that there was no major impact on the city's utilities although one fifth of the population was made homeless. Serious though the damage had been, Berlin was not 'wrecked from end to end' and the morale of the people was as resilient as had been that of London during the Blitz. None of this was known at the time as it proved very difficult to obtain good

reconnaissance photographs because of the almost continuous cloud cover. Ecstatic claims of success were therefore made by the Command and the media on very flimsy evidence.

Even if this optimism had proved justified, it could not hide the unpalatable truth that the Battle of Berlin was becoming increasingly difficult to sustain in terms of casualties which eventually amounted to 5.4 per cent, or one sortie in 20. The series started well enough when only nine of the 444 despatched failed to return from the first raid on the 18th November. But losses started to mount as the night fighter defences became increasingly adept at surmounting the obstacles of 'Window' and radio jamming aids, and increasingly the success of the raid depended upon the ability of the fighter controller to 'guess' the target. If he was right, the fighters could concentrate in that area and pick-off the bombers as they ran-in or departed the target, often silhouetted against the glare of the explosions beneath. Sometimes he was deceived, as when he decided on the night of 5th February 1944 that the target was Berlin when the bombers were actually heading for Stettin some 75 miles to the north east and escaped with only small losses. Casualties nevertheless increased steadily: on the first of four attacks in December the rate rose to 8.7 per cent and in the following month the average rate was 6.1 per cent. This increasing loss rate culminated in a staggering 9.1 per cent on what proved to be the final sortie against Berlin on the 24th March. In this raid, an increasingly efficient flak organisation accounted for a high proportion of the casualties. Although losses were unacceptably high, it was not until nearly a week later that a raid on Nuremberg brought to a close this chapter in Bomber Command operations.

Sir Arthur Harris had not destroyed Berlin and brought the war to an end by the 1st April as he had claimed possible in a letter to the Air Ministry on 7th December 1943. In fact, despite the courage and fortitude of Bomber Command crews during this torrid winter, the Battle of Berlin, unlike those of the Ruhr and Hamburg, had ended in defeat. The 'Pointblank' directive agreed by the President and Prime Minister at their conference in May had in the end proved as essential a requirement for the sustained operations of Bomber Command as it had been for 8th Air Force earlier in the year. We should now, therefore, take a longer look at the Luftwaffe's increasingly effective eye in the night.

Flt Sgt R. McDonald – 158 Squadron

On the night of the 15th February 1944 en route to Berlin in our Halifax 'O' Orange, we ran into flak over Denmark. Our port inner engine burst into flames and the aircraft went into a vertical dive. Our skipper, Bill Hogg, regained control after 10,000 feet, but our port outer was now on fire. He extinguished the fires, feathered the props and jettisoned the load, but could not maintain height. Not sure whether we were over sea or land, we decided to stay with the aircraft.

The starboard inner was now faltering as we skimmed a house and crashlanded in a snow covered field. The nose burst open on impact as did the overloaded fuel tanks and one engine tore loose. But miraculously there was no fire and all seven of us stepped out of the wreckage.

Although the total number of Bomber Command aircraft lost remained at a peak until the middle of 1944, the loss rate in percentage terms started to decrease quite sharply after the Nuremberg raid of March 1944 reflecting the increasing number of missions mounted.

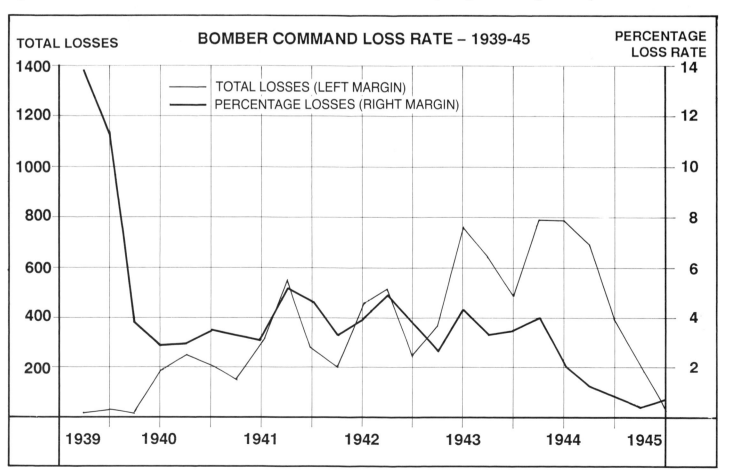

'Boar Hunt'

The German night fighter defences, which in 1939 were virtually non-existent, had slowly developed through the Himmelbett system in 1941 to a reasonable degree of effectiveness by 1942. But the increasing weight of Bomber Command attacks tended to nullify the developing expertise of the few night fighter aces who were still largely dependent upon good weather conditions for success until, as 1943 approached, it was apparent that more imaginative tactics were needed if the fighter defences were not to be completely overwhelmed. Technology was also starting to play a much wider role in the night fighter war. Telefunken had been experimenting with an airborne radar in the Spring of 1941 and early in 1942 the first Ju 88Cs were fitted with the Lichtenstein Airborne Interception (AI) radar with its imposing aerial array suspended inelegantly on the nose of the aircraft. The Me 210 which was intended to replace the Bf 110 was a costly failure, but an improved version of the Bf 110, the 'G' model, and the slow but heavily armed Dornier Do 217 with four cannon and four machine guns were soon being fitted with the new eye in the sky.

One innovative development known as 'Schrage musik' was the introduction of two 20 mm cannon installed in the rear cockpit section of the Bf 110 G which could be fired upwards at an angle of about 75 degrees through a reflector sight. The fighter tracked astern and well below the bomber, which might be silhouetted in the moonlight, and then pull-up in the blind spot beneath the belly. The first indication the bomber crew had of their unwelcome guest was the heavy shells thudding into the highly vulnerable underside of the wing which contained the petrol tanks. The British were unaware of 'Schrage musik' for many months, for the effect on the aircraft was almost identical to a direct hit by flak.

Despite these advances, by mid 1943 the Luftwaffe was being overwhelmed at night. In May General Kammhuber could marshal little more than 300 serviceable aircraft although to a certain extent this was compensated by improved flak defences, now equipped with 105 and 128 mm guns. In the Ruhr alone, the deployment of guns was almost doubled. However, Hitler was in the main obdurately resistant to pleas to bolster the defences, blindly putting his faith in a counter offensive of which the Luftwaffe was by now incapable: 'You can only smash terror with terror. You have to counter-attack. Anything else is useless'. In the event, Bomber Command losses continued to fall and with the advent of 'Window' fell to less than 3 per cent in the major onslaught on Hamburg in August. Despite the improvement in the flak defences, the main need was to bring an increasing number of fighters into action.

Major Hans-Joachim Hermann, an experienced bomber pilot who had been given command of a Bf 109 Geschwader, firmly believed that the single seat fighter should be re-introduced to the night role. His idea was to concentrate the Bf 109s over the expected target thereby enabling the pilot to visually acquire the bombers in the beams of the searchlights or the reflected glare of fires and target markers. The key was to identify the target in sufficient time to position the fighters before the bombing actually began. The tactic was known as 'Wilde Sau' (Wild Boar) operations. Although the introduction of 'Window' complicated the fighter controller's task in respect of close control, it had far less impact on 'Wild Boar' operations; all that was required was a perceptive controller who could see through the feints and deviations of the bomber stream and accurately predict their final destination. Sometimes, of course, the concept completely misfired with the fighters aimlessly circling some dark and peaceful city whilst the bombers made free elsewhere, as happened on the Nuremberg raid in March 1944. There were, however, snags in using the Bf 109 at night as the Luftwaffe had discovered in 1939. Its blind flying instrumentation and navigation aids were limited and its very short endurance meant that many 'Wild Boar' missions ended in a hectic scramble to the nearest airfield. Crashes were numerous and at this stage of the war the Luftwaffe was losing more fighters in this way than were victims of the bomber's guns. General Kammhuber was sceptical, he was still reluctant to abandon his precious Himmelbett system completely, but for a time at least, 'Window' forced even the twin engine fighters to adopt the 'Wild Boar' tactics.

The Luftwaffe control rooms, called by the Germans 'Battle Opera Houses', were by now far more sophisticated than those available in the original Himmelbett system. Superficially resembling the Sector Operations Rooms of the Battle of Britain era, the tracks of bomber formations were filtered and displayed as light spots on large frosted glass screens. Controllers directed small groups of fighters against individual targets until the pilot's own Lichtenstein radar picked-up the

---

Wg Cdr J.H. Dyer – 61 Squadron

An entry in my logbook reads "Lancaster 'J' of 61 Squadron south of Stettin, height 22,000 feet, was fired on by a Me 210. Both gunners returned fire and saw smoke pouring from the enemy aircraft which fell away below. The Me 210 was claimed as destroyed. CONFIRMED BY BOMBER COMMAND".

The story now moves forward more than a quarter of a century to a hot, sunny afternoon in Naples. After a dull day of work at a NATO Air Order of Battle Conference I was enjoying a glass of cool beer with the Chairman, a Colonel in the German Air Force. The conversation almost inevitably went back to World War II. I learnt to my complete surprise that in a flying career which spanned almost all fronts from 1939 to 1945, the only time that Hans Munt had been shot down was by a Lancaster which he also claimed to have destroyed over Stettin in January 1944. A comparison of our logbooks soon confirmed that it was his Me 210 and our Lancaster which were involved in the incident. He had in fact baled out and celebrated his escape over a champagne breakfast. We had been pleased enough to settle for a beer or two after our crash landing in England!

target. 'Window' however not only cluttered the Wurzburg ground radar, but also badly interfered with the airborne radar as well. The Freya search radar on the other hand was not normally affected by 'Window' and the solution adopted was a form of broadcast control, a running commentary on the estimated position and track of the bomber stream which could still be identified with reasonable accuracy by an experienced sector controller. This broadcast enabled the night fighter crews to locate the bomber stream after which they had to acquire their own individual target. The fighters insinuated themselves into the bomber stream, picking-off their targets almost at will with five or more kills from a single sortie not unusual. This tactic was known as 'Zahme Sau' (Tame Boar). When both 'Wild' and 'Tame Boar' tactics were in use, the flak was restricted to a predetermined height of about 15,000 feet above which the fighters were given free rein.

Despite Hitler's obdurance, Erhard Milch, who had become responsible for aircraft production after Udets suicide in November 1941, tried to bolster the number of available fighters and for a time was successful. The total of day fighters increased, but even then they had to be supplemented by the twin engine fighters to meet the increasing weight of the 8th Air Force daylight raids. Goering was by now totally out of favour with Hitler, the Chief of the General Staff, Jeschonnek, committed suicide in August and Kammhuber was dismissed in September. By the end of the year, the night fighter operational strength fell to 240, exacerbated by a shortage of trained pilots. The successes which were achieved now depended on improved technology and fortunately for the Germans there were some significant advances at this time. The fire power of the fighters was increased, the Bf 110 was equipped with two 30 mm cannon as well as four 20 mm cannon and four 21 cm rockets. The Lichtenstein SN-2 radar was as yet impervious to jamming and two devices were introduced called 'Naxos' and 'Flensburg' which allowed fighters to home onto the bomber's H2S radar and 'Monica' tail warning radar respectively. These devices, allied with a new ground radar which was also resistant to 'Window', allowed the night fighters to continue to score steadily and at the time of the Battle of Berlin, the German night fighter defences enjoyed their longest period of sustained success, culminating in the heavy casualties which Bomber Command sustained at the end of March in the raid against Nuremberg. With the concentration on the support of 'Overlord', the heavy bombers only infrequently visited Germany after Nuremberg, but when they began to do so again in the Autumn, the Luftwaffe night fighter defences were already in rapid decline.

The Lichtenstein SN-2 radar array on the nose of a Bf 110 G-4.   IWM

CHAPTER SEVEN

Years of Fulfilment — 1944-45

The Nuremberg Raid — 30th March 1944

1943 had been a year of mixed fortunes for both sides. Despite the improvements in the Reich air defences, the Allies had dropped four times as many bombs on Germany as they had achieved in 1942. But on the debit side of the balance, the 'intermediate' objective of 'Pointblank' to defeat the German fighter defences had not been achieved: after Schweinfurt and Berlin the bomber forces had undoubtedly been forced onto the defensive. The high hopes following the successful Ruhr and Hamburg phases of Harris' crusade across Germany had proved a false dawn and the year had ended on a particularly sour note for the Combined Bomber Offensive. In the first place it could hardly be called combined, perhaps not even complementary: the pressing need of the Americans was to defeat the Luftwaffe to enable the 8th Air Force to pose a credible threat at all, whilst the British were doggedly hammering away at German cities in what proved to be almost the final fling of the area bombing offensive.

That the blunt instrument was not achieving the desired result and becoming increasingly costly in terms of casualties was only too evident to the Air Ministry in the early months of 1944 and once again they returned to the theme of a more selective bombing policy. In fact, by March Harris had been issued with a new list of priority objectives which did not specifically include Berlin and which he would have perceived as a return to the policy of 'panacea' targets, but which was in reality yet another re-iteration of 'Pointblank'. Harris, however, was to have one more tilt at area bombing before his attention was directed into other channels.

Nuremberg is perhaps most associated today with two political events of a very different if interrelated character: Hitler's infamous Nazi Party rallies of the pre-war years and the post war retribution in the form of the Nazi War Crimes Tribunal. Situated in northern Bavaria, it was a delightful medieval city with many beautiful buildings concentrated in the old town, the Altstadt, and celebrated in times past for the manufacture of toys. With a population of about half a million, Nuremberg also contained important engineering factories and thus had industrial as well as political importance. Furthermore, there were unsubstantiated reports in Bomber Command files that the morale of the population was fragile. In nearly every

respect, therefore, it met all of Harris' criteria for an area target. Interestingly, it lay midway, just 50 miles distant, from two cities which were on the Air Staff's priority list — Schweinfurt and Regensburg. If, therefore, conditions were right for attacking Nuremberg, they were just as likely to be suitable for these priority targets: it is an incontrovertible example of the way that Harris paid scant regard to the bombing directives given to him by the Air Ministry at this time, and which later in the year was to come inevitably to a head.

The weather always played a necessarily dominant role in the choice of target and the meteorological forecast for the night of the 30th March clearly pointed towards a target in southern Germany. Convection cloud was forecast for north Germany, a clear space to the south, and a good prospect of high frontal cloud lying across northern Bavaria which would provide cover for the bombers without obstructing the target. If, however, the skies were clear, the outbound leg would be bathed in the light of a half moon — this was destined to become of great significance. Sir Arthur Harris was in no doubt at his morning briefing and quickly selected Nuremberg, an area target which had not received the attention of Bomber Command for the previous seven months. Two meteorological flights during the day confirmed the presence of cumulous cloud in the north, but reported only low level stratocumulus with some thin cloud above in the area of Nuremberg. This was rather different from the morning forecast and did not augur well for the long leg across Germany to the target, but to the surprise of many did not alter Harris' decision to mount a full scale raid that night.

Route selection was also controversial. The more usual plan was to devise a succession of short legs avoiding known areas of flak concentration and fighter holding points, a tactic which also made it difficult for the German fighter control organisation to establish the intended target and marshal their fighters accordingly. On this occasion, the bombers were to make a dog leg south of the Ruhr, but then to follow a steady course of some 275 miles to a point north of Nuremberg before turning towards the target. Several potential targets would be threatened on the way and then bypassed. Mosquito decoy raids were tasked against Aachen, Cologne and Kassel to the north of the bomber stream, all credible targets, and a major diversion of 50 mine laying Halifaxes in the Heligoland area was intended to keep the north German fighter bases engaged. There were other minor diversions, all of which could be expected to play some part in deceiving the enemy defences. Apart from the suspect long leg, it was a credible plan, typical of the complex deception measures now second nature to Bomber Command. Although the decision to proceed was subsequently strongly criticized and the raid would doubtless have been cancelled if caution was the sole criteria, this attitude was alien to the temperament of both Harris and the bomber crews alike.

It was another night of maximum effort and the first of 790 bombers took off soon after nine o'clock. The force comprised 569 Lancasters, 212 Halifaxes and 9 Mosquitos. Assembling this mass of aircraft into a stream which would cross the target within just 17 minutes is inevitably a complex affair, but this was achieved without undue difficulty about midway across the North Sea and the snake, some 70 miles in length, headed for the first turning point near Charleroi, straddling levels either side of 20,000 feet. A little over 50 aircraft had already turned-back with technical problems: although it sounds a lot, this was an average figure for this size of raid and excludes some crews who would press-on despite defects. Two had crashed on take-off.

As so often, the key to a successful mission depended upon the success of the diversionary raids – would the fighters be drawn away to challenge the minor operations leaving the main

By the time of the Nuremberg raid at the end of March 1944, the Lancasters usually formed the major component of all large scale operations over Germany.   IWM

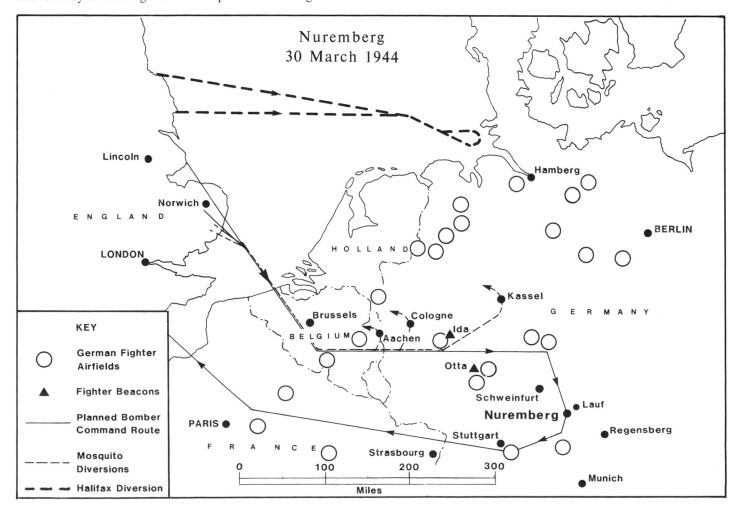

Nuremberg
30 March 1944

Lincoln

Norwich

E N G L A N D

LONDON

Hamberg

BERLIN

HOLLAND

Kassel

Brussels   Cologne

B E L G I U M   Aachen   Ida

G E R M A N Y

Otta

Schweinfurt

Nuremberg   Lauf

PARIS

Stuttgart   Regensberg

F R A N C E   Strasbourg

Munich

KEY

○ German Fighter Airfields

▲ Fighter Beacons

—— Planned Bomber Command Route

– – – Mosquito Diversions

▬ ▬ Halifax Diversion

0   100   200   300

Miles

force to proceed with relative safety? It was not an easy decision for the German fighter control organisation. It was always difficult to estimate the size of the force when the raiders were dispersing copious quantities of 'Window', and to add to the confusion the Mosquitos were dropping markers over the decoy targets to simulate the start of a major raid. In the event, three factors conspired to turn the Nuremberg raid into a disaster. The fighter controllers were not seriously misled by the decoys and virtually all available fighters converged on the main raid. Secondly, two radio beacons, codenamed 'Ida' and 'Otta', to which German fighters homed like moths to a light, lay conveniently either side of the long leg. Finally, the promised high cloud had not materialised and the bomber stream was exposed to a clear moonlight night. To add to their problems, vapour trails were evident down to lower levels than normal.

Over 200 night fighters homed in from all corners of Germany in good time to catch the stream in perfect weather conditions for night interception. Using 'Tame Boar' tactics, the fighters infiltrated into the bomber stream which had now become somewhat scattered because the wind was not quite as forecast, and in little over 200 miles no less than 59 bombers were shot down on the long leg. Although a few fell to flak, the majority succumbed to Bf 110s and Ju 88s with some crews credited with four or more victims, and as usual it was the more experienced pilots who were the most successful. If the level of training and experience in the night fighter squadrons had been higher, there is little doubt that the carnage could have been far worse. Mosquito 'Serrate' night fighters accompanying the bombers made no impact whatsoever and only the pathfinders at the head of the stream escaped relatively unscathed. The bomber stream now enjoyed their one slice of luck, for the fighter controllers misjudged the intended target and four gruppes of Bf 109 'Wild Boar' aircraft which could have engaged the bombers over Nuremberg were not brought into play. Even so, many of the night fighters observed the turn to the south and 20 more aircraft were destroyed during the final leg and run-in to the target.

The absence of cloud cover had contributed greatly to the casualties suffered on the way to Nuremberg, its presence was now largely to thwart the accurate bombing of the target itself for the 650 or so aircraft which remained in the force. The plan had envisaged 'Newhaven' visual marking with 'Wanganui' sky marking as an emergency fallback. Nine Mosquitos and 92 Lancasters were tasked with the marking, most of which had escaped the holocaust which had beset the main force. Unfortunately, solid cloud now covered the target and visual marking was impossible, leaving the bomb aimers no alternative to marking on H2S. This was never likely to be as accurate as visual or Oboe marking, but at Nuremberg the problem was exacerbated by the fact that the nearby town of Lauf had a similar ground/river configuration. Furthermore, as the inaccurate forecast wind had driven several aircraft north of track, it was not entirely surprising that there was confusion in the marking. In fact, two distinct areas were marked, one correctly over Nuremberg itself, but with a larger concentration

---

Flt Lt F.P.G. Hall DFC – 76 Squadron

I had made my first trip of 8 hours to Nuremberg on the 27th August 1943. My 26th on the 30th March 1944 was rather more spectacular. We were in the last wave and fighters were seen to be up in strength as we crossed the Rhine. Aircraft were continually falling out of the sky on fire and I gave up logging them. One minute after leaving the target we were shattered as cannon fire suddenly hit us from underneath putting the starboard inner engine out of action. The navigation table was covered in debris, the wireless set hit, the starboard wing, bomb bay and fuselage on fire. The pilot dived twice to put out flames and we all tackled the fires with extinguishers, eventually successfully. As if this was not enough, 12 minutes later we were approached by a fighter from dead astern, but we took evasive action and he passed 50 yards over the tail receiving full blasts from both gunners.

Fuel was now disappearing fast from a broken fuel pipe and so we made straight for the nearest part of the French coast. We crossed the Channel safely and headed for Ford, but this airfield was full of circling aircraft so we continued on to Tangmere. The Engineer had to take an axe to the undercarriage uplock housing to manually release the jammed starboard leg. We landed, but swung off the runway as the tyres were burst. A fuel check after landing showed that we had only 5 minutes fuel remaining.

The Squadron Engineer flew down from Holme on Spalding Moor the following morning to confirm that the aircraft was beyond repair, indeed, he couldn't understand why the starboard wing had not folded. But our only injury was found the following morning when the Wireless Operator discovered his cigarette case had been flattened by a cannon shell and he had a bruise on his right hip!

I had never seen so many aircraft attacked, on fire and falling, or so many attacks by fighters so early in a trip. I felt sure that my 26th trip was going to be my last.

(The pilot and Flt Lt Hall were awarded immediate DFCs.)

---

10 miles to the east over Lauf. The main force, the majority of which in any case arrived five minutes later than the scheduled zero hour of 0105, now had a choice of targets to bomb as the sky markers had drifted in the wind. A few chose correctly, but the majority selected the incorrect cluster to the east with some settling for the black hole in the middle. With the well known factor of creep-back now coming into play, comparatively few bombs fell on Nuremberg itself; many more were scattered to the north and east. Over 100 aircraft never bombed Nuremberg at all, mistaking Schweinfurt for their real target. Very little damage was done to the city and none at all to the main industrial units: the vulnerable old town did not succumb to the incendiaries. Lauf and some of the suburbs received more substantial damage, but there were few civilian casualties.

The bombers were widely scattered by the time they departed the target area. Many of course had not reached

Individual aircraft by 1944 were compiling impressive totals of operational raids; 'N' for 'Nan' of No 100 Squadron had just completed 100 sorties when this picture was taken.   IWM

Nuremberg at all and turned for home some 50 miles to the north. Fortunately, the night fighters had almost exhausted their effort, but even so 10 more bombers were lost to flak or fighters, a Halifax and a Lancaster collided and two more crashed into the sea. The fickle weather had one more trick to play, for snow showers and low cloud were now covering much of eastern England and many aircraft had to be diverted; several crashed or crash landed.

The final toll only became fully apparent the next day. Ninety four aircraft had not returned from the mission and another 14 had crashed in England or off the coast. Over 700 airmen were missing with the unusually large number of 545 killed. It was Bomber Commands most expensive major raid of the war with a loss rate of 13.6 per cent, but even this did not match some of the loss rates of the Americans in their daylight raids. Following the loss of 78 aircraft on the Leipzig raid and another 73 against Berlin only six nights before Nuremberg, the first three months of 1944 had been a severe setback to Bomber Command. The Battle of Berlin by which Harris had vowed to end the war had turned into a clear victory for the Luftwaffe – it was not to be their last success, but from now on the trend began to move in favour of the Allies.

'Big Week' – and 'Big B'

Schweinfurt had proved the most significant milestone yet in the 8th Air Force's commitment to the Combined Bomber Offensive and put at risk the American contribution to 'Pointblank', a policy to which Bomber Command as we have seen had paid only intermittent attention since its inception. It also led the USAAF higher command to review its contribution to the strategic offensive and influenced the decision to divert a considerable part of the force earmarked for the 8th to the newly formed 15th Air Force in Italy. Even so, such was the pace of America's military build-up that the size of the 8th's bomber force was to double between October 1943 and June 1944.

However, it was the weather rather than any definitive change in policy which conditioned VIII Bomber Commands activity during the Winter months. A constant blanket of cloud seemed to shroud north west Europe for most of the period,

severely restricting the opportunities for visual bombing. A few aircraft were now equipped with Oboe and H2S and used in the pathfinding role, but these were dogged with technical malfunctions causing missions either to be abandoned or bombs dropped in the wrong locations. During December a new operational task was undertaken under the code name of 'Noball', the bombing of V-I launch sites and storage areas in the Pas de Calais. But in sum, 8th Air Force achieved very little in the last two months of 1943 although losses to enemy action were also reduced, a welcome respite after the disastrous raids of August and October. Of increasing concern, however, was the number of aircraft lost in accidents due to technical failures or inexperienced crews. A particularly intractable problem in both the B-17 and the B-24 was runaway propellers which could quickly cause the aircraft to become uncontrollable if the feathering unit failed.

The turn of the year also saw a refashioning of the command structure. A new organisation called the United States Strategic Air Forces in Europe (USSTAF) was set-up at Bushey Park to co-ordinate the activities of the 8th and 15th Air Forces and the 8th moved to VIII Bomber Command's headquarters at High Wycombe, the latter command being disbanded. There was also a change of leadership with General Eaker, who felt perhaps that he was being made a scapegoat for the misfortunes of the Autumn, moving to a command in the Mediterranean. General Carl Spaatz took over the new command at Bushey Park and the legendary General James Doolittle was translated to 8th Air Force from North Africa.

1944 started in much the same vein as the previous year had ended with the weather generally proscribing activity. The P-51 Mustang was now entering operational service in greater numbers to complement the Lightnings and shorter range Thunderbolts and it was now becoming feasible once again to mount long range missions into Germany if only the weather would relent. One major operation was possible on the 11th January against aircraft factories at Oscherleben and Halberstadt, but the weather interfered with the join-up of the fighter escort and no less than 34 B-17s were shot down out of the 1st Division's 174 aircraft attacking the Fw 190 plant at Oscherleben. Despite over half of the force being recalled when it was realised that the weather was not co-operating, 60 bombers in all were lost in the two raids with many more damaged.

The third week of February saw a high pressure system at last settling over central Europe and the frustrated commanders of 8th Air Force decided to make a supreme effort to regain the initiative. It subsequently became known as the 'Big Week' and

Top: Although 8th Air Force was restricted to day bombing, aircraft often departed on their mission before dawn as shown by this picture of a B-17 taking off. IWM

Below: 8th Air Force concentrated on aircraft production facilities during 'Big Week' in February 1944. These B-17s are bombing Weiner Neustadt where there was a large Messerschmitt factory. IWM

was the most sustained assault yet in pursuance of the 'Pointblank' directive. Although the loss rate had dropped significantly from a high of nine per cent in October to just over three during the Winter months, it was quite clear that the Luftwaffe fighter units had plenty of life in them yet.

Nearly a thousand bombers were marshalled for the first raid of 'Big Week' on the 20th February. The whole stream headed for Brunswick after which they dispersed for individual targets, all aircraft factories. Several intense encounters with the Luftwaffe ensued, but 835 fighters had been tasked as escort, losing only 11 against a claim of 61 enemy aircraft destroyed. The bomber losses were only 21 and several groups reported good bombing conditions, the Bf 109 factory at Leipzig being particularly hard hit. The following day saw almost a thousand bombers launched again, but weather conditions were poor and results, using H2S, variable. However, it was another comparatively quiet day for casualties, the weather for once clearly hampering the ground defences. A major effort was mounted again the following day, but weather conditions forced the recall of both the 2nd and 3rd Divisions. There were also two unfortunate accidents on this day when one aircraft bombed Nijmegen by mistake causing 850 Dutch casualties and another bomb accidentally released over England killed three people. Although only 99 aircraft found their targets, useful damage resulted to aircraft factories at Aschersleben and Bernburg. Casualties rose dramatically again to 41 because the fighter escort, hampered by weather, was only able to escort the 1st Division intermittently.

After a days respite, 800 bombers were tasked again on the 24th. The Luftwaffe also changed its tactics on this occasion, intercepting the mainstream early over Holland and using rockets, aerial mines and cable towed bombs in addition to their by now more conventional head-on attacks. The Liberators suffered heavily on this occasion and in all 49 bombers were lost. Despite these losses, yet another force of over 800 bombers was assembled on the 25th to attack aircraft factories at Furth, Regensburg and Augsburg. Good results were achieved for a loss of 31 aircraft. The weather closed in again on the following day and 'Big Week' was over; 3,300 sorties had been flown, but over 400 aircraft had been lost or damaged beyond repair. Some parts of the German aircraft industry had taken a severe battering, but the dispersal of factories mitigated the overall damage and the Jagdgeschwader had by no means yet been defeated. The Luftwaffe was increasingly dependent, however, upon their most experienced fighter pilots, some of whom were now building a creditable score of victories, and 'Big Week' took its toll of their diminishing numbers.

One target which the 8th had not yet attempted was Berlin. Bomber Command of course had been visiting the city regularly since 1940 and the American crews were becoming increasingly impatient to add this prestige target, known to them as 'Big B', to their list. The Mustang was now available in sufficient numbers to escort the bombers all the way, and after one abortive attempt on the 3rd March, the first B-17s penetrated to the capital on the following day. In fact, the force had been

The advent of the P-51 Mustang brought Berlin into the 8th Air Force target lists for the first time in March 1944. This aircraft of the 357FG is landing at Leiston in Suffolk. IWM

recalled because of weather, but one combat wing of three groups failed to receive the message and although bombing accuracy was poor in bad weather, only four aircraft were lost. Although the Germans may have been caught by surprise on this first occasion, they were now fully alerted to this new daylight target and waiting for the next raid which predictably came two days later. Nearly 800 bombers escorted by the same number of fighters set-off on a clear, cold day, and some of the heaviest fighting yet seen was experienced by the leading 1st Division. The main casualties, however, were experienced by the 3rd Division in the middle of the stream when an alert fighter controller recognised that they were unescorted. Whilst the 2nd Division in the rear escaped relatively unscathed, in all 69 bombers were shot down and 105 severely damaged. The 350th Bombardment Squadron lost no less than ten of its aircraft and other squadrons were almost as severely depleted.

Shaken, but not deterred, General Doolittle launched another 600 bombers to Berlin two days later. Unlike the previous occasion when bombing results were poor, this mission produced some very accurate results, but at the cost of another 37 bombers shot down. A smaller force went yet again the next day, this time losing only nine; the fighters too were becoming exhausted. The weather now intervened and only one more raid was attempted in the remaining days of March. It had been a testing period and February and March 1944 produced some of the heaviest American casualty figures of the war. But there was

now a flood of new aircraft and crews to replace those lost and damaged and in February the 8th Air Force at last overtook Bomber Command in terms of the numbers of aircraft and crews available for combat. The tide was definitely turning, but new tasks were ahead: the long promised second front was soon to be opened and both the USAAF and the RAF had major roles to play.

A Welcome Diversion – Operation 'Overlord'

In mid 1943, with the undeniably successful attack on Hamburg, it appeared that Bomber Command had turned the corner in its strategic onslaught upon the industrial might and morale of the Third Reich. But the Winter raids against Berlin and other major cities, culminating in the disastrous attack on Nuremburg on the 30th March 1944, had again tilted the balance in the opposite direction. The German night fighter was beginning to establish a dangerous primacy which suggested a reappraisal of Harris' tactics was necessary.

Despite the unacceptable losses, however, Bomber Command was at last attaining the strength and power for which

This dramatic picture shows a B-17, a German fighter (top left) and another bomber exploding after a direct hit by flak. IWM

it had been so earnestly waiting since the dark and distant days of 1940 when circumstances had dictated a policy no more aggressive than distributing paper across the length and breadth of Germany. After April 1944, the average daily availability of heavy bombers never dropped below one thousand of which two thirds were Lancasters. The number of Stirlings in the front line was steadily reducing – it was to be withdrawn altogether by October – and the more capable Mk III Halifax was replacing the earlier models. Mosquitos, of which there were on average 120 available every day by October, were playing a small but increasingly valuable role both in pathfinding and independent bomber operations. The 8th Air Force was also at last achieving its latent potential, producing more than one thousand bombers a day from April 1944, with 15th Air Force operating from bases in central Italy providing a valuable diversion in the 'soft underbelly' of Europe. A new strategy was nevertheless required despite this rapidly developing capability, for although hindsight has shown that the Luftwaffe's strength rested on extremely flimsy foundations, it was by no means overwhelmed by the Spring of 1944. Fortunately, an alternative policy was available, indeed the developing political scenario would have dictated a change of direction even if it had not been desirable on other grounds.

It will be recalled that 'Pointblank' had never been seen as an end in itself although the interim objective of neutralising the Luftwaffe air defences had tended to overshadow its underlying

intention which was to prepare the ground for the invasion of Europe. In 1943 the Combined Bomber Offensive had been intended to achieve air superiority, a disruption of the German industrial and military base and a decline in morale, all necessary preconditions for a successful land invasion. Although none of these pre-requisites had been totally achieved at the beginning of 1944, the invasion could not be further delayed. The land conquest of Europe could not be left to the Russians as Churchill had long recognised and the United States, although somewhat reluctantly supporting the indirect approach through Italy, was anxious that the Second Front should be launched as soon as possible. The immediate tactical requirements of Operation 'Overlord' thus increasingly came into direct confliction with the strategic objectives of 'Pointblank'. The direct support of the invasion was too large a task for the tactical air forces alone and it was inevitable that at least some part of the strategic force would need to be diverted to this end. Given Harris' and, to a slightly lesser extent, Spaatz's single minded devotion to the strategic cause, it was hardly to be expected that this change of direction would be achieved without some acrimony.

Planning for 'Overlord' had been proceeding in something of a vacuum throughout most of 1943 under Lieutenant General F

Some of the preliminary planning for Operation 'Overlord' was accomplished at the Quebec Conference in August 1943 attended by General Arnold and ACM Sir Charles Portal who struck up a good working relationship throughout the war. IWM

AM Sir Trafford Leigh-Mallory, here seen with General Montgomery's Chief of Staff, General de Guingand, was responsible for air operations in support of 'Overlord'. IWM

E Morgan. At this time, the main air requirement was seen as the maintenance of air superiority over the landing beaches and it thus seemed appropriate to give this task to a fighter specialist, Air Marshal Sir Trafford Leigh-Mallory, the favoured Group Commander in the Battle of Britain and currently the Commander-in-Chief Fighter Command. The American contribution was to be provided by the 9th Air Force, hesitantly being brought together throughout 1943, but in direct competition with the 8th Air Force for the inadequate supply of fighters arriving from the United States. Command and control, given the sensitivities always surrounding this vital function, inevitably caused difficulties and the delay in appointing a Supreme Commander did not help to clarify the situation. Leigh-Mallory had been appointed Commander-in-Chief of the Allied Expeditionary Air Force at the Quebec conference in August 1943 although 9th Air Force did not come under his command until December. General Eisenhower was at last appointed as the Supreme Commander in December 1943 and took as his deputy Air Chief Marshal Sir Arthur Tedder with whom he had worked harmoniously in the Mediterranean theatre. At this stage no conclusions had been reached as to how the strategic air forces might be assimilated into the structure. The responsibilities of Leigh-Mallory and Harris to Portal also inevitably clouded the issue. The respective roles of Tedder, Leigh-Mallory, Harris and Spaatz thus remained equivocal and each had his own idea of the primary objectives.

Leigh-Mallory produced an ambitious and comprehensive plan in March 1944 which envisaged far more than just attaining air superiority over the bridgehead. Whilst making some concessions to the continuance of 'Pointblank', its main feature was an extensive assault on the railway system within northern France to disrupt the ability of the Germans, benefitting from interior lines of communication, to reinforce their defensive posture. The aim was to isolate the Wehrmacht in France whilst at the same time, by the mounting of an extensive deception operation, conceal the actual location of the invasion thrust. In this latter aim it was entirely successful and Leigh-Mallory's plan was undoubtedly a sensible and constructive ingredient of the overall strategy. But it could not be implemented without the extensive assistance of the strategic bomber forces, still at this time concentrating their effort against the heartland of Germany itself. It was, nevertheless, a plan hardly likely to commend itself to either Harris or Spaatz.

Despite the losses in the opening months of 1944, Harris saw no reason to depart from his by now well established strategy of an area offensive against the main industrial cities. He was appalled at the thought of allowing Germany a respite from the sustained assault that he could now mount with around a thousand bombers every day that the weather was suitable. He argued, as fiercely and persuasively as ever, that allowing the German industrial base to recover from the pounding it had received throughout 1943 would in itself harm 'Overlord' which even now he only reluctantly conceded was necessary. Furthermore, he fell back upon one of his original arguments in support of area bombing, his force simply could not hit at night

General Eisenhower, here seen with AM Sir Arthur Tedder and General Montgomery, was given control of the strategic bomber forces in the lead up to 'Overlord'. IWM

the precision targets demanded by the Leigh-Mallory plan.

Spaatz opposed the plan on rather different lines. He still saw the primary requirement as the neutralisation of the Luftwaffe, not only by destroying the aircraft factories, but increasingly, with the advent of the Mustang, in drawing the German fighters into combat and destroying them in the air. To achieve this he had to force the Luftwaffe to fight by attacking targets they could not ignore, and he saw the old 'panacea' – synthetic oil plants – as the means to this end. Spaatz too, although he phrased his arguments rather more diplomatically than Harris, was equally opposed to any substantial diversion of effort to prepare for and support the landings in Normandy.

However, there can be little doubt, persuasive though their arguments were, that it was inconceivable that the prospects of 'Overlord' could in any way be jeopardised by the lack of air support. The reinvasion of Europe had been the central plank of the Allies policy since the Casablanca Conference. Massive resources had been devoted, particularly by the Americans, to the development of an infrastructure of troops, marine craft, support arms and administrative organisations to promote a Second Front in Europe, and despite the many distractions and diversions en route, it was an inevitable and inescapable commitment. It was going to happen, and Harris and Spaatz were going to be compelled to support it no matter where their own inclinations might have led them. Even so, the way forward was not trouble free and in the end Eisenhower, loyally and skilfully abetted by Tedder, had to deploy all his many attributes of co-ordination, diplomacy and authority before agreement was eventually reached.

It was not until all the various concepts had been examined at

a historic meeting on the 25th March that the communications plan was adopted, in the words of the official historian, 'more in a spirit of desperation than of optimism'. In one of his more maverick moods, Mr Churchill now objected to the plan on the grounds of the potential casualties among the civilian population in the occupied countries, but was brusquely overruled by Roosevelt who insisted that the decision must be left to the military commander.

Spaatz, a more subtle man than Harris, continued to work on Eisenhower and eventually persuaded him that the oil plan was complementary to rather than in opposition to the communications plan, and in the end the strategic element of the latter fell largely upon Bomber Command – ironically so as they were apparently the less able of the two strategic air forces to implement a precision bombing campaign. Harris, however, had achieved a well justified reputation for pursuing his own course irrespective of higher direction, but this was unexpectedly countered in April by the transfer of the control of the strategic bomber force from Portal to Eisenhower, an arrangement which would last until September when the precarious toehold in Europe was at last secure. In practice, despite Harris' worst fears, the diversion to 'Overlord' was not only to provide welcome respite to Bomber Command, but in a number of ways was to be positively beneficial. Moreover, Harris also proved to be unusually deferential to the Supreme Commander, a loyalty he consistently withheld from his own chief, Portal.

The Renaissance of Precision Bombing

Bomber Command had abandoned precision bombing in 1941 not because, at that time, it preferred the mass destruction of cities, but because it was recognised, albeit belatedly, that the means to hit precise targets at night simply did not exist with the technology available. For three years, therefore, it had pursued a policy of saturation area bombing with the objective of generally disrupting the German economic and social systems. Inevitably many individual industrial and communications sites important to the German military and industrial base were damaged in the process, but the impact was variable, a consequential effect rather than the fulfilment of a definitive objective. Sir Arthur Harris had become totally converted to the area concept and genuinely believed that although precision had been achieved in special operations such as the dams and Peenemünde raids, it was not a viable objective for the main stream of Bomber Command.

The Air Staff, and Portal in particular, was not so sure. They believed, with some justification, that Harris' view was coloured by his own conception of the strategic role of Bomber Command and for this reason devalued the advances in navigation and bomb aiming techniques and the increasing accuracy in target marking pioneered by the Pathfinder Force. Portal proposed, therefore, in February 1944 that a trial should be held to determine just how accurately the Command could hit a precise target, and what better choice than marshalling

yards in France which were at the heart of the 'Overlord' communications plan. Six specific sites were mentioned – Trappes, Aulnoye, Le Mans, Amiens, Coutrai and Laon – all nodal points in the network of communications from Germany which sustained their forward troops in the Channel areas.

Under the forceful direction of Don Bennett, the Pathfinder Force had made remarkable progress in developing their techniques for marking an area target and reinforcing or adjusting the point of aim as necessary during a prolonged large scale raid. It was less suited and did not have the resources necessary to support a series of smaller simultaneous raids on a larger number of precision targets where it was important that the whole force bombed accurately; for whereas stray bombs in Germany might achieve some useful collateral damage, in France and the Low Countries they would more probably kill friendly civilians. We have already noted Mr Churchill's concern regarding this aspect of the communications plan.

Nevertheless, conventional methods of marking were used for the first phase of the 'Overlord' plan which began on the 6th March with a raid against Trappes. Mosquitos from the

Trappes marshalling yard in northern France was one of the targets used to assess the accuracy of Allied bombing in April 1944. The success is apparent from this recce photograph taken on the following day. RAFM

Pathfinder Force provided the marking by blind Oboe techniques and it was not until the fourteenth and last of the initial series on the 10th April against Aulnoye that a master bomber was used to visually assess and correct the marking accuracy. The results were reasonably encouraging and five marshalling yards were adjudged to be effectively destroyed although photographic reconnaissance disclosed that 25 per cent of bombs were still falling well outside the estimated average error of 640 yards. Whilst a phenomenal improvement on the bombing accuracy observed in 1942, clearly still greater accuracy was required both to economise on effort and, more particularly, to avoid unnecessary risk to the French population.

Nevertheless, the results were sufficiently impressive to justify Portal's faith in the Bomber Command contribution to the 'Overlord' plan and for the next three months their effort was almost entirely directed against objectives in France, not

V-1 (Crossbow sites) were a regular diversion for Bomber Command in 1944. This site in the Pas de Calais is being attacked by Halifaxes in July before they were overrun by the advancing Allied armies. IWM

only communications, but V-I sites and other military targets. The most significant aspect, however, of this phase was the impact it had on the techniques for precision bombing. These proved to be of vital importance when the strategic campaign was recommenced against Germany in July. For all practical purposes, it transformed Bomber Command from an area to a precision force and enabled their effort to be directed eventually against the jugular vein of the German war effort, the synthetic oil plants.

An important decision in April was the employment of No 5 Group as an independent force using its own marking techniques. Two pathfinder Lancaster squadrons, Nos 83 and 97, were attached to the Group, but of greater significance was the experience of No 617 Squadron which had pioneered precision bombing. Furthermore, the Squadron was now commanded by the outstanding bomber pilot of the war, Wing Commander Leonard Cheshire. Cheshire recognised that marking accuracy was usually a factor of the height above the target and developed with the Mosquito a system in which the aircraft dived at the target at an angle of about 30 degrees and,

using the gun site for aiming, released red spot markers from very low level. These were reinforced by Lancasters from a higher level and above this the main force bombed in comparative safety on markers which should have been laid very precisely. The technique was tried against an aircraft factory in Toulouse on the 5th April and photographic evidence disclosed that every building on the site had been destroyed or badly damaged. Evaluation of subsequent raids showed that the average bombing error could now be reduced to only 285 yards. However, even when accurately marked in the first instance, the target could soon disappear in the haze of smoke and glare, making identification and remarking difficult. Cheshire now developed an ingenious offset technique by which the markers were dropped about 400 yards from the target and a false wind vector fed to the main force. The latter then aimed as usual at the markers, but because of the wind offset set in the bomb

It was by no means a rare occurrence for an aircraft to be struck by bombs from above in both 8th Air Force and RAF operations. This picture shows a Liberator of No 37 Squadron which was damaged in this way over Monfalcone in Italy. RAFM

sight, their bombs actually fell on the target rather than the markers. The master bomber, who was quite frequently Cheshire himself, then corrected the accuracy as necessary throughout the raid. The technique was later extended to targets in Germany with considerable success at Brunswick and Munich and only marginally less accurately against that old favourite, the ball bearing factory at Schweinfurt. Other long established techniques were modified during this period and it is not too strong to say that Bomber Command made a quantum leap forward in the efficiency and accuracy of its operations in the three months from April to June 1944. It vindicated the views of the Air Staff and even caused Harris himself to express surprise at the accuracy achieved. It came as less of a surprise to the crews of Bomber Command who did not doubt their ability to carry-out the task if an enlightened visionary could identify the method. Such a man was Leonard Cheshire, supported by the most innovative and vigorous of the Group Commanders, AVM Ralph Cochrane.

The same aircraft after landing. RAFM

No man contributed more than Gp Capt Leonard Cheshire to the development of precision bombing techniques in the second half of the war.
IWM

Flt Lt F. Fish – 153 Squadron

On the night of 31st October 1944 our target was Cologne with a total of 493 aircraft. On our run in to the target to bomb, we suddenly heeled over to starboard, and thinking that it was flak under our port wing which had lifted us up, just straightened and continued. I noted in the log that we bombed at 2108 and were holed in our starboard wing. The Wireless Operator (who was keeping a look-out in the astrodome over the target) now revealed that he had seen a 1000lb bomb coming straight at us from above. When asked in no uncertain terms why he had not shouted a warning, he replied "I was too paralysed to speak". We eventually agreed that perhaps this was understandable. When we examined the aircraft the following day, we discovered that by a miracle it had missed the starboard petrol tank by about three inches. Fortunately the bomb had not completed its arming cycle and did not explode. I suspect that we must have lost quite a few of our own aircraft in this way.

Target Systems

Throughout the war so far, the accessibility of those target systems upon which the planners would most liked to have concentrated had frequently been inhibited by operational factors beyond the control of the force commanders. Their choice had been constrained by many factors of which the most important were the inability of Bomber Command to destroy precise targets at night, the continuing battle which the 8th Air Force was forced to wage against the fighter defences to stay alive, and the demands upon both to concentrate on short term objectives in times of perceived crisis. The latter constraint existed to a limited extent almost to the end of the war, for example the need to neutralise the V-2 sites, but by the middle of 1944 the strategic bomber forces at last had the strength, the expertise and the relative invulnerability to bring their immense striking power to bear upon whatever target system was judged by the planners to prove most beneficial towards a rapid conclusion of the conflict. It had taken five long years of unrelenting effort, of frustration and disappointment, controversy and rancour, of problems undreamed of by those who before the war had seen the employment of the strategic bomber in such simple terms. It is thus appropriate at this stage to consider the major target systems in more detail to assess their relative claims to primacy, for even now controversy still bedevilled the employment of the bombers.

Three main target systems may be identified; oil, communications and industrial/economic objectives. There were of course other objectives which did not fit neatly into any of these categories of which the direct support of ground forces was the most important in 1944. But our analysis may be confined to these three which were the focus for discussion and often dissension after the end of the direct commitment to 'Overlord'.

Along with the railways, the advent of the internal combustion engine had revolutionised warfare in the twentieth century, leading directly to the development of the aeroplane and the tank, the two machines which dominated the course of the Second World War. But in consequence, the dependence upon fuel oil had merely replaced that upon forage which had sustained the mobility and striking power of armies in previous generations which were so reliant upon the horse. Whereas these armies could hope to a large extent to live off the land over which they were fighting, oil was not so readily available, and one of the key factors limiting Germany's military potential was the lack of an indigenous source of crude oil. One of the most significant advantages to Hitler of the Ribbentrop-Molotov pact of 1939 had been the ability to import oil from Russia, and nearby Romania, Austria and Hungary were other valuable sources of supply. Even so, this potential weakness was very evident to both sides from the outbreak of war and oil had been the first of the 'panacea' targets in 1941.

Germany had sought to redress its weakness by the creation of plants for the production of synthetic oil and substitute products such as methane gas. The synthetic plants and the refineries for crude oil had been widely distributed throughout

Germany and her dependent territories such as Czechoslovakia and Silesia which were thought originally to be beyond the range of air attack. A significant number, however, were as close as the Ruhr and central Germany, which were demonstrably well within the reach of the Allied bombers, and two thirds of the production of aviation spirit came from just seven synthetic plants. Their destruction in 1944 would for all practical purposes have driven the Luftwaffe from the skies. It is also probably true to say that, as with other parts of their military/industrial base, the Germans did not fully appreciate the vulnerability of their oil supplies until it was too late.

This lack of awareness certainly did not afflict the Ministry for Economic Warfare and the Joint Intelligence Committee who had never ceased to stress the importance of the oil plants and, furthermore, had generally accurately established which were the most critical. Nevertheless, the problem remained that hitherto they had been a difficult objective to hit effectively by day and almost impossible at night. As a result, despite rapidly increasing consumption, Germany's stock of oil had steadily increased until by May 1944 it stood at nearly 1.4 million tons, over one third of which was aviation spirit. However, once the strategic forces had the ability to strike at these relatively small installations, it only required the collective will to single them out as the most profitable target system to shorten the war. The Americans of course had been more concerned throughout 1943 and early 1944 to counter the threat of the Luftwaffe; but as we have already seen, General Spaatz strongly pressed the case for attacking oil in the early part of 1944 and actually commenced a sustained offensive in May. At this time Bomber Command was heavily involved in the pre 'Overlord' plan, but Harris too started to give spasmodic attention to oil targets from June onwards.

The initial raids by Bomber Command were far from promising. On three nights a total of 832 Lancasters and Halifaxes were dispatched to four targets in the Ruhr valley – Gelsenkirchen, Sterkrade, Wesseling and Buer. On the first of these against Gelsenkirchen on the 12th June, using the conventional Oboe blind marking technique, only 15 of the 271 aircraft dispatched hit the target although the damage was considerable. The bombers were severely harassed by night fighters and 21 (9.3 per cent) failed to return. The second raid four nights later against Sterkrade in unfavourable weather conditions suffered even higher casualties, 31 aircraft lost in return for some damage to the plant. Similar weather conditions prevailed on the 21st June and the force was briefed to drop on H2S if the markers could not be seen. They were not and, predictably, little damage was caused. The weather did not inhibit the night fighters and no less than 45 Lancasters were destroyed: in the Wesseling raid, the loss rate was a massive 28 per cent. In all four raids, 93 aircraft had been lost and not surprisingly this did little to enhance Harris' opinion of the oil option. However, there was no reason to believe that the same losses would not have resulted from conventional area attacks and thus no justification for abandoning the target system, only reviewing the method of attack.

The American attack on oil had been initiated by 15th Air Force in April with raids against the oil plants at Ploesti which had been the focus of the costly operation the previous August. By June 1944 their output had been cut by half and by August the oil fields had been overrun by the Russians. The 8th Force joined in with a massive raid of 886 bombers on the 12th May against five separate targets in Central Germany. Despite the brisk attention of German fighters who claimed 46 aircraft, bombing from 18,000 feet in clear skies was accurate and considerable damage achieved at all targets. An even larger raid was mounted on the 28th of 1,282 aircraft, of which nearly a third were Liberators, against seven targets. And so it continued throughout the Summer. Although there were many diversions, oil plants across the length and breadth of Germany were attacked at every opportunity with the 15th Air Force, freed of its commitment to Ploesti, concentrating on refineries in Austria and Hungary.

The results exceeded even the planners most optimistic expectations. In June, the German output of petrol and aviation spirit dropped to half that produced in April and by September it had dropped to less than a quarter. Desperate efforts were made by the Germans to protect the plants, particularly those producing aviation spirit, and a virtual wall of heavy flak now surrounded the most important sites. Albert Speer also ordered a supreme effort to repair the damaged plants and some were put back into production time and time again. For a while this effort showed some return, production actually rose again in October and November as the onset of bad weather made bombing conditions more difficult. This period was also that in which Harris most neglected his primary objective and returned to the area bombing of cities. By this time oil production in the Ruhr had been dramatically reduced, but plants farther east, particularly in Poland which 8th Air Force could not reach in the shorter days of Winter continued to produce substantial amounts of aviation spirit.

In December, however, Harris at last turned his full attention to oil targets and concentrated on the remaining plants in the east, assisted by 15th Air Force who attacked targets in Silesia. Leuna and Politz were heavily and successfully bombed and in February the Russians began to overrun the most easterly installations. By this time the supply of aviation spirit had dropped to a trickle and the Luftwaffe was reduced to little more than the occasional sortie. Although motor fuel was not quite so badly affected, the Ardennes offensive in December had largely exhausted reserves. From March 1945 onwards there was no further production of aviation spirit at all and the few remaining stocks of other fuels were being rapidly consumed. Even this source became increasingly limited as the bombers now turned their attention to the storage depots.

There can be no doubt that the final concentration against oil which had started almost a year before made a decisive contribution to the Allied victory, assured though it already may have been. Furthermore, driving the Luftwaffe from the skies, which had largely been achieved by September 1944, opened-up other strategic targets which could be attacked with near

impunity. Although Bomber Command made a substantial contribution towards the end of the campaign, it was really the combined efforts of 8th and 15th Air Forces which had paved the way. If only Harris had not prevaricated for so long, it is conceivable that the Ardennes offensive would not have been possible and the war ended several months earlier. The first 'panacea' target had undoubtedly shown the sound judgement of the planning staff, but it had taken five long years to deliver the proof.

Even so, not all the Allied leaders were entirely united in the 'oil plan'. Sir Arthur Tedder's preference was for the main weight of attack to be brought against the communications systems, often described as the 'transport plan', although he too recognised that attacking oil targets was one of its principle constituents. Tedder's experience in Sicily and Italy as a tactical air force commander had impressed upon him the extent to which the enemy's ground operations depended upon the availability and reliability of a comprehensive transport system. He saw little different in the situation in north west Europe: the war he believed would be brought to a successful conclusion by

The supply of oil became critical for Germany in the latter half of 1944. This B-24 is bombing a refinery at Shulau near Hamburg. IWM

the defeat of the enemy's military forces and the occupation of their territory. The air forces, strategic and tactical, could best be used to facilitate their advance.

But whereas the production and refining of oil was contained within a hundred or so well defined sites, there was a plethora of possible communications targets. Again, whilst oil was clearly a strategic rather than a tactical target, communications could fit into either category, the distinction often itself becoming blurred. There was always a risk, therefore, that the concentration of effort would become so diffuse that neither objective would be satisfactorily achieved. Furthermore, whereas the intelligence and planning committees were generally in agreement as to how the oil offensive should be tackled, they were often at odds in grading the importance of strategic transport targets. Much incidental damage had already been inflicted upon railway marshalling yards in the course of area bombing, but this had not been part of a scientifically

The onslaught continues. Industrial objectives were the third major target system in the last year of the war. This B-17 is attacking the Ordnance Plant at Bottenhausen on the 2nd October 1944. IWM

planned campaign and the size and flexibility of the German network had mitigated most of the effects in the longer term. It was also generally recognised that concentrated attack on clearly defined nodal points within the transport system was more effective than widespread but indiscriminate damage which could often be bypassed.

The dependence of rail transport upon coal was self evident, as of course were most heavy industrial enterprises within Germany. But whereas coal mines are not easy targets for attack, disruption of the onward transportation of coal would be a double edged sword, an attack upon industry as well as communications. Sealing-off the Ruhr, therefore, a major producer as well as consumer of coal could prove decisive to Germany's war effort. However, the isolation of the Ruhr meant not only an attack on the railway system, for Germany was blessed with an abundance of natural navigable waterways supplemented by a network of canals. Far more than any other country in Europe, Germany depended upon water transport to supply and support its industrial base. The Dortmund-Ems and Mittelland Canals connecting the Rhine, Ems and Weser were

key components of the system connecting the Ruhr to north east Germany. On the railways, there were also a number of important viaducts on the three main routes to the east. These two key components were to feature in some of the most impressive and successful attacks of the war.

In support of the tactical offensive, a number of key communication areas were identified running all the way down the heart of Germany from Hamburg to Ulm. In this context, the wide front of Eisenhower's advance posed considerable difficulties of selection and concentration and the Ardennes offensive in December 1944, which on the face of it had not appeared to suffer unduly from transport problems, caused acute controversy as to the effectiveness of the whole 'transport plan'. In fact, post war study disclosed that the communications network had been severely degraded, particularly in the Ruhr. The distribution of coal was seriously curtailed and by

December the situation appeared to Albert Speer to be as critical as the supply of oil. Attempts were made to bolster the flak defences, but it was far more difficult to build a wall round a transport system than it was to protect a few key oil plants.

In February 1945, when Bomber Command was once again embroiled in its area offensive, a determined attempt was made to complete the sealing-off of the Ruhr with more spectacular raids on the Bielefeld and Arnsberg viaducts. This final effort achieved complete success, but it was accomplished only one week before the area was overrun by the Allied troops. The strategic benefits should not therefore be over exaggerated although the cumulative degradation was obviously significant. In the final months of the war it became even more difficult to assess the effectiveness of the 'transport plan', but the fact that large quantities of tanks and other weapons were discovered in store as the territory was overrun emphasises the severe difficulties which faced the communications system. That the 'transport plan' had a major impact upon Germany's ability to continue the war is undoubted, but its effects were slower and more difficult of achievement than in other key areas, particularly oil, and in the end the tactical benefits were perhaps of greater significance than the strategic.

There were a number of reasons why the oil and communications plans were not pursued with the weight and concentration which would have ensured a quicker result. One of the more important was the diversion of effort towards our third major target system, direct attack upon Germany's industrial capacity. Despite the formal priority given to oil and communications, a greater tonnage of bombs was actually dropped in the last year of the war on other target systems. Area bombing was possible on many occasions when the weather precluded an attack on precision targets and sometimes preferred when it did not, and although the Americans never deviated from their professed policy of precision bombing, many of their operations during this period were in practice of an area nature. However, even in the context of area bombing, the new-found accuracy was such that an attack on an industrial town was likely to destroy or damage the factories and their internal communications as well as generally disrupting electricity and gas supplies. In this period, the boundary between area and precision bombing was thus becoming as blurred as that between strategic and tactical operations.

Bomber Command once again concentrated upon the Ruhr which had been such a thorn in its side during the early war years, and its area operations here interacted with the precision attacks on oil and communications such that the impact upon each type of target system tends to become almost indistinguishable. In any event, the Ruhr's industrial base had been almost totally destroyed before the Allied armies overran the area in March 1945. Many factories had ceased production by the end of 1944, including the great Krupp works, and those which were still functioning were gravely inhibited by the inability to move raw materials and finished products out of the area. In fact, many of the raids in the Spring of 1945 were largely unnecessary, merely stirring the rubble of long abandoned factories. Nevertheless, it was probably the direct attack upon industrial centres rather than the severance of communications which eventually destroyed the economic heartland of Germany.

On the other hand, in other parts of Germany, it was the loss of communications rather than direct attack which caused the greater restriction on military industrial output. The main industrial targets selected were designed to restrict the flow of equipment and weapons to all three elements of the German armed services. In the case of the army, factories producing tanks and motor vehicles and ordnance depots were regularly visited, but these attacks had little strategic value after the end of 1944 as the Germans had neither the means to transfer their products to the front or the fuel to employ them if they reached their destination. Attacks on aircraft factories were even less productive, for although the threat of the jet fighter was very apparent, lack of fuel and the shortage of trained pilots prohibited this vitally important development ever realising its potential. It is, however, easier to recognise this with hindsight and such was the potency of this revolutionary new form of defence that it is understandable that no chances were taken in this area. The German's ability to continue to prosecute the war at sea was, however, a very real threat and concerted efforts were made to destroy the U boat factories and their associated assembly sites, which were much more vulnerable. Of great significance in this context was the component factories, particularly those producing the accumulator batteries, and three out of the four were either destroyed or badly damaged by the end of 1944.

There is no doubt that direct attack upon the industrial power of Germany was very effective during the last year of the war with its concomitant disruption of essential services and the weakening of the morale of the civilian population, particularly in the Ruhr and the Rhineland. Nevertheless, it was not in the end decisive. Severe shortages in specialised areas though there undoubtedly were, it was not a deficiency of weapons, ammunition, tanks or aircraft which so curtailed the fighting efficiency of the German armed forces in 1945, it was the shortage of fuel to employ them which in the end crippled the military arm of the Wehrmacht. The primary target systems, oil and communications, above all the former, were the decisive objectives and, in retrospect, there can be little doubt that if even greater effort had been expended on these two alone, the conflict might have drawn to a close a few months earlier than May 1945.

Controversy Again

We have examined the various options for the employment of the strategic bomber forces from mid 1944 onwards in some detail because they were no longer constrained by operational and technical considerations to anything like the same extent as hitherto, thereby opening-up a whole range of options to help bring the war to a swift conclusion. Virtually all recognised the importance of the synthetic oil plants and it might be thought that the battle in future would principally rest between the strategic air forces of Britain and the United States on the one hand and the Luftwaffe on the other. In fact, the major battle ground was drawn between Sir Charles Portal and Sir Arthur Harris in one of the most vigorously contested controversies of the war.

As we have seen, control of the strategic air forces had been transferred to General Eisenhower in April 1944, which in practice meant Sir Arthur Tedder, and so the latter's views on the employment of air power were crucial at this time. Tedder, despite his advocacy of the 'transport plan', was well aware of the importance of the oil plants and in fact directed Harris to pursue this objective in June. All the intelligence leads pointed towards the criticality of oil and the efforts the Germans were making to bring damaged plants back into production: there was a widespread view that Germany would not be able to continue the war beyond December if the whole weight of the strategic air forces could be thrown against the oil industry. The Air Staff also was moving firmly in this direction. To Harris, however, it was just another 'panacea' target, a concept he totally abhorred,

and doubtless his views were coloured and reinforced by the heavy losses for limited returns in the four raids he mounted in June against oil targets.

Unfortunately, the Allied leadership now entered one of its least decisive phases with many competing interests clouding the horizon. First of all were the requirements of the ground forces who had become very used to bomber support and reluctant to attempt any major, or even minor, enterprise unless they were provided with overwhelming air support involving the strategic as well as the tactical air forces. They had in Tedder's words become 'drugged with bombs', and as direction of the strategic air forces rested with the Allied Supreme Commander, their needs were usually in the forefront of target planning. This determined Portal to regain control of the strategic forces and led to a period of unseemly wrangling between the British and American Chiefs of Staff which only ended with an untidy compromise in September. At the same time, much considera-

The battleship Tirpitz was located and photographed in the north Norwegian Fiords in September 1944 and damaged, but not sunk, by Lancasters of Nos 9 and 617 Squadrons.   IWM

tion was given again to another attack on the morale of the German people, and although discounted for the time being, was influential eventually in the massive assault upon Dresden in February 1945. This latter thinking was very much in accord with that of Harris who still firmly supported general area bombing.

After much indecision and prevarication, the Air Staff at last issued a formal directive to Harris that, subject to the exigencies of weather and tactical feasibility, the first priority was to be accorded to the campaign against oil. But the subsequent wording, not by any means for the first time, contained within it something for everybody. The second priority was communications, Tedder's primary option, and there was also mention of 'important industrial areas'. Sir Arthur Harris once again had quite a lot of scope to play it his way.

In the latter half of 1944, benefitting from the new confidence and expertise which was an indirect consequence of the

The same two Squadrons finally sank the Tirpitz *in Tromso Fiord in November. This picture of the capsized ship shows the port propeller.*

IWM

diversion in support of 'Overlord', Bomber Command launched some of its most spectacular precision raids of the war. Ships, in transit, or even in port, had not proved to be the easiest of targets for the Command, but in September an opportunity arose to redress the balance: the battleship *Tirpitz* had been located in the Altenfiord in north Norway. Too far away to mount a heavy attack even from Scotland, Nos 9 and 617 Squadrons transitted to Archangel in the Soviet Union from whence they launched 27 Lancasters on the 15th September using 'Tallboys'. Although badly damaged, the *Tirpitz* was still afloat and eventually moved to Tromso. Here she was finally sunk by the same two squadrons on the 12th November.

No 617 Squadron was also involved in another spectacular raid on the 23rd September when it wrecked an aqueduct on the Dortmund-Ems canal. Two months later, when the structure had been restored, Bomber Command destroyed it again, repeating the medicine twice more before the New Year. These examples show the extent to which Bomber Command had become a precision force by the latter half of 1944. Although it would be incorrect to suggest that the whole of Bomber Command had reached the same pitch of perfection as the elite

squadrons, the improvement in target marking was making significant advances possible across a wide spectrum of operations.

The Command mounted a massive effort against Germany in October, over 13,000 sorties with a bomb weight more than twice that delivered previously in any single month. One third of the sorties were in daylight and the loss rate dropped to under one per cent. Subsequent evaluation disclosed, however, that only six per cent had been dropped on oil targets and the second priority, communications, had received no more attention. In fact, the major part of the tonnage was still being devoted to attacks on cities. Whilst precision attacks on oil plants and communications demanded more favourable weather conditions than area bombing, it was difficult for Portal to believe that Harris was paying more than lip service to the Air Staff directive. Tedder too was increasingly apprehensive regarding the application of the strategic forces although his priorities were still rather different to those of Portal. He believed that the quickest method of ending the war in Europe was the co-ordinated employment of air and land forces; there should be no attempt to defeat Germany by strategic air forces alone, but their effort should be closely directed, albeit in a strategic sense, to facilitate the advance of the armies. For Tedder, the weight of attack should have been concentrated against communications.

There now ensued an increasingly vituperative correspondence between Portal and Harris as the former, at first gently, reminded the Commander-in-Chief of the Air Staff's priorities. As the flow of letters developed, Harris' views regarding the primacy of general area bombing were ever more openly expressed. What is more, he left little doubt that he intended to pursue the campaign in his way irrespective of any directives he received from the Air Staff. Sir Arthur Harris by this time had enormous prestige, not only within his own Command but with the public at large, as a result of the widespread publicity accorded to the feats of the bomber crews. Harris, almost uniquely among senior field commanders had also carefully cultivated a direct line to the Prime Minister. His reputation was not without foundation, for he had raised Bomber Command from the depths of depression in 1942 and sustained it through its most difficult years. Nevertheless, no individual commander can openly ignore a direction from higher authority, and despite his reasoned arguments, some more logical than others, this is exactly what Harris was doing towards the end of 1944. Whilst stating his views ever more forcibly, Portal fell short of the ultimate step of sacking his

An unusual picture of a Mosquito in USAAF markings. The Special Operations Group – 'The Carpetbaggers' – operated this B Mk XVI.
WWE

recalcitrant subordinate. It was, perhaps, a mistake, but Harris' standing was so high at that time that it could only have resulted in an unseemly and public quarrel in which Portal may have come-off second best.

Although controversy may rage for ever on this question, there are sound grounds for believing that Harris' view was wrong at this stage of the war. Despite Bomber Command's concerted effort, Germany had not been brought to its knees by general area bombing, the impact of which, as was to be confirmed after the war, was even less effective than believed at the time. Nor had the morale of the political leaders, the military, or the public at large been so affected that there was an overwhelming demand for the conflict to end. As it was, through weak and vacillating direction, Harris was allowed to pursue his own course which, although causing widespread destruction within German cities, was not actually hastening the end of a war moving inexorably towards a conclusion on the battlefields of Germany. It was not until the final weeks of the campaign against oil that Harris at last made a significant, indeed in the end, a vital contribution.

The Apogee of American Air Power

After 'Big Week', the American strategic bomber force developed into a weapon of awesome size and destructive power. More aircraft, more crews, an ever expanding fighter escort capability, tactical innovations and refinements, confidence and experience – all contributed to an overwhelming might which first crushed the Luftwaffe and then pounded oil, communications and industrial targets almost at will across the length and breadth of Germany. But at first the 8th Air Force did not have it all its own way, there were alarms, disappointments and still on occasion serious losses.

In March 1944, General Doolittle, although indicating that the tide was turning, still felt the need to reinforce the view that the destruction of the German Air Force remained the 'immediate goal'. It has in consequence been argued that the bomber at this period was merely being used as bait to entice the Luftwaffe into combat with the escort fighters, but whilst it is true that the fighter groups relished the opportunity, it is too simplistic to claim that the massive bomber force available to General Spaatz was engaged only in a gigantic 'Circus' operation. Although, as we have seen, target selection was a complex affair, all commanders were determined to exact the maximum utility from the weight of bombs now available even if they could not always agree where they would cause most effect.

This massive build-up of aircraft brought with it its own problems. By June 1944 there were no less than 43 Bomber and 15 Fighter Groups in three Air Divisions, all compressed into an area south of the Wash and north of London. Assembling such a force into a compact defensive formation was a complex and difficult affair, rather more so than co-ordinating a Bomber Command stream at night in which every aircraft flew independently to arrive over the designated assembly point at a precise time to fit into the pattern. Battle weary Liberators called 'Assembly Ships', painted in bizarre colours and festooned with lights, acted as a kind of 'whipper-in' until the individual aircraft, now normally grouped in boxes of 12, were in their appointed position in the formation. Collisions, usually with fatal results, were by no means infrequent; in five days in March six aircraft were lost in this way. Another self inflicted hazard was being struck by bombs dropped from an aircraft flying higher in the formation. Whilst it is understandable that formation discipline could sometimes break down in the heat of battle, bombing an aircraft below in broad daylight suggests a break-down in crew co-operation with so many eyes available to search the sky. Aircraft crashes were also too frequent: on the morning of the 20th May, whilst only two aircraft were lost in the raid itself, eight aircraft were destroyed in take-off crashes, one collision costing 21 lives. Flying discipline at the beginning and end of a mission was not always as strict as it should have been.

Although the bomber's equipment, techniques and tactics were still being refined, the most important development in early 1944 concerned the 8th Air Force's fighter groups. Instead of simply providing a close escort to the bombers to fend-off attackers, the fighters now adopted a much more aggressive posture, ranging ahead of the bomber force and breaking away to pursue any enemy aircraft detected, often down to their own airfields which would be straffed for good measure. Air superiority was now an achievable aim with the introduction of the long range Mustang and an improved P-47 Thunderbolt.

On the bomber front, 8th Air Force had adopted the RAF's pathfinding technique with each division having a designated pathfinder squadron. Another innovation was the introduction of weather scouting aircraft, Mosquitos and Mustangs which flew ahead of the main force and relayed back weather information. An improved version of H2S called H2X enabled the 8th to depart from its normal practice of visual aiming and to bomb through cloud cover. Although never actually admitted as such, this was in practice a resort to area bombing techniques with the lack of accuracy that entailed, but it did enable missions to be flown on many days when weather would otherwise have caused an abort, increasing the pressure on the Luftwaffe defences. To combat the increased accuracy of radar laid flak, electronic warfare was pursued vigorously with the installation of the RAF's 'Mandrel' and the USAAF's own 'Carpet' noise jammers. 'Window' was also liberally spread to confuse the anti-aircraft gun radars.

Some ventures were less successful. One pioneered in June was for bombers to fly on to Russia after attacking East German targets; reminiscent of the method adopted for the Schweinfurt/Regensberg raid in 1943 when some of the bombers caried-on to North Africa. This had a political as well as a tactical value, but B-17s at Poltava on the 21st June were caught on the ground at night by He 111 and Ju 88 bombers and 44 out of 72 were destroyed, albeit with little loss of life. A more successful shuttle mission was flown in August before the arrangement was abandoned. Also in August, a short lived attempt under the code name 'Aphrodite' to use unmanned radio guided B-17s carrying 20,000lbs of high explosive against 'V' sites threatened

The American fighter pilots escorting the bombers increasingly adopted a more aggressive approach in 1944. Lt Col 'Gabby' Gabreski of the 56FG (P-47Ds) shot down his 25th victim, a Bf 109, on the 12th June over France.   IWM

after two spectacular crashes to cause more damage to the Suffolk countryside than to the targets in France.

Despite these understandable difficulties, the most impressive feature of 1944 was the sheer weight of attack which the 8th Air Force could now bring to bear. In February, a total of 700 bombers a day ranging to a dozen targets became a regular occurrence and in April the total reached 900. On the 7th May the one thousand bomber milestone was passed for the first time. Over 12 times as many missions were mounted in June 1944 as had been possible in the same month of the previous year. Unlike Bomber Command, the transfer of overall command to General Eisenhower had little impact on the type of mission mounted with aircraft production usually featuring prominently in the target lists. As we have seen, however, oil targets increasingly appeared from May onwards and when conditions were not suitable for missions over Germany, 'Noball' attacks on 'V' weapon sites were regularly mounted.

The German day fighters throughout the Spring and Summer of 1944 were a diminishing threat, but there were times when they were tempted from their lairs in force. Such an occasion was a 700 bomber raid against Berlin on the 29th April when over 300 fighters caught a badly strung-out formation and despatched over 60. There were also missions when the bombers were unescorted for a part of the time and again the Luftwaffe exacted a heavy toll when this happened. The Germans sometimes tracked the bombers back to their bases in England

when it was apparent that they would be landing at dusk. On the 22nd April, a group of Me 410s caught the B-24s of the 3rd Division in these conditions; 11 were either destroyed in the air or bombed on the ground, including one shot down by mistake by British anti-aircraft fire. An increasing number of aircraft, 19 on the 20th June alone, were landing into internment in neutral Sweden or Switzerland, usually as a result of damage sustained, but occasionally in circumstances which appeared less than genuine. The increasing losses sustained to flak were real enough and 131 were attributed to this cause in April, the month in which more American bombers were lost than at any period in the war. The Germans were now devoting far greater resources to their anti-aircraft arm with over a million men and women manning these weapons, the majority of which were the highly effective 88 mm radar laid high altitude guns grouped in batteries of up to 24. By the Summer, flak had become a far greater threat in the eyes of the bomber crews than German fighters.

But these losses have to be put into perspective, for although the absolute total of aircraft lost had increased, this was mainly a reflection of the numbers employed. Nearly 30,000 missions were flown in both June and July and the casualty rate amounted to less than four per cent compared with up to ten per cent in the previous year. The results were also becoming impressive; the attacks against the synthetic oil plants and aircraft factories were beginning to take their toll, although the Luftwaffe's problems centred more on the number of experienced pilots and inadequate training rather than a shortage of aircraft and oil at this stage. On the other hand, no such problem afflicted the Allies, in July they could muster some 3,000 fighters against less than half that number available to the Luftwaffe.

The Luftwaffe fighter arm, however, had another brief flurry of activity in September, assembling some 400 aircraft against

Below
The arrival of the jet powered Me 262 generated considerable apprehension, particularly within the 8th Air Force, but its potential was in the event not fulfilled.   IWM

Bottom
One of the top scoring American fighter pilots was Captain Don Gentile of the 4FG (P-51Bs) who first came to England to fly with the 'Eagle' Squadron in December 1941.   IWM

raids which now amounted to nearly 1,500 bombers still concentrating against oil and aircraft production targets. But although they achieved some success, it was not on the scale of the previous year and they themselves suffered heavily from the predatory Mustangs ranging far and wide above and ahead of the bomber force.

That the Germans were building a jet fighter had been known from intelligence sources for some months and their arrival in the sky was awaited with considerable apprehension. In fact, the first sighting in July was not of a jet, but the rocket powered Me 163 although this aircraft never posed a real threat to either bombers or fighters because of its inherent technical limitations. The far superior twin jet powered Me 262 appeared in September, but despite a significant speed advantage over the Mustangs and Thunderbolts, it was less manoeuvrable and their pilots at this stage appeared reluctant to engage in combat. In practice the menace of the jet fighter never really materialised and although there were a few largely ineffectual combats, the jets were generally used for picking off stragglers in the bomber stream.

The final major flurry in German fighter activity appeared in November when about 300 aircraft engaged bombers over a four day period. Goering had conceived a plan to launch a massive force of a thousand fighters against a single American raid, but the plan miscarried and was eventually abandoned. Despite achieving some success against the American fighters, the Germans were outnumbered and ill trained and suffered heavy losses. In December 1944 the Wehrmacht played its final card, the counter offensive in the Ardennes. In retrospect we can see that it was but a pin-prick against the inexorable tide of the advancing Allied armies even though it was regarded with considerable apprehension at the time. In response, the Allies mounted their largest bombing raid of the war on Christmas Eve when 2,034 8th Air Force aircraft were launched against airfields and communications targets in the rear of the German offensive. The raid was extremely effective with only limited opposition, but Bf 109s shot down nine B-17s including one carrying the force commander, Brigadier General Fred Castle.

Before, however, turning to the climax of the strategic bombing offensive in 1945, we need to digress slightly to consider the continuing fortunes of the light bomber which had led such a chequered existence in the fateful days of the Battle and the Blenheim in the early years of the war.

The Light Night Striking Force

Although Bomber Command had been quite content to transfer operational control of No 2 Group to the 2nd Tactical Air Force in June 1943, it had the foresight to retain the two Mosquito squadrons, Nos 105 and 139, which were transferred into Bennett's No 8 Group. They formed there the nucleus of the Light Night Striking Force (LNSF) which by the end of the war was to grow to 13 squadrons with over 200 aircraft of various marks.

The premier task of No 8 Group was of course pathfinding

and the Mosquito made an invaluable contribution to this role. But although some of the squadrons specialised in this task, notably Nos 109 and 139, all at some time participated in an independent bombing role. The great attribute of the Mosquito was its versatility and this was nowhere more apparent than in its time with the LNSF. Initially because of the small numbers available, the Mosquitos were generally employed on nuisance or spoof raids. These were designed to actuate the Reich's air defence and air raid warning system and to draw the fighters attention away from the main force raids. Later, with increasing numbers of aircraft, the LNSF was able to keep most of Germany awake at night by small scale scattered raids, with formations proceeding from one target to another dropping just a few bombs on each. Dispensing 'Window', a small force could thoroughly confuse the air defence organisation even though the weight of bombs dropped was insufficient to cause significant damage.

Throughout the last two years of the war, the Mosquito was almost invulnerable to fighters when operating at night. Bombing from heights around 25,000 feet at over 300 knots, no German night fighter crew could hope to shoot down a Mosquito unless the pilot was caught unawares, which but rarely happened. Although the jet fighter was very occasionally encountered, it never posed a real threat to the LNSF. The Mosquito was not, however, quite so immune from heavy flak which could now range up to 40,000 feet; many aircraft returned with some flak damage although this was rarely lethal. Throughout this phase of the Mosquito's bombing operations, the overall loss rate was just under one per cent.

The number of Mosquito squadrons slowly increased during 1944 and the variety of their operations likewise expanded. Their normal load ranged from six 500lb (two carried externally) to four 1,000lb bombs, but a major innovation in 1943 was the modification of the Mosquito to carry the 4,000lb bomb – the 'cookie'. The first 'cookie' was dropped by a Mosquito on Dusseldorf on the 4th February 1944 and by April they were carrying this formidable weapon all the way to Berlin. Sometimes a small force of Oboe or H2S equipped pathfinder Mosquitos marked a target for a larger force of Mosquito bombers, the size of formations steadily growing until figures approaching 100 were frequently recorded and once exceeded.

The LNSF ranged widely across Germany throughout 1944. Night high level raids were its routine task, but during the last 18 months it regularly turned its hand to other more specialised operations. We have already noted the spectacular raid on Amiens prison in February 1944; in May No 692 Squadron was laying mines from low level in the Kiel Canal, on D-Day Mosquitos were both marking targets and conducting a major raid on a marshalling yard at Osnabruck, a few days later they were mounting precision attacks on oil production plants. In November the LNSF flew its first daylight raid, and although the German fighter threat had begun to fall away, the Mosquitos were escorted by RAF Mustangs – a formidable combination. On the first of January 1945, four squadrons were tasked with attacking railway tunnels on the west German border, a 4,000lb

The Mosquitos of No 8 Group were increasingly used in an independent bombing role from 1943 onwards. This is a B Mk XVI of No 571 Squadron. RAFM

delayed action bomb being tossed into the tunnel mouth from 200 feet. These are just a few examples of the remarkable versatility of this outstanding bomber.

Throughout this period, however, the LNSF's favourite target was Berlin, indeed this became known as the 'milk run' to the Mosquito crews. Throughout 1944, ever larger raids visited the Reich capital and by early in the following year this had built-up to a crescendo. During the first four months of 1945, 3,988 Mosquito sorties were made to the capital for the loss of just 14 aircraft, with raids frequently perpetuated throughout the night to achieve the maximum disruption. From the 20th February, the capital was attacked on 36 consecutive nights, with many aircraft carrying the 4,000lb bomb. On the 21st March, the heaviest Mosquito raid upon Berlin, some aircraft visited the city twice in the same night with different crews. The LNSF raided Berlin for the last time on the 21st April; thereafter as the war drew to its close, the Mosquitos concentrated on attacks on airfields and on Kiel when even at this stage the U boat was considered a potent threat.

The LNSF was one of the major success stories of Bomber Command operations. For two years, with minimal loss, it harassed industrial and other targets night after night throughout Germany, often in weather conditions which were unsuitable for the heavy bombers. The Mosquito flew almost as many bomber sorties as the Wellington, twice that of the Stirling and nearly half as many as the Halifax, many more of which were in operational service. Its loss rate overall was only 0.63 per cent. With the Lancaster, the Mosquito justifiably earned its place in Bomber Command's hall of fame.

The Climax of The Strategic Offensive – 1945

At the beginning of 1945, Bomber Command and 8th Air Force, complemented by 15th Air Force and RAF squadrons operating from Italian airfields, reigned virtually unchallenged in the skies of Europe. Whilst Sir Arthur Harris had been able to mount a thousand bomber raid in 1942 by dredging aircraft from training units and every other conceivable source, the daily average of available aircraft amounted to no more than about 500 of which the majority were still the twin engined Wellington. By January 1945 the daily average had increased to 1,420, consisting entirely of four engine heavy bombers and Mosquitos. By April this figure had risen to 1,609, over a thousand of which were Lancasters. Even more strikingly, the tonnage of bombs which could be lifted in 1945 was more than ten times that which was available to Harris in the Spring of 1942 when he assumed command. Bombing accuracy had improved by similar margins; by the end of 1944, 96 per cent of aircraft which reached the target area were dropping their bombs within three miles of the target, most much closer. 8th Air Force was even more formidable, providing no less than 1,826 aircraft daily at the beginning of 1945, a total which by April had grown to 2,018. Furthermore, with the demise of the Luftwaffe, the loss rate had dropped to negligible proportions; this vast armada of lethality could now range across the whole of Germany, release its weapons with an accuracy seemingly beyond attainment only two years before, and return almost unscathed to prepare for another mighty effort the following day. Only the weather remained untamed, almost the only constraint on an otherwise untrammelled ability to pound Germany to defeat, if not annihilation. How was this awesome power to be used?

The divergence of views on the employment of the strategic air forces which had characterised 1944 had left an aura of anti-climax at the end of the year which had been heightened by the fleetingly successful German counter-offensive in the Ardennes in December. All of the senior commanders were conscious of the fact that the latent power of the strategic bomber force had not been exploited to best effect since 'Overlord' in June. There had been too many competing objectives, leading to a dispersion of effort and an inevitable dilution of effect. The oil plan had proved the most successful despite Harris' reluctance to support it fully, but the communications offensive favoured by Tedder had been only sporadically supported and almost everybody, except the ground forces themselves, felt that the tactical demands of the land offensive were siphoning away too high a proportion of the bombers which were better suited to achieving strategic objectives. In fact, the division between strategic and tactical targets had become blurred with a decreasing number which could be defined as truly strategic.

This graph shows dramatically how the striking power of Bomber Command and 8th Air Force increased from the beginning of 1944, subsiding only after March 1945.

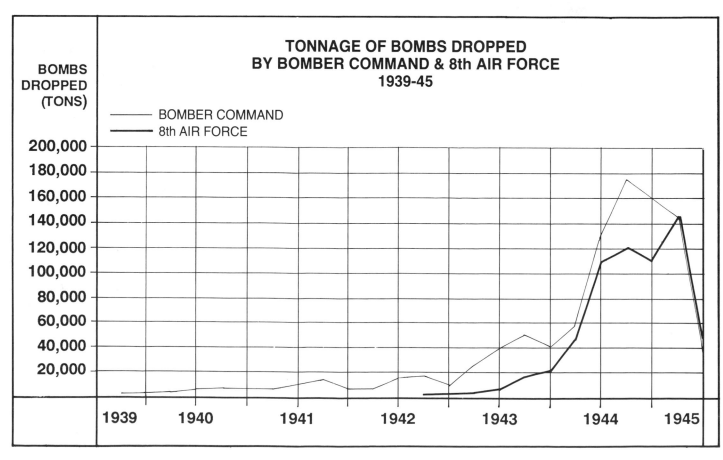

BOMBS DROPPED (TONS)

TONNAGE OF BOMBS DROPPED BY BOMBER COMMAND & 8th AIR FORCE 1939-45

BOMBER COMMAND
8th AIR FORCE

200,000
180,000
160,000
140,000
120,000
100,000
80,000
60,000
40,000
20,000

1939   1940   1941   1942   1943   1944   1945

That old adversary, the Krupps factory at Essen, had finally been destroyed by the end of 1944. This photograph was taken in April 1945.   IWM

Communications targets were still being attacked as the war drew to its close. This is the Bielefeld Viaduct after attack by No 617 Squadron on the 14th March 1945.   IWM

The advance of German technology was also disquieting. Although the V-I sites in France had been overrun, the V-2 rocket against which there was no defence appeared a very real menace, the introduction of the jet fighter had threatened to re-open the issue of air superiority, and the Schnorkel equipped submarine challenged again the control of the sea lanes. Of even greater moment, looming ominously in the background was the threat of atomic weapons. For the first time in this war, the advent of technologically advanced weapons might still just tip the balance in favour of a combatant who in every other respect was on the verge of defeat. We know now that these fears were largely unwarranted. Hitler had failed to devote the necessary resources to the development of these radical new weapons with the result that they had arrived too late to affect the outcome of the struggle. But this was by no means so evident even in January 1945 and the feeling was prevalent that this war had still to be won. Germany was not simply going to slide into ignominious surrender.

Not surprisingly, the potential threat of the jet fighter to daylight operations weighed particularly strongly in General Spaatz's thinking and the 'intermediate' objective of 'Pointblank', the destruction of the Luftwaffe and its supporting aircraft industry, became once again for the USAAF a 'principle objective for attack'. The Joint Intelligence Committee on the other hand adhered strongly to the oil plan. But there were other considerations; the renewed Russian offensive in the east pointed towards the destruction of tank factories, for only by a rapid replacement of its many losses could the Wehrmacht hope to stem the advance on land. The Russian successes also raised again the possibility of a massive attack against German morale which it will be remembered had been the subject of much debate in the Autumn of 1944 but, with the exception of Sir Arthur Harris, had largely lain dormant in most minds ever since. It was now linked to supporting the Russian advance and the deliberations which ultimately led to the destruction of Dresden were firmly underway. At this time, however, it was Berlin itself which was regarded as the primary objective, although Chemnitz, Leipzig and Dresden were all mentioned as worthwhile targets for attack in support of the Russians. Meanwhile, oil and communications remained officially the primary objectives, with tactical support of Eisenhower's advancing armies a continual source of diversion.

In January 1945, therefore, the many competing strategies were as active as ever. In addition to pursuing the oil plan, General Spaatz was obsessed by the menace of the jet fighter, Tedder still actively pursuing the destruction of the communications infrastructure, and Harris the devastation of German industrial power. At the same time, for motives varying between an assault on morale, the destruction of communications and the support of the Russian advance, they were all contemplating a massive attack on the cities of East Germany. Sir Charles Portal was particularly indecisive at this time, for although he still generally adhered to the oil plan, his minutes reflect a hesitant flirtation with most of the other objectives which were under consideration, thus allowing the operational commanders considerable latitude to exploit their own individual whims. Harris, as usual, was never hesitant in taking advantage of this vacillation and there is no doubt that of all the competing strategies, the attack on Berlin and the other East German cities was to him the most attractive option, for it was much more closely attuned to his strategic priorities.

Warrant Officer W.G. Pearce R.A.A.F. – 156 Squadron

On the 20th February 1945 we were detailed to mark the synthetic oil refinery at Reiszholz in the Ruhr Valley. Still some way short of the target we were caught up by an enemy fighter (later identified as a Ju 88 using upward firing cannon) and the starboard inner exploded and caught fire. The captain soon decided our position was untenable and ordered us to bale out: we didn't need to be told twice. I discarded my flying helmet and oxygen mask (we were at 18,000 feet), picked up my parachute pack from the floor and started to make my way to the rear door on the starboard side of the aircraft, just forward of the tailplane. I can still remember sitting on the main wing strut, fumbling to attach the parachute pack to the clips on the front of the harness. This is where the lack of oxygen began to take effect and I can remember thinking I had better get moving.

When I eventually reached the door the mid-upper gunner was there before me. He had made the fatal mistake of picking up his parachute pack by the shiny handle, the ripcord, and it had opened in the aircraft. He had, however clipped it to his harness and gathered the canopy in his arms. I watched him jump and saw the canopy which was torn from his grasp by the slipstream pass over the top of the tailplane and his body beneath. His body was found later on the ground, still attached to his parachute: he had been killed by the impact when dragged back into the tail by his entangled canopy.

Now it was my turn to leave the aircraft, by now somewhat light-headed from the lack of oxygen and not too concerned by my predicament. I can still remember looking at the fire in the wing and thinking 'that sure is burning well'. The next moment I fell out of the aeroplane, and after tumbling for what seemed an age thought 'well I had better pull it now'. I was overcome by a feeling of absolute loneliness, but the cold and the lower altitude soon brought me back to my proper senses. But I could now hear other aircraft swishing past me and was frightened of what would happen if one of them hit me: this did not happen of course. They soon passed and I was left hanging in complete silence.

As I drifted down towards a cloud bank I could see a searchlight running around on the underside of this cloud. Again I was frightened of being picked up by this light and becoming target practice for an anti-aircraft battery: again my fears were groundless as the light was switched off before I entered the cloud bank. Below the cloud the darkness was even more complete and I couldn't see the ground. I realised I was drifting backwards and remembering my parachute drill I tried to correct; I wasn't very successful and I hit the ground in an untidy heap. There was very little wind and my parachute quickly collapsed, I had landed in the middle of a paddock, but had hurt my left shoulder and the arm was virtually useless.

Dresden – An Aberration?

The British and American raids on Dresden between the 13th and 15th February 1945 proved by far the most controversial of the war and have come to symbolise the debate about the morality of air bombardment of cities. Operation 'Thunderclap' was first envisaged in July 1944 when a minute to the Prime Minister from the Chiefs of Staff suggested that 'an all-out attack by every means at our disposal on German civilian morale might be decisive'. The plan produced by the Air Ministry to concentrate the assault on Berlin was in the event shelved, but raised again in a slightly different context in January 1945. This time the emphasis was placed on harrying the German retreat on the Russian front with particular emphasis on Berlin, Breslau and Munich. The Joint Intelligence Committee expressed support and Sir Arthur Harris proposed that the plan should also embrace Chemnitz, Leipzig and Dresden. After an intervention by Mr Churchill on the 26th January, Bomber Command was directed on the following day to mount a major raid on East German cities 'with the object of exploiting the confused conditions which are likely to exist … during the successful Russian advance'.

The ancient capital of Saxony, Dresden was another of those beautiful medieval German towns packed with old timbered houses bordering a maze of narrow streets as well as grander public buildings of a later age. Its peacetime population of about 600,000 was swollen to perhaps as many again by an influx of refugees from the East and Allied prisoners of war. Dresden was a cultural rather than a major industrial centre, but it was also an important communications nodal point for troops transitting between the Western and Eastern Fronts. Nevertheless, it cannot be denied that an assault against Dresden was an attack on German morale rather than upon a target of significant industrial, military or economic importance. As such, it followed in the pattern of Allied policy which, with varying degrees of emphasis from 1941 onwards, had regarded economic disruption and civilian morale as legitimate targets for attack: it was emphatically not a new policy cobbled together for the dying days of the war.

The raid was led by nine Mosquitos to mark the target from 1000 feet using Loran, an American development of Gee with a much longer range. The city was to be attacked in two waves, the first of 245 aircraft at 2205 pinpointing the old town with the aim of creating a conflagration similar to that suffered by Hamburg 18 months earlier. The second wave of 529 Lancasters would arrive three hours later led by H2S equipped pathfinders. A massive deception raid of 368 Halifaxes was mounted against an oil refinery at Bohlen as well as spoof raids by small groups of Mosquitos. The raid went very much according to the plan except that the second wave pathfinders had difficulty identifying their precise aiming point, the railway marshalling yards, because of smoke haze. Their more general marking simply widened the area of destruction within the city. The fighter opposition was very light and only five aircraft were lost, a casualty rate of just over 0.5 per cent, low even at this stage of

the war for such a deep penetration into Germany. Although the 8th Air Force followed-up with medium scale raids on the two succeeding days, they did little more than stir the rubble and frustrate the recovery cycle.

The initial raid was devastatingly effective. There was a strong wind blowing which fanned the fires started by the incendiaries of the first wave and large parts of the city were consumed in a firestorm which was even more destructive than that at Hamburg. In many areas more than 75 per cent of the houses were totally destroyed and many people died from suffocation as the tongues of fire sucked the oxygen from the air. Estimates of the number of people killed varied widely from 35,000 to over 400,000. The true figure will never be known, the circumstances of the raid and the ensuing outcry have inhibited a dispassionate appraisal of the results, but I think we may discount the highest figures which were usually associated with 'political' hyperbole.

Sergeant W. Morris – R.A.S.C.

I had been a prisoner of war in Dresden for some months before that dreadful night of 13th February 1945. It was a beautiful city with parks and grand houses – it seemed virtually untouched by war. I quite liked the people of Dresden, they were more softly spoken, civilised people than I had met elsewhere in Germany. The Russians had reportedly already bypassed the city and the people were convinced that the war was all but over. They were certainly more frightened of being caught up in the Russian advance than of any threat from the air. It must have been about 2200 that I first heard the aircraft, they were so low that I could see them quite clearly. I was on the outskirts of the city and no bombs fell near me, but there was a strong wind blowing and they dropped the incendiaries so that the fires started upwind and then raced through the city. It was as bright as day and I could see the fires burning on the surface of the river and the markings of the aircraft still flying overhead. There seemed to be no opposition. They were now dropping high explosives and I saw the railway station receive a direct hit and blow up.

The American bombers came the next day, but there didn't seem much left to destroy. Many Russian prisoners were killed in the bombing, but most of the British survived and we were drafted into the city to help clear up. There was rubble everywhere, and even three weeks after the raid the bricks underneath the rubble were still hot to the touch. We came across bodies everywhere as we cleared up the rubbish. There was a network of cellars under the city interconnecting from house to house and the people had obviously used these for protection. Many had apparently died of suffocation as the flames racing overhead had sucked out all the oxygen from the air. One German I met, who had been away from Dresden at the time of the bombing, committed suicide when he saw the state of the city in which his family had been trapped – he knew they could not have survived. It was a sad experience, I wish now it had never happened.

The question of the morality of area bombing has tended to focus on Dresden and it was undoubtedly one of the most destructive single raids of the war. Even some of those who accepted the validity of the concept questioned the need to pursue this form of attack at this late period. Certainly, it did not succeed in bringing the conflict to a premature close, the morale of the people had become almost irrelevant at this stage of the war. Bewildered armies, by now bereft of meaningful direction from Hitler's bunker, simply blundered on until they were defeated in detail. A mass rising of the people or the emergence of alternative leaders had become near impossible in a country devastated by aerial assault and the two converging Allied armies. If a nation is to be cowed into surrender, it must be achieved whilst the organisational infrastructure is still in place to effect an orderly cessation of hostilities. The Third Reich had passed beyond this stage by February 1945.

Nevertheless, it was less easy to recognise this so clearly at the time. There had been little public disavowal of area bombing until after the event – the newspapers and radio broadcasts revelled in the exploits of Bomber Command, often with grossly exaggerated versions of the destruction caused, and only isolated voices were raised in disquiet. There was undoubtedly a profound sense of retribution among the great mass of the population: after London, Liverpool and Coventry, the Germans were only getting what they deserved, and hadn't they started it in the first place! In any case, London had but recently suffered the indiscriminate assault by the 'V' weapons. There is an element of hypocrisy in many of the voices raised in the aftermath of Dresden: the dreadful destruction of that city was no more than the culmination of a four year old policy which had been vigorously criticised from time to time for its lack of effectiveness, but rarely for its immorality. Indeed, the concept of the nation at war had been assiduously fostered by all combatant countries in the twentieth century and any clear distinction between the men fighting at the front and the women working in the munitions factories was rigorously denied. The advent of the aeroplane had irrevocably changed the face of war: all faced the same risk and all must be responsible for the excesses of their leaders. It is simply impossible to separate the women and the children from the consequences of modern warfare: if nation states cannot live in peaceful co-operation, all must endure the heavy hand of deterrence and retribution. Those responsible for directing the war in January 1945 when the Dresden raid was conceived had only just recovered from

The bombers were used for supply dropping towards the end of the war. In the first 3 days of May 1945, 400 B-17 sorties delivered 800 tons of food to Holland.   IWM

the set-back of the Ardennes and still faced the potential threat of the V-2, the U boat and the jet fighter. It was believed, with some justification, that many more Allied lives would be lost before success was theirs. The attack on Dresden should be evaluated dispassionately in the light of the situation as it was seen at the time.

After Dresden, bombing operations built-up to a short lived crescendo with communications targets in support of the advancing allies featuring strongly in the daily raid plan. The 8th Air Force in March mounted the highest monthly total of operations of the war with over 30,000 sorties, breaking the record which had stood from the previous June. Displaying the inherent flexibility of air power, the bombers were also increasingly used for supply dropping sorties for allied troops and civilian refugees.

In 1945 the opposition rapidly crumbled; operations involving over a 1,000 aircraft returned without loss from enemy action although there were still too many accidents and collisions to mar the overall picture. There were flurries of opposition on isolated occasions with the Me 262 beginning to play a more prominent and sometimes the only defensive role. On the 18th March when over 1,300 bombers were sent to Berlin, the jets claimed eight aircraft and the flak, which although short of ammunition was still active, another 16. There was, however, no doubt that by this time both the 8th Air Force and Bomber Command could range freely over Germany both by day and night. The 'intermediate' objective of 'Pointblank' had finally been achieved.

Mission Complete

At the end of March 1945 it was quite clear that the long and arduous struggle was drawing to a close. The military, industrial and economic system of Germany was in chaos, the Allies in the west were across the Rhine and the Russians on the threshold of Berlin, the final battle for which was to begin on the 16th April. Despite the faltering way in which they had been pursued, the oil and communications plans, particularly the former, had been overwhelmingly successful.

It was, therefore, the appropriate moment to consider whether there was any point in continuing the strategic bomber offensive. Indeed, it was argued that any further destruction would actually be counter productive. Although armies in the twentieth century did not depend for their sustenance on pillaging the land they overran, they did not carry with them sufficient food and other essentials of life to sustain the indigenous population. Buildings and materials which were needed to shelter an advancing army had to a large extent been sequestered already by a homeless population. Roads, railways and canals which would be needed to regenerate the economy after the soldiers laid down their arms were also an essential feature of the lines of communication which would soon stretch from London to Berlin. Almost overnight, the pressing requirement became to protect and sustain the infrastructure and economy rather than to destroy it.

Flt Lt F.W. Powell DFC – 640 Squadron

On the night of 7th February 1945, we took off in a Halifax Mk III from Leconfield. I was on my 41st operation and our target was Goch in support of the British XXX Corps. A short while after leaving the target we received some unwelcome attention from flak batteries below which was particularly disconcerting as we were by then over friendly territory. I fired off a Verey cartridge in the colour of the period which only attracted increased attention from below; the firing only stopped after I had fired two more signals. We had barely recovered from this intrusion when we heard a series of explosions as cannon shells thundered into the fuselage with both the rear and mid-upper gunners confirming that we had been attacked by a Me 262, identified by its jet exhausts as it flashed past from underneath on our starboard side. Convulsed by smoke and the smell of cordite, the aircraft was now in a dive and I recall wondering just how long it would be before the aircraft hit the ground and praying that death would be swift. But after what seemed an interminable period, the pilot levelled out and said he thought he had regained control.

Examination of the aircraft showed that the control cables to the starboard ailerons and rudder were either severed or badly damaged. The skipper ordered us to prepare to bale out, but the engines were still functioning properly and we decided to try to make the emergency strip at Manston. We now found a new problem as we could not raise Manston and it took another 20 minutes to repair the damaged aerial. By now we had overflown Manston and with damage to the controls could not easily turn back. We pressed on to Woodbridge who to our relief gave us permission to land.

Inspection of the aircraft showed that we had been hit by 30mm cannon shells from below from the rear turret to the bomb bay, but by a miracle all had missed the crew positions. We concluded that the 262 had been lurking in the area and had been alerted to our presence by the Verey signals we had made to our 'friendly' flak.

Although somewhat concerned when we first heard at the end of '44 that the jet fighter had become operational, our cause for alarm was to a degree unfounded as the Me 262 did not prove very satisfactory as a night fighter. If the initial strike was not successful, its speed restricted its manoeuvrability and we could usually escape in the darkness or cloud cover.

On the 28th March the Prime Minister, in an unfortunately worded note which he was forced by irate Chiefs of Staff to reissue in revised form on the 1st April, asked for a review of the area bombing campaign. Albeit with some reservations, they were generally in sympathy with Mr Churchill's views and on the 6th April Sir Arthur Harris was directed to stop the area bombing of industrial centres and cities. Some attacks on communications targets would have to continue to facilitate the advance of the Allied armies, particularly on the Eastern Front.

One exception to the general rule was the naval town of Kiel which still concealed a concentration of submarines which even at this late stage could wreak havoc on Allied shipping.

On the 16th April, in a message to Harris which he suggested might be published as an order of the day, Sir Charles Portal formally signified the conclusion of the strategic bombing offensive:

'The tasks given to the British and American strategic air forces in Europe were to disorganise and destroy the German military, industrial and economic systems and to afford direct support to our forces on land and sea. In the first of these tasks we are now at the point of having achieved our object.'

Sporadic operations continued, but the final raid of the war was authorised on the night of the 2nd May when 125 Mosquitos bombed the naval base at Kiel. The bombing, using Oboe, was devastatingly accurate, no opposition was encountered and all aircraft returned safely to their bases. It was a poignant contrast to the very first raid of the war nearly six years earlier when a far less capable twin engine bomber, the Blenheim, had departed from the same East Anglian airfields to bomb ships at Wilhelmshaven. On that earlier occasion 15 aircraft were dispatched, five were lost, and no significant damage was achieved. Bomber Command had moved on a long way in those dark and frustrating intervening years.

The 8th Air Force's strategic bombing campaign over mainland Germany formally ended on the 11th April when 1,300 bombers attacked the whole gamut of strategic targets: marshalling yards, oil storage areas, ordnance factories and supply depots. Although medium scale missions continued for a while against targets in southern Europe and port facilities at Bordeaux, the American campaign quickly wound down. The final American mission was against the Skoda factory at Pilsen in Czechoslovakia on the 25th April when an unfortunate radio broadcast warning to the civilian population alerted the local flak batteries which claimed six B-17s. Six days previously, the last B-17s to be shot down by fighters had succumbed over Prague when six were claimed by Me 262s.

From that distant day in July 1942 when the first B-17 group had tentatively arrived in Britain, the 8th Air Force had grown to a massive 2,500 bombers and nearly 1,000 fighters. They had dropped nearly 700,000 tons of bombs in that time, the majority within the last year of the war. The rivalry between the B-17s and the B-24s continued to the end, but both could justifiably claim that their mission was fulfilled. Slowly, too slowly for most, the bomber groups drifted back to the United States, but their presence had forged a relationship between the United States Air Force and the Royal Air Force which has extended to this day. Indeed, on the very day that I pen these words, RAF Tornado bombers and Jaguar ground attack aircraft are joining together with USAF F-15s and F-16s in the deserts of Saudi Arabia, once again to protect the fragile branch of freedom against another ambitious dictator.

The U boat pens finally succumbed in 1945 with the advent of the 'Grand Slam' bomb which in this example at Farge, near Bremen, had penetrated 15 feet of concrete.

IWM

Bomber Command had the task of repatriating POWs at the end of the war. This Lancaster of No 635 Squadron is at Lubeck on the 11th May 1945.

IWM

Farewell. A B-24 leaves RAF Valley in Wales on return to the USA in June 1945.

IWM

=====================APPENDIX=====================

British Pathfinder Operations (as at March 1944)*
ISSUED BY
LUFTWAFFENFUHRUNGSSTAB IC/FREMDE LUFTWAFFEN WEST

Preface

The success of a large-scale night raid by the RAF is in increasing measure dependent on the conscientious flying of the Pathfinder crews. The frictionless functioning of the attack is only possible when the turning points on the inward and outward courses, as well as the target itself, are properly marked. Lately, these attacks have been compressed into about four minutes for each wave averaging 120-150 aircraft.

Dense and high-reaching clouds, which hide the sky markers over the target, and exceptionally strong winds which blow the markers away quickly, represent an unpredictable barrier to Pathfinder operations and can often appreciably decrease the efficiency of an attack.

Another reason for the failure of a raid may lie in the partial failure of the first Pathfinders, the Initial Markers, to arrive, since experience has shown that succeeding Pathfinders, in spite of being equipped with H2S and blind marking equipment, have allowed themselves to be influenced, to a certain extent, by the Initial Markers.

A. Development

1. The concentrated large-scale RAF raid on Cologne on 30/31 May 1942, during a full-moon night and with an alleged strength of more than 900 aircraft, was the first attempt to imitate the 'Focal Point' raids initiated by the German Air Force during this strategic air war against the British Isles during the years 1940 and 1941.

The lessons taught by this first large-scale raid, the increasingly high losses and the fact that the 'Hyperbola' (Gee) navigation system could only be used in certain conditions, forced the AOC-in-C of Bomber Command to develop new systems of attack.

Using the German system of 'Illuminators' and 'Fire Raisers' as a model, the use of Pathfinders was developed towards the middle of August 1942 in order to bring on to the target all the aircraft, some with inexperienced, others with only medium-trained crews, and to allow the dropping of the bombs without loss of time.

2. Air Vice Marshall Bennett, at present still in command of these special units, was appointed Chief of the Pathfinder formations. This 35-year-old Australian – known as one of the most resourceful officers of the RAF – had distinguished himself as long ago as 1938 by a record long-range flight to South Africa in a four-engined seaplane which was launched in the air from a Sunderland flying boat (composite aircraft). In 1940, Bennett established the Transatlantic Ferry Command with aircraft of the Hudson type. As an example of his personal operational capabilities, an attack may be cited which he made on the German Fleet base at Trondheim. Bennett's appointment as commander of the Pathfinder Formations is also based on the fact that he has written two standard books on astro-navigation.

3. The use of Pathfinders in the first large-scale raids was comparatively primitive. Several particularly experienced crews were sent out first as 'Fire Raisers' ahead of the Main Bomber Force and, in order to facilitate and ensure the location of the target, moonlit nights were especially favoured.

Shortly after the formation of these Pathfinder groups, however, the principle of raids during moonlit nights was dropped and raids in dark cloudless periods began to take place.

Bennett strove to render the raids independent of the weather and at the same time to make it easier for the less experienced crews to locate the target.

4. At first there were only four bomber squadrons, equipped with Stirlings, Halifaxes, Lancasters and Wellingtons, and in January 1943 these units were organised into 8 Bomber Group, the Pathfinder Group.

The grouping of the Pathfinders into a Bomber Group of their own made it possible to standardise the equipment and the training, to put new ideas into operation and immediately to evaluate all experiences.

*This remarkable German Intelligence document, kindly provided by Group Captain Mahaddie, shows that by March 1944 the Germans had a very clear and accurate picture of the scope and techniques of the RAF's Pathfinder force.

During the course of 1943, the number of Pathfinder squadrons was increased to meet the increased demands and, among others, several Mosquito Squadrons were detailed to the Pathfinder Group.

B. Organisation and Equipment

1. 8th Bomber Group at present consists of five Lancaster Squadrons, one Halifax Squadron, four Mosquito Squadrons (including two special bomber squadrons with 'Bumerang' (Oboe) equipment); One Mosquito Met Flight.

For further information concerning the organisation of these units, see 'Blue Book Series, Book 1'; *The British Heavy Bomber Squadrons.*

2. In addition to the normal navigational aids (see also 'Blue Book Series, Book 7; *British Navigation Systems*) the aircraft carry the following special equipment:

a) Four-engined aircraft (Lancaster and Halifax):
'Rotterdam' (H2S) for location of target and bombing without ground visibility.
'Hyperbola' navigation instrument (Gee).
Identification Friend-Foe (IFF).
Acoustic night-fighter warning instrument 'Monica'.
Visual night-fighter warning instrument (cathode ray oscilloscope) 'Fish Pond'.
Provision for bomb release in the cockpit as well as in the navigation cabin.

b) Twin-engined aircraft (Mosquito):
'Hyperbola' navigation instrument (Gee).
Special equipment according to mission, for example 'Bumerang' (Oboe).
The existence of Mosquitos equipped with H2S has not as yet been definitely established. According to latest information available, this special equipment does not seem to have been installed in the Mosquito.

3. The crews are no longer composed mainly of volunteers as was formerly the case. Owing to the great demand and the heavy losses, crews are either posted to Pathfinder units immediately after completing their training, or are transferred from ordinary bomber squadrons. As in the past, however, special promotion and the Golden Eagle badge are big inducements to the crews.

At first Pathfinder crews had to commit themselves to 60 operational flights, but because there were not sufficient volunteers, the figure was decreased to 45.

After transfer to a Pathfinder Squadron, a certain probationary period is undergone. The crews are not appointed Pathfinders and awarded the Golden Eagle until they have proved themselves capable of fulfilling the requirement by flying several operations (about fourteen) over Germany.

4. There is a special Pathfinder school (NTU Upwood Special School). All new crews, however, are sent on a special navigational course lasting 8-14 days at a Navigational Training Unit where particularly experienced instructors, who have already completed their Pathfinder tours, train the crews in the operation of the special equipment and put the final polish on their already good navigational training.

New Pathfinder crews fly training flights over Great Britain. These are usually made South-West from the Cambridge area, course then being set for the Isle of Man. On the return flight a large city, such as Birmingham or Manchester is approached, dummy bombing using H2S is carried out, and target photographs are brought back to the home base. Flights of this kind are flown to a strict time schedule, just as in the case of a large-scale raid on Germany or the Occupied Western Territories, and are taken into consideration in the assessment of the crews as Pathfinders. If on several occasions the schedule is not adhered to, the crew is transferred to an ordinary bomber squadron.

C. Pathfinder Operations

1. General

The operational tactics of the Pathfinders have been under constant development ever since the earliest days, and even now cannot be considered as firmly established or complete. New methods of target location and marking, as well as extensive deceptive and diversionary measures against the German defences are evident in almost every operation.

Whereas the attacks of the British heavy bombers during the years 1942-43 lasted over an hour, the duration of the attack has been progressively shortened so that today a raid of 800-900 aircraft is compressed into 20 minutes at the most. (According to captured enemy information, the plan for the raid on Berlin on 15/16 February 1944 called for about 900 aircraft in five waves of four minutes each).

In spite of the increased danger of collision or of dropping bombs on other aircraft which must be taken into account, the aim has been achieved of allowing the German defences, the Commands as well as the defence weapons themselves, only a fraction of the time available to them during raids in the past. The realisation of these aims was made possible by the conscientious work of the Pathfinder group and by the high training standard (especially regarding navigation) of the crews.

The markers over the approach and withdrawal courses serve as navigational aids for all aircraft and above all they help them to keep to the exact schedule of times and positions along the briefed course. Over the target, the markers of the Pathfinders enable all aircraft to bomb accurately without loss of time.

2. Markers

Up to date, the following markers have been identified:

Target Markers

a) Ground markers, also called cascade bombs, are red, green and yellow. Weather conditions govern the setting of the barometric fuse whereby the ground marker container is detonated at a height varying from 800 to 5,000 metres, releasing 60 flares which fall burning and burn out on the ground.

Ground markers are mainly dropped in the target area, but they are also sometimes used as route markers. Ground markers are also dropped in 10/10ths cloud in order to illuminate the cloud base from below. When the clouds are thin, the crew can see the glare without difficulty.

b) Sky markers are parachute flares, of which several are usually placed simultaneously. As a rule, the flares used are red from which at regular intervals quick-burning green flares ('dripping green stars') drop out. Besides these, green sky markers with red stars and, although comparatively seldom, green sky markers with yellow stars are also used.

The bomb-aimers are for the most part briefed to drop their bombs into the middle of a group of sky markers. This corrects the opinion held until now that two sky markers are set, one to indicate the point of bomb release and the other to indicate the target.

c) White and yellowish flares are used chiefly to illuminate the target. They are also sometimes used as dummy markers.

During raids in the autumn of 1943 the enemy attempted to mark a target approach corridor by setting numerous flares. It may be assumed that he dropped this system because of the heavy losses inflicted by German single-engined night-fighters in the target area.

Route Markers

a) As track markers or indicators, sky markers are used in 10/10ths cloud.

b) Ground markers (spotfires) are red, green or yellow; red and yellow are mainly used.

A ground marker does not split up into different traces, but burns with a single bright light for three to eight minutes.

New kinds of markers, as yet not clearly identified

The enemy has often tried to introduce new kinds of markers with varying lighting effects.

a) Among others, a quick-falling flare bomb was observed lately. After it hit the ground, a 90-metre high column of sparks was observed, which slowly descended in many colours. Confirmation, however, is not yet available.

b) To designate the beginning and the end of the attack, a large reddish-yellow 'Fireball' has often been observed. Red flares fall from the fireball and at low heights these again split up into green stars. The light intensity of these bombs is unusually high.

c) The so-called red 'Multi-Flashes' are apparently used as route markers. They have been observed sparkling to the ground at intervals of 2-3 seconds.

d) The enemy seem to have stopped using enormous 1,800 kg size flare bombs. The reasons for this could not be determined.

3. Execution of Pathfinder Operations

Dividing of the Pathfinder crews

a) At present, Pathfinder crews are divided into the following categories:

> Blind Markers
> Blind Backers-up
> Visual Backers-up
> Visual Markers
> Supporters, Pathfinder Main Force

About 15% of the bombers used for a large-scale operation are Pathfinders. For example, out of a total strength of 900 aircraft, 120 would be Pathfinders, of which about 20-25 would be blind markers, 30-45 would be blind and visual backers-up and 60-70 would be Pathfinder main force.

b) Blind markers – It is the duty of the blind markers to locate the target using H2S and to set ground or sky markers, or both, according to weather conditions, at zero hour minus 2 to 5 minutes.

The blind marker crews alone are responsible for the success or the failure of the raid. They are more strictly bound to the time schedule than all the other aircraft taking part in the raid. They are not allowed to drop their markers if the schedule is deviated from by more than one or two minutes, or if the instruments fail. In such cases the blind marker aircraft automatically becomes part of the Pathfinder main force and must drop its HE bomb load exactly at zero hour.

With smaller targets it is the duty of the blind markers to set flares over the target area in order to illuminate it.

Another duty of good blind marker crews during the initial stages of the attack is not only to set new markers, but also to re-centre the attack. Experience has shown that the first aircraft of the main force drop their bombs near the markers but that succeeding aircraft tend to drop them short of the target area during the progress of the attack. It is the duty of the blind markers detailed for this purpose to bring the bombing back to the original target by re-setting the markers past the first aiming point in the direction of withdrawal.

For several months past, the blind markers have had a further duty. In several operations it was repeatedly shown that errors in the navigation of the main force occurred owing to inaccurate wind forecasts. Experienced Pathfinders were therefore instructed to transmit their established wind calculations to England by W/T. Each group picks up these reports and transmits them every half hour to the airborne bombers.

c) Blind backers-up – The duties of the blind backers-up are similar to those of the blind markers, except that they fly in the bomber stream. Thus, they drop their markers during the attack, also in accordance with a strict previously laid-down time schedule. Blind backers-up are used to set ground markers and, above all, sky markers which are always renewed by means of the H2S and never visually.

d) Visual backers-up – In order to give new Pathfinder crews a chance to gain experience for future operations as visual or blind markers, they are allowed to set new markers visually; these, however, are always of a different colour. Theoretically, these markers should be on, or very near to, the original markers, but as in practice this is very seldom the case, the impression given is that of the target being framed by markers.

e) Visual markers – An attack on a small or pin-point target (definite industrial installations, dockyards, etc) necessitates still more accurate marking than is possible by the blind markers. The visual markers, therefore, locate the target visually from medium heights, sometimes from as low as 1,500 metres, and then release their ground markers on the centre of the target in order to concentrate the attack of the high-flying bombers.

f) Supporters – New crews who come from training units or other squadrons and who are to be trained as Pathfinders fly their first operations in the Pathfinder main force. They carry only mines or H.E. bombs, arrive excactly at zero hour, and try to create the conditions necessary to allow the incendiary bombs of the succeeding waves to take full effect.

Route Markers

Route markers are set by good blind marker crews and are renewed during the approach of the 'Bomber Stream' by further good blind marker crews. Ground markers (Spotfires) are sometimes set visually, and sometimes by instruments, but sky markers used as track markers or indicators are set only by means of H2S.

The routes of approach and withdrawal are generally identified by three markers set at especially prominent points or turning points. The colours of these markers for any single night raid are usually the same, either red, green, yellow or white. It has often been observed that the route markers do not always lie exactly on course. They are set somewhat to one side so that the approaching bombers are not unnecessarily exposed to the danger of German night-fighters.

Target Markers

The target markers used will differ according to weather conditions. Up to date, the following methods of attack and target marking have been recognised:

a) The 'Paramata' attack under a clear sky and with good visibility. Ground markers are used only.

b) The 'Wanganui' attack with 8-10/10ths cloud cover. Sky markers only.

c) The 'Musical Paramata' attack with 5-8/10ths cloud cover. Mainly ground markers, but some sky markers.

d) The 'Newhaven' attack, in which the target area is illuminated by means of parachute flares, coupled with several ground markers.

e) The 'Musical Wanganui' attack with 8-10/10ths cloud cover. Mainly sky markers, but some ground markers. This system of target marking has been used to a great extent lately during bad-weather operations.

Dropping the Markers

The setting of the Pathfinder markers requires a great deal of experience. For this reason, training flights with markers of all kinds are often carried out over Great Britain, serving for practical experiments with flares as well as for training purposes.

When the target area is already illuminated by previously dropped flares, the ground markers are released visually by means of the ordinary bomb-sight.

In cases where 10/10ths cloud or dark conditions are found over the target area, H2S is used for dropping all markers.

A great deal of experience is required for the setting of blind markers. Close co-operation between the navigator and the H2S operator (see 'Blue Book Series, Book 7'; *British Navigation Systems* for the difference between the two) who sit side by side in the navigation cabin is the first essential for the precise setting of markers by means of H2S. Above all, drift must be calculated before the markers are set so that the main attacking force only has to navigate on the markers themselves.

Navigation

The basis for all Pathfinder navigation is dead reckoning, and all other systems are only aids to check and supplement this. H2S equipment is valueless without dead reckoning because the ground is not shown on the cathode ray tube screen as it is on a map.

To facilitate the location of the target, an auxiliary target, which experience shows to give a clear picture on the cathode ray tube, is given during the briefing. This auxiliary target should be as close to the actual target as possible, in order to eliminate all sources of error. Cities, large lakes, or sometimes even the coastline features are used as auxiliary targets.

The course and the time of flight from the auxiliary target to the actual target are calculated in advance, taking the wind into consideration. The H2S operator then knows that the main target will appear on the screen a given number of seconds after the auxiliary target has been identified.

4. Mosquito Pathfinder Operations

The Mosquito aircraft have special duties as Pathfinders, concerning which the following information is available:

a) Setting ordinary markers 15 to 20 minutes before the beginning of the actual attack, in conjunction with other 'Lancaster' Pathfinders, over an auxiliary target.

b) Setting dummy markers along the coast and at other places to indicate a false course and a false target.

c) Dropping so-called 'Fighter Flares' which are imitations of the white and yellow flares dropped by German flare-carrying aircraft, to attract and divert German night-fighters.

These dummy markers are often three to five minutes flight from the target, or are sometimes placed at points off the approach and withdrawal courses, although always in some sort of relationship to these.

d) Dropping 'Window' from great heights. This is so timed, after taking wind conditions into consideration, that a cloud of

'Window' will be over the target when the first four-engined Pathfinders get there. This is made necessary by the fact that the target must be approached in straight and level flight, without evasive action, in order to get a good H2S picture. It is supposed to eliminate to a great extent aimed fire by the flak.

e) Release of single H.E. bombs 20 to 30 minutes after the main attack and observation of the results of the main attack.

f) Identification of pin-point targets for succeeding Mosquito waves by setting ground markers with the aid of 'Bumerang' (Oboe). The succeeding Mosquitoes then drop their bombs visually on the marked target.

D. Conclusions

1.　Strong criticism from amongst their own units was at first levelled against the British Pathfinder operations, but they were able to prevail because of their proven successes in 1943/44.

2.　The original assumption that the majority of bomber crews would be less careful in their navigation once they became used to the help of the Pathfinders, and that therefore the total efficiency and success of raids would diminish, has hitherto not been confirmed. The navigational training and equipment of the ordinary British bomber crews have also been improved.

3.　The operational tactics of the Pathfinders cannot be considered as complete even today. There are in particular continual changes of all markers and marking systems.

4.　The trend of development will be towards making possible on one and the same night two or more large raids on the present scale, each with the usual Pathfinder accompaniment.

Distribution
Units of the R.d.L. and Ob.d.L. Luftflotten down to operational Gr Flakabteilungen and Ln. Regiments.

Although the majority of bomber losses were claimed by the fighters, the anti-aircraft defences became increasingly successful as the war progressed. This B-17 of the 379BG was shot down near Assen on the 26th November 1943 by the 8th Motorised Flak Division – it was their 184th victim.　IWM

BIBLIOGRAPHY

Anderson, W, *Pathfinders*, Jarrolds 1946.

Babington Smith, C, *Evidence in Camera*, Chatto and Windus 1958.

Bennett, D, *Pathfinder*, Muller 1958.

Bowyer, M, *2 Group RAF*, Faber and Faber 1974.

Boyle, A, *Trenchard*, Collins 1962.

Craven, W. and Cate J, *The Army Air Forces in World War II*, University of Chicago Press 1949.

Frankland N, *The Bombing Offensive against Germany*, Faber 1965.

Freeman R, *The Mighty Eighth*, Arms and Armour 1986.

Galland, A, *The First and the Last*, Methuen 1955.

Gibson, G, *Enemey Coast Ahead*, Michael Joseph 1946.

Green, W, *Warplanes of the Third Reich*, Macdonald and Janes 1970.

Harris, Sir Arthur, *Bomber Offensive*, Collins 1947.

Hastings, M, *Bomber Command*, Michael Joseph 1979.

Hinsley, F, *British Intelligence in the Second World War*, HMSO 1981.

Irving, D, *The Destruction of Dresden*, Kimber 1963.

Jackson, R, *Before the Storm*, Arthur Barker 1972.
Storm from the Skies Arthur Barker 1974.

Jones, N, *Origins of Strategic Bombing*, Kimber 1973.

Jones, R, *Most Secret War*, Coronet 1979.

Lawrence, W, *No 5 Bomber Group RAF*, Faber and Faber 1951.

Longmate, N, *The Bombers*, Hutchinson 1983.

Middlebrook, M, *The Battle of Hamburg*, Allen Lane 1980.
The Peenemunde Raid, Allen Lane 1982.
The Schweinfurt-Regensburg Mission, Allen Lane 1983.
The Nuremberg Raid, Allen Lane 1973.
The Berlin Raids, Viking 1988.

Mitcham, S, *Eagles of the Third Reich*, Airlife 1988.

Moyes, P, *Bomber Squadrons of the RAF and their Aircraft*, Macdonald 1964.

Murray, W, – *Luftwaffe – Strategy for Defeat*, Allen & Unwin 1985.

Norris, G, *The Royal Flying Corps*, Muller 1965.

Overy, R. J, *The Air War 1939-1945*, Europa Publications 1980.

Price, A, *Instruments of Darkness*, Macdonald and Janes 1967.

Richards, D, *Portal of Hungerford*, Heinemann 1977.

Richards, D. and Saunders H. St. G, *Royal Air Force 1939-1945 – HMSO 1954 (3 Volumes)*.

Robertson, B, Lancaster: The Story of a Bomber, Harleyford Publications 1964.

Rumpf, H, *The Bombing of Germany*, Muller 1964.

Saundby, Sir Robert, *Air Bombardment*, Chatto and Windus 1961.

Saward, D, *The Bomber's Eye*, Cassell 1959.
Bomber Harris, Doubleday 1984.

Slessor, Sir John, *The Central Blue*, Cassell 1956.

Tedder, Lord, *With Prejudice*, Cassel 1966.

Speer, A, *Inside the Third Reich*, Weidenfeld and Nicolson 1970.

Terraine, J, *The Right Of The Line*, Hodder and Stoughton 1985.

Thetford, O, *Aircraft of the RAF Since 1918*, Putnam 1957.

Verrier, A, *The Bomber Offensive*, Batsford 1968.

Webster, C. and Frankland N, *The Strategic Air Offensive Against Germany 1939-1945*, HMSO 1961 – (4 Volumes).

White, C. M, *The Gotha Summer*, Robert Hale 1986.

AHB Narratives – AHB/II/116/14,16,17 and 19
AHB/II/117/1(B)

Statistical Summary of 8th Air Force Operations, European Theatre AFSHRG.

INDEX